EYEWITNESS TRAVEL GUIDES

WASHINGTON, DC

Main contributors:
SUSAN BURKE AND ALICE L. POWERS

DK PUBLISHING

LONDON • NEW YORK • MUNICH
MELBOURNE • DELHI

PROJECT EDITOR Claire Folkard
ART EDITORS Tim Mann, Simon J.M. Oon
SENIOR EDITOR Helen Townsend
EDITORS Emily Anderson, Felicity Crowe
US EDITOR Mary Sutherland
DESIGNERS Gillian Andrews, Eli Estaugh,
Elly King, Rebecca Milner
DTP Sam Borland, Maite Lantaron
PICTURE RESEARCHERS Brigitte Arora, Katherine Mesquita
PRODUCTION Mel Allsop

CONTRIBUTORS
Susan Burke, Alice L. Powers, Jennifer Quasha, Kem Sawyer

PHOTOGRAPHERS
Philippe Dewet, Kim Sayer, Giles Stokoe, Scott Suchman

ILLUSTRATORS
Stephen Conlin, Gary Cross, Richard Draper, Chris Orr &
Associates, Mel Pickering, Robbie Polley, John Woodcock

Reproduced by Colourscan, Singapore
Printed and bound by South China Printing Co. Ltd., China

First American Edition, 2000
4 6 8 10 9 7 5 3

Published in the United States by Dorling Kindersley Publishing, Inc.,
375 Hudson Street, New York 10014

Reprinted with revisions 2002, 2003

Copyright © 2000, 2003 Dorling Kindersley Limited, London

Published in Great Britain by Dorling Kindersley Limited.

A CATALOGING IN PUBLICATION RECORD IS AVAILABLE
FROM THE LIBRARY OF CONGRESS.

ISSN 1542-1554
ISBN 0-7894-9576-7

THROUGHOUT THIS BOOK, FLOORS ARE REFERRED TO IN ACCORDANCE WITH
AMERICAN USAGE, I.E., THE "FIRST FLOOR" IS THE FLOOR AT GROUND LEVEL

See our complete product line at
www.dk.com

◁ **The White House**

CONTENTS

**HOW TO USE THIS
GUIDE** *6*

Fountain in Dumbarton Oaks

INTRODUCING
WASHINGTON, DC

**PUTTING
WASHINGTON, DC
ON THE MAP** *10*

**THE HISTORY OF
WASHINGTON, DC**
14

**WASHINGTON, DC
AT A GLANCE** *28*

**WASHINGTON, DC
THROUGH THE YEAR**
34

**View toward the Lincoln Memorial
from Arlington National Cemetery**

Columns from the US Capitol building, now in the US National Arboretum

Senate Bean Soup

Map seller outside the National
Gallery of Art on the Mall

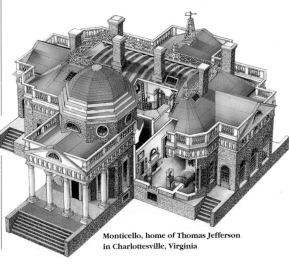

Monticello, home of Thomas Jefferson
in Charlottesville, Virginia

HOW TO USE THIS GUIDE

THIS GUIDE helps you to get the most from your stay in Washington, DC. It provides detailed practical information and expert recommendations. *Introducing Washington, DC* maps the city and the region, sets it in its historical and cultural context, and gives an overview of the main attractions. *Washington, DC Area By Area* is the main sightseeing section, giving detailed information on all the major sights, with photographs, illustrations and maps. *Farther Afield* looks at sights outside the city center, and *Beyond Washington, DC* explores other places within easy reach of the city. Carefully researched suggestions for restaurants, hotels, entertainment, and shopping are found in the *Travelers' Needs* section, while the *Survival Guide* contains useful advice on everything from changing money to traveling on Washington's Metrorail system.

FINDING YOUR WAY AROUND WASHINGTON, DC

The center of Washington has been divided into five sightseeing areas, each with its own chapter, color-coded for easy reference. All sights are numbered and plotted on an area map for each chapter.

The area shaded pink is shown in greater detail on the Street-by-Street map on the following pages.

2 Street-by-Street map *This gives a bird's-eye view of the heart of each sightseeing area. Interesting features are labeled. There is also a list of "star sights" that no visitor should miss.*

The Visitors' Checklist provides detailed practical information.

1 Area Introduction *This describes the history and character of the area and has a map on which the sights have been plotted. Other key information is also given.*

Each area has color-coded thumb tabs

Locator Map

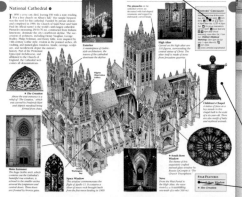

A suggested route takes in the most interesting and attractive streets in the area.

3 Star sight map *These are given two or more full pages. Historic buildings are dissected to reveal their interiors. Where necessary, sights are color-coded to help you locate the most interesting areas.*

Stars indicate the sights that no visitor should miss.

WASHINGTON, DC AREA MAP

THE COLORED AREAS shown on this map (inside the front cover) are the five main sight-seeing areas used in this guide. Each is covered in a full chapter in *Washington, DC Area by Area* (pp38–121). They are highlighted on other maps throughout the book. In *Washington, DC at a Glance (see pp28–33)*, they help you to locate the top sights. The *Street Finder (see pp208–213)* shows the sights from these five areas on a detailed street map of Washington.

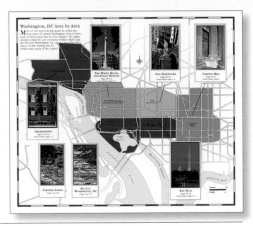

4 Detailed information *All the important sights are described individually. They are listed in order, following the numbering on the area map.*

Practical information is provided in an information block. The key to the symbols used is on the back flap.

The Introduction outlines the areas covered in this section and their historical context.

A map of the city shows the location of the Farther Afield sights in relation to the city center.

5 Farther Afield *This section covers those sights that lie just outside central Washington and are easily accessible from the city center.*

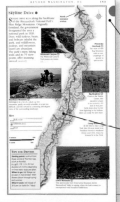

6 Beyond Washington *Places worth visiting that are situated within a day's travel of Washington are described here. They include interesting cities, historic towns, and national parks.*

Special sights, such as this national park, are highlighted with maps or detailed illustrations.

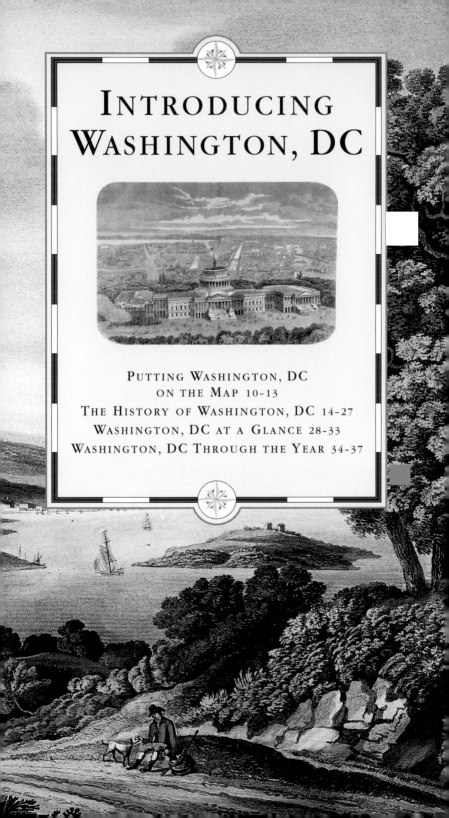

INTRODUCING WASHINGTON, DC

Putting Washington, DC on the Map

WASHINGTON, DC is situated near the East Coast of North America, surrounded by the state of Maryland and separated from Virginia by the Potomac River. It covers an area of 108 sq km (67 sq miles) and has a population of 570,000. As the capital of the United States, and seat of federal government, the city is a major focus of American life. It is a very popular tourist destination, attracting millions of visitors each year. The beautiful countryside of Maryland and Virginia is also easily reached from the capital city.

Satellite view of Washington, DC, with the Potomac River

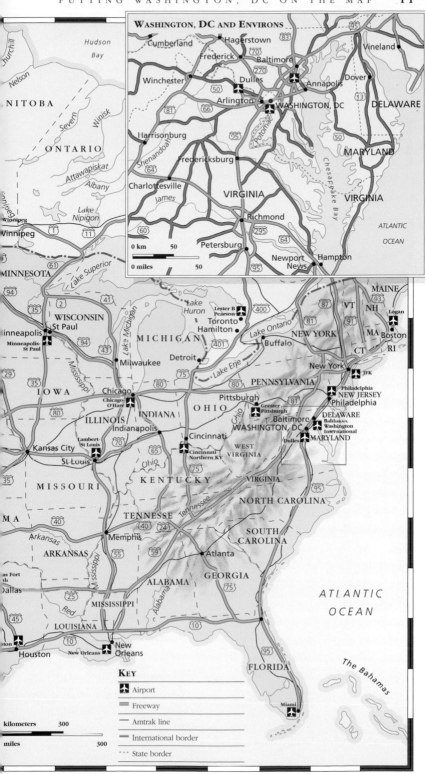

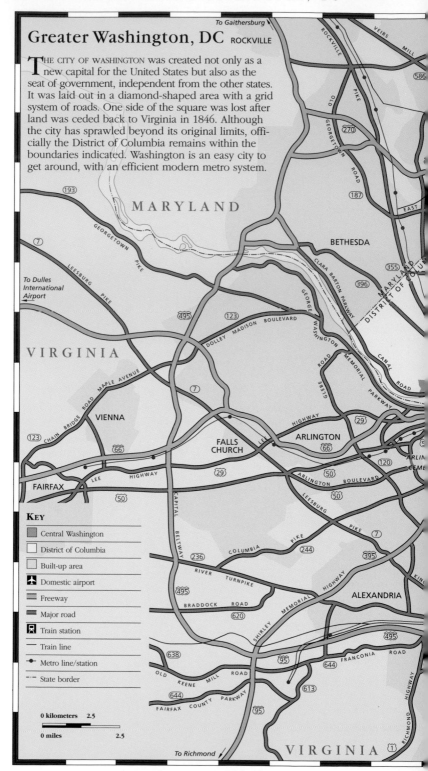

Greater Washington, DC

THE CITY OF WASHINGTON was created not only as a new capital for the United States but also as the seat of government, independent from the other states. It was laid out in a diamond-shaped area with a grid system of roads. One side of the square was lost after land was ceded back to Virginia in 1846. Although the city has sprawled beyond its original limits, officially the District of Columbia remains within the boundaries indicated. Washington is an easy city to get around, with an efficient modern metro system.

To Gaithersburg

ROCKVILLE

VEIRS MILL

ROCKVILLE PIKE

OLD GEORGETOWN ROAD

270

586

193

M A R Y L A N D

187

EAST

GEORGETOWN PIKE

BETHESDA

7

LEESBURG PIKE

CLARA BARTON PARKWAY

355

396

To Dulles
International
Airport

GEORGE WASHINGTON MEMORIAL PARKWAY

CANAL ROAD

MARYLAND
DISTRICT OF COLUMBIA

495

123

DOLLEY MADISON BOULEVARD

V I R G I N I A

ROAD

GLEBE ROAD

7

MAPLE AVENUE

CHAIN BRIDGE ROAD

VIENNA

HIGHWAY

29

ARLINGTON

123

66

FALLS
CHURCH

LEE

66

120

ARLIN
CEME

LEE HIGHWAY

29

ARLINGTON BOULEVARD

50

FAIRFAX

50

LEESBURG

50

KINC

KEY

	Central Washington
	District of Columbia
	Built-up area
✈	Domestic airport
═	Freeway
▬	Major road
🚆	Train station
—	Train line
●—	Metro line/station
-·-	State border

CAPITAL BELTWAY

PIKE

7

236

COLUMBIA

PIKE

244

395

RIVER TURNPIKE

495

BRADDOCK ROAD

620

SHIRLEY MEMORIAL HIGHWAY

ALEXANDRIA

495

0 kilometers 2.5

0 miles 2.5

638

95

FRANCONIA ROAD

644

644

OLD KEENE MILL ROAD

613

RICHMOND HIGHWAY

FAIRFAX COUNTY PARKWAY

95

To Richmond

V I R G I N I A

1

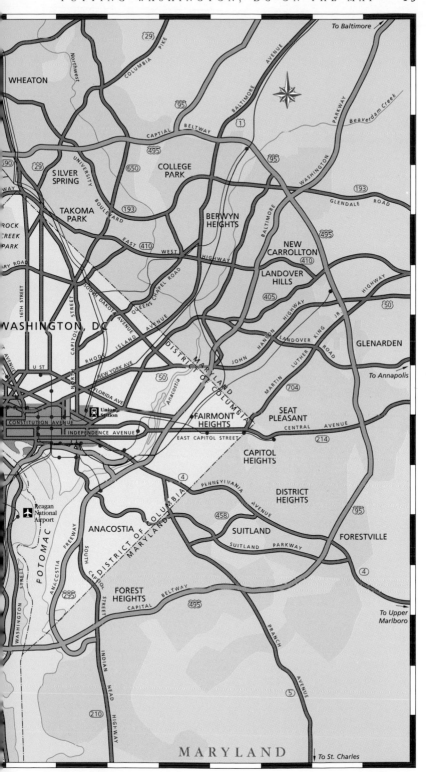

THE HISTORY OF WASHINGTON, DC

NATIVE AMERICANS *settled in what is now the District of Columbia as long as 6,000 years ago. Archeologists have discovered traces of three villages in the area; the largest was called Nacotchtanke. Its people, the Anacostines, settled along the Potomac River and a smaller tributary now named the Anacostia River.*

ENGLISH SETTLEMENT

In December 1606 Captain John Smith of the Virginia Company, under the charge of King James I of England, set sail from England for the New World. Five months later he arrived in the Chesapeake Bay and founded the Jamestown colony. A skilled cartographer, Smith was soon sailing up the Potomac River. In 1608 he came to the area that would later become Washington.

The English settlers who followed supported themselves through the fur trade, and later cultivated tobacco and corn (maize). The marriage in 1614 between John Rolfe, one of the settlers, and Pocahontas, daughter of the Indian chief Powhatan, kept the peace between the English and the Indians for eight years. Struggles over land ownership led to massacres in 1622. The English finally defeated the Indians in 1644, and a formal peace agreement was made in 1646.

The settlement of Jamestown, Virginia, in 1607

The first Africans arrived in the region in 1619 and worked as indentured servants on plantations. They were given food and lodging as payment for serving for a fixed number of years. However, within the next 40 years the practice changed so that blacks were purchased for life, and their children became the property of their master. As the number of plantations grew, so did the number of slaves.

In the late 1600s another group of settlers, this time Irish-Scottish, led by Captain Robert Troop, established themselves here. Along the Potomac River two ports, George Town (later Georgetown) and Alexandria, soon became profitable centers of commerce. Here planters had their crops inspected, stored, and shipped. In both towns streets were laid out in rectangular patterns. With rich soil, plentiful land, abundant labor, and good transportation, the region rapidly grew in prosperity.

TIMELINE

1607 Captain John Smith founds Jamestown settlement in Virginia

1619 The first Africans arrive in American colonies

Captain John Smith (1580–1631)

1751 George Town is established

1748 Tobacco merchants granted land for the town of Alexandria

1646 The Indians and the English reach a peace agreement in the Tidewater and Potomac region

1634 Lord Baltimore founds Catholic colony in Maryland

1600   1650   1700   1750

◁ **George Washington by Rembrandt Peale, painted 1824–5**

REVOLUTIONARY YEARS

Some 100 years after the first settlers arrived, frustration over British rule began to grow, both in the Potomac region and elsewhere in the 13 American colonies. In 1775, the colonies began their struggle for independence. On April 19, shots were fired at Lexington, Massachusetts by American colonists who wanted "no taxation without representation," thus beginning the War of Independence.

On July 4, 1776, the Declaration of Independence was issued as colonists attempted to sever ties with Britain. Revolt led to revolution, and the newly formed United States won an important victory at Saratoga, New York in 1777. The French came to the aid of the Americans and finally, on October 19, 1781, the British, led by Lord Cornwallis, surrendered at Yorktown, Virginia. This ended the war and assured the independence of the United States. The peace treaty was signed in Paris on September 3, 1783. Britain agreed to boundaries giving the US all territory to the south of what is now Canada, north of Florida, and west to the Mississippi River.

The Continental Congress, a legislative body of representatives from the newly formed states, appointed a committee to draft the country's first constitution. The result was the Articles of Confederation, which established a union of the newly created states but provided the central government with little power. This later gave way to a stronger form of government, created

Meeting in New York of first delegates of Congress to discuss location for a new capital city

Lord Cornwallis

by the delegates of the Federal Constitutional Convention in Philadelphia in May, 1787. George Washington was unanimously chosen to be president. He took office on April 30, 1789.

A NEW CITY

The Constitution of the United States, ratified in 1788, allowed for the creation of a seat of government, not to exceed 10 square miles, which would be ruled by the United States Congress. This area was to be independent and not part of any state. At the first meeting of Congress in New York City in 1789, a dispute arose between northern and southern delegates over where the capital should be located. Secretary of the Treasury Alexander Hamilton and Secretary of State Thomas Jefferson worked out an agreement whereby the debts incurred by northern states

TIMELINE

1781 The British surrender at Yorktown

1783 The US and Britain sign the Treaty of Paris

1787 The Federal Constitutional Convention meets in Philadelphia

1793 President Washington lays the Capitol's cornerstone

| 1775 | 1780 | 1785 | 1790 | 179 |

Articles of Confederation

1775 The first battles of the American Revolution are fought at Lexington and Concord

1789 Delegates gather in New York City to discuss a location for the capital

1791 President Washington obtains land for the capital city

1792 Construction beg on the President's Ho (later the White House

during the Revolution would be taken over by the government, and in return the capital would be located in the south. George Washington chose an area that incorporated land from both Maryland and Virginia, and included the towns of Alexandria and Georgetown. It was to be known as the city of Washington. At Suter's Tavern in Georgetown, Washington convinced local residents to sell their land for £25 an acre. He chose a surveyor, Andrew Ellicott, and his assistant Benjamin Banneker, a free African-American, to lay out the streets and lots. Washington also accepted the offer of Major Pierre Charles L'Enfant to create a grand design for the new capital city *(see p65)*.

In 1800 the government was moved to Washington. President John Adams and his wife Abigail took up residence in the new President's House, designed by James Hoban, which was later renamed the White House by Theodore Roosevelt. The city remained empty of residents for many years while the building works took place.

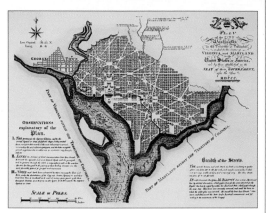

Ellicott's engraved map of 1792, based on L'Enfant's plan

WAR OF 1812

Tension with Britain over restrictions on trade and freedom of the seas began to escalate during James Madison's administration. On June 18, 1812, the US declared war on Britain. In August 1814, British troops reached Washington and officers at the Capitol fled, taking the Declaration of Independence and the Constitution with them. First Lady Dolley Madison escaped from the White House with Gilbert Stuart's portrait of George Washington.

On August 24, the British defeated the Americans at Bladensburg, a suburb of Washington. They set fire to the War Department, the Treasury, the Capitol, and the White House. Only a night of heavy rain prevented the city's destruction. The Treaty of Ghent, which finally ended the war, was signed on February 17, 1815 in the Octagon.

The British attack on Washington, DC in August 1814

1814 The British set fire to Washington

1802 Robert Brent appointed first mayor of Washington

1812 US declares war on Britain

1815 President Madison signs the Treaty of Ghent with Britain

1800	1805	1810	1815

1800 The seat of government is transferred from Philadelphia to Washington

1804 President Jefferson initiates the Lewis and Clark expedition which resulted in the discovery of America's West Coast

The signing of the Treaty of Ghent

The Baltimore and Ohio Railroad's "Tom Thumb" locomotive racing a horse-drawn car

REBIRTH

With the end of the War of 1812 came a period of renewed optimism and economic prosperity in Washington. Washingtonians wanted to make their city a bustling commercial capital. They planned to build the Chesapeake and Ohio Canal to connect Washington to the Ohio River Valley and thus open trade with the west. Construction on the Baltimore and Ohio Railroad line also got under way. As the population grew, new hotels and boarding-houses, home to many of the nation's congress-men, opened up. Newspapers, such as the *National Intelligencer,* flourished.

In 1829 an Englishman called James Smithson bequeathed a collection of minerals, books, and $500,000 in gold to the United States, and the Smithsonian Institution was born.

Construction began on three important government buildings, each designed by Robert Mills (1781–1855): the Treasury Building, the Patent Office, and the General Post Office building. Also at this time, the Washington National Monument

Chained slaves walking past the unfinished Capitol building

Society, led by George Watterston, chose a 600-ft obelisk to become the Washington Monument, again designed by the architect Robert Mills.

SLAVERY DIVIDES THE CITY

Racial tension was beginning to increase around this time, and in 1835 it erupted into what was later known as the Snow Riot. After the attempted murder of the widow of architect William Thornton, a botany teacher from the North was arrested for inciting blacks because plant specimens had been found wrapped in the pages of an abolitionist newspaper. A riot ensued, and in the course of the fighting a school for black children was destroyed as well as the interior of a restaurant owned by Beverly Snow, a free black. As a result, and to the anger of many people, black and white, laws were passed denying free blacks licenses to run saloons or eating places.

Nothing has been more divisive in Washington's history than the issue of slavery. Many Washingtonians were slaveholders; others became ardent abolitionists. The homes of several

TIMELINE

1828 President John Quincy Adams breaks ground for the Chesapeake and Ohio Canal

James Smithson (1765–1829)

1844 The invention of the telegraph speeds the distribution of news from Washington

| 1825 | 1830 | 1835 | 1840 | 18 |

1829 James Smithson leaves a fortune worth more than $500,000 to the United States

1835 Baltimore and Ohio Railroad links Washington and Baltimore. Racial tension leads to the Snow Riot

1846 Construction of the Smithsonian Castle begins. Alexandria i retroceded to Virginia

1827 The Washington Abolition Society is organized

abolitionists and free blacks, as well as black churches, were used as hiding places for fugitive slaves. On an April night in 1848, 77 slaves attempted to escape the city, and boarded a small schooner on the Potomac River. But the following night they were captured and brought back to Washington, where they were sold at auction. The incident served only to heighten the tension between pro-slavery and anti-slavery groups. Slavery was abolished in Washington in 1862.

THE CIVIL WAR

In 1860, following the election of President Abraham Lincoln, several southern states seceded from the Union in objection to Lincoln's stand against slavery. Shots were fired on Fort Sumter in Charleston, South Carolina on April 12, 1861, and the Civil War began. By the summer, 50,000 volunteers arrived in Washington to join the Army of the Potomac under General George B. McClellan. Washington suddenly found itself in the business of housing, feeding, and clothing the troops, as well as caring for the wounded. Buildings and churches became makeshift hospitals.

Black residents of Washington celebrating the abolition of slavery in the District of Columbia

Many people came to nurse the wounded, including author Louisa May Alcott and poet Walt Whitman.

Thousands of northerners came to help the war effort. They were joined by hordes of black people heading north to escape slavery, so that by 1864 the population of Washington had doubled that of 1860, reaching 140,000.

After skirmishes on July 12, 1864, witnessed by Lincoln himself at Fort Stevens, the Confederates retreated. By March 1865 the end of the war appeared to be close at hand. Parades, speeches, and band concerts followed Confederate General Robert E. Lee's surrender on April 9, 1865. Yet the celebratory mood was short-lived. Disturbed by the Union Army's victory, John Wilkes Booth assassinated President Lincoln at Ford's Theatre during the third act of *Our American Cousin* on April 14, 1865. Lincoln was taken to the house of tailor William Peterson, across the street from the theater, where he died the next morning (see p90).

Victory parade through Washington, DC to celebrate the end of the Civil War in April 1865

POST CIVIL WAR

The Freedmen's Bureau was created to help provide African Americans with housing, food, education, and employment. In 1867 General Oliver Otis Howard, commissioner of the bureau, used $500,000 of the bureau's funds to purchase land to establish a university for African Americans. He was president of this institution, later named Howard University, from 1869 to 1873.

On February 21, 1871, a new "territorial government" was formed to unite Georgetown, the city of Washington, and the County of Washington into the District of Columbia. A governor and a board of public works were appointed by President Ulysses S. Grant. Alexander "Boss" Shepherd, a member of the board of public works, paved streets, installed streetlights, laid sidewalks, planned parks, and designed an advanced sewerage system. But the District's debts rose uncontrollably. As a result, Congress quickly tightened its reins and established home rule. It took over some of the District's debts, and appointed three commissioners to work within a set budget.

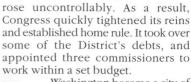

Frederick Douglass

Washington became a city of contrasts, attracting both rich and poor. One of the most distinguished literati in the city was Henry Adams, best known for his autobiographical work, *The Education of Henry Adams*. He lived on Lafayette Square next door to John Hay, Secretary of State and also a man of letters. One of Washington's most prominent African Americans, Frederick Douglass, lived at Cedar Hill, across the river in Anacostia. Born a slave in Maryland, he escaped north to freedom where he started an abolitionist newspaper. During the Civil War he became an adviser to President Lincoln.

Many lived well, including the growing middle class, which moved to the new suburbs of Mount Pleasant and LeDroit Park, yet a large number of the poor made their home in Washington's hidden alleys.

A NEW CENTURY

In 1901 Senator James McMillan of Michigan spearheaded a plan to improve the design of Washington by partaking in the "city beautiful" movement, in vogue at the time. L'Enfant's plan was finally completed, and the Mall between the Washington Monument and the US Capitol was laid out. Architects Daniel Burnham,

The Library of Congress under construction

Suffragettes demanding a hearing for imprisoned leader, Alice Paul

attracted small businesses, theaters, nightclubs, and restaurants. It became home to many successful musicians and writers; Duke Ellington and the opera star Madame Evanti lived here, as did poets Langston Hughes and Paul Dunbar. Alain Locke, a professor of philosophy at Howard, and Jean Toomer, author of *Cane*, were also residents.

Charles F. McKim, and others planned the building of a memorial to honor President Abraham Lincoln.

When the US entered World War I in 1917, growing numbers of women came to Washington to fill the posts vacated by men. Suffragettes took to the streets to campaign for the right to vote. The National Women's Party, led by Alice Paul, picketed the White House to urge President Wilson to endorse a constitutional amendment to give women the vote.

African Americans in Washington were not only banned from voting but also faced discrimination in housing and education. After a local black battalion was excluded from a World War I victory parade, tension mounted. On July 20, 1919, riots erupted on the streets and did not stop for four days. Although discrimination continued, the 1920s were a period of commercial, artistic, and literary success for the black community. The area around U Street and Howard University

ROOSEVELT USHERS IN A NEW DEAL

Following the stock market crash of 1929, federal workers received salary cuts, and many other Washingtonians lost their jobs. As a result, President Roosevelt created the "New Deal," an ambitious public works program to reduce unemployment. People were paid to do a range of tasks, from planting trees on the Mall to completing some of the city's edifices, such as the Supreme Court, the government office buildings of the Federal Triangle, and the National Gallery of Art.

Roosevelt's wife, Eleanor, was a champion of the poor and a tireless reformer. In 1939, when Marian Anderson, the African American singer, was denied permission by the Daughters of the American Revolution to perform at Constitution Hall, Eleanor Roosevelt arranged for her to sing at the Lincoln Memorial instead, to a crowd of 75,000.

President Franklin D. Roosevelt with First Lady Eleanor

Marian Anderson (1897–1993)

After the US entered World War II in December 1941, Washington's population soared. Women from all across the country arrived in the capital, eager to take on government jobs while the men were overseas. They faced housing shortages, and long lines as they waited to use rationing coupons for food and services. The city also offered a respite for soldiers on leave. Actress Helen Hayes, a native Washingtonian, opened the Stage Door Canteen where celebrities provided food and entertainment.

Soldiers on patrol after the death of Martin Luther King, Jr.

THE CIVIL RIGHTS MOVEMENT

In 1953 the Supreme Court's ruling in the Thompson Restaurant case made it illegal for public places to discriminate against blacks. With the passage of other anti-discrimination laws, life in Washington began to change. In 1954, the recreation department ended its public segregation. In the same year, on May 17, the Supreme Court ruled that "separate educational facilities are inherently unequal."

On August 28, 1963, more than 200,000 people arrived in the capital for the "March on Washington" to support civil rights. From the steps of the Lincoln Memorial, Marian Anderson

John F. Kennedy, Jr. salutes his father's casket at Arlington Cemetery in 1963

sang again and Reverend Martin Luther King, Jr. shared his dream in words that would echo for generations (see p91).

In November 1963, the nation was stunned by the assassination of President John F. Kennedy in Dallas, Texas. An eternal flame was lit at his funeral in Arlington Cemetery by his widow, Jaqueline. Five years later, on April 4, 1968, Martin Luther King was shot. Killed at the age of 39, he is revered as a hero and a martyr.

Anti-Vietnam protesters in Washington in 1969

The opening of the Kennedy Center for Performing Arts in 1971 indicated the growing international character of the city. Several art museums with impressive collections (the East Wing of the National Gallery of Art, the Hirshhorn, the National Museum of American Art, and the National Portrait Gallery) also opened to enrich the city's cultural life. The construction of the Metro helped alleviate traffic problems. The embassies, the foreign banking community (the World Bank,

TIMELINE

1940 First plane lands at National Airport

1945 The first atomic bomb is dropped on Hiroshima, ending World War II

1963 Martin Luther King gives "I Have a Dream" speech

1973 Washingtonians gain the right to elect a mayor

1969 250,000 anti-Vietnam War protesters march

1950

1960

1970

1941 The National Gallery of Art opens. After Japan attacks Pearl Harbor, the US enters World War II

Dr. Martin Luther King, Jr. (1929–68)

1964 Washington residents vote in a presidential election for the first time

1974 President Richa Nixon resigns followi criminal investigati

the International Monetary Fund, and the Inter-American Development Bank), and the increasing number of immigrants, provided a cosmopolitan flavor.

HOME RULE

Residents of the District of Columbia have never been given full representation in American politics, as they have no senator. (Until the 23rd Amendment of 1961 they could not even vote for president – the 1964 election was the first in which they took part.) In 1967, with people clamoring for a greater say in local government, President Lyndon Johnson replaced the system of three commissioners, set up by Congress in 1871, with an appointed mayor and a city council who were given greater responsibility in policy and budget issues. The result was the city's first elected mayor in over 100 years, Walter E. Washington. Residents were permitted to elect a non-voting delegate to Congress in 1971, and the Home Rule Act of 1973 allowed the people to elect both mayor and city council.

In 1978 Marion Barry succeeded as mayor. Born in Mississippi and raised in Tennessee, he came to Washington in 1965 to work for civil rights. He was the city's mayor for 16 of the next 20 years, but toward the end of his tenure, a large deficit and dissatisfaction with city politics developed. Middle-class families, both white and black, were beginning to flee the increasingly crime-ridden city for the safety of the suburbs.

Fireworks lighting the Washington Monument during the 2000 celebrations

Marion Barry, Washington's mayor for 16 years

In 1995 Congress stripped the mayor of much of his power and appointed a five-person "financial control board" to oversee the city's affairs. The election in 1998 was won by Anthony Williams, an outsider who offered a fresh outlook and financial stability. Congress returned to the mayor much of the authority it had taken away. Within months of taking his new office it appeared that Mayor Williams was turning the city around. The budget was operating with a surplus, the population had stabilized, and unemployment was down.

The new millennium augurs a smoothly run government and a capital city renowned for an efficient transportation system, a rich cultural life, and a community that is proud of its diversity. The new administration under Mayor Williams has transformed the city's image. No longer dubbed the crime capital of the United States, Washington, DC has once again become a mecca for tourists and a safer, cleaner place for its residents.

1976 Metro opens. National Air and Space Museum opens

1993 Opening of the US Holocaust Memorial Museum

President Bill Clinton (1946–

2001 September 11 Terrorist attack on the Pentagon

1980   1990   2000

1982 Dedication of the Vietnam Veterans Memorial, designed by Maya Ying Lin

1998 Anthony Williams elected mayor

1999 Impeachment, trial, and acquittal of President Bill Clinton turns all eyes to Washington, DC

1978 Marion Barry elected mayor for the first of four terms

The American Presidents

Benjamin Har
(188...

THE PRESIDENTS OF the United States have come from all walks of life; at least two were born in a log cabin - Abraham Lincoln and Andrew Jackson. Others, such as Franklin D. Roosevelt and John F. Kennedy, came from privileged backgrounds. Millard Fillmore attended a one-room schoolroom and Jimmy Carter raised peanuts. Many, including Ulysses S. Grant and Dwight D. Eisenhower, were military men, who won public popularity for their great achievements in battle.

Chester A. Arthur
(1881–5)

Millard Fillmore
(1850–53)

Zachary Taylor
(1849–50)

James K. Polk
(1845–9)

Franklin Pierce
(1853–7)

W.H. Harrison
(1841)

Rutherford B. Hayes
(1877–81)

Andrew Johnson
(1865–9)

George Washington
(1789–97) was a Revolutionary War general. He was unanimously chosen to be the first president of the United States.

James Madison
(1809–17), known as the Father of the Constitution, was co-author of the Federalist Papers.

| 1775 | 1800 | 1825 | 1850 | 1875 |

| 1775 | 1800 | 1825 | 1850 | 1875 |

John Adams
(1797–1801), a lawyer and historian, was the first president to live in the White House.

James Monroe
(1817–25)

John Quincy Adams
(1825–9)

John Tyler
(1841–5)

James A. Garfield
(1881)

Martin Van Buren
(1837-41)

Ulysses S. Grant
(1869–77)

**Grov...
Clevela...**
(1885–

James Buchanan
(1857–61)

Thomas Jefferson
(1801–9), architect, inventor, landscape designer, diplomat, and historian, was the quintessential Renaissance man.

Andrew Jackson
(1829–37) defeated the British at the Battle of New Orleans in the War of 1812.

Abraham Lincoln
(1861–5) won the epithet, the Great Emancipator, for his role in the abolition of slavery. He led the Union through the Civil War.

illiam cKinley 897–1901)

Harry S. Truman (1945–53) made the decision to drop the atomic bombs on Hiroshima and Nagasaki in 1945.

KEY TO TIMELINE

▢ Federalist
▢ Democratic Republican
▢ Whig
▢ Republican
▢ Democrat

Woodrow Wilson (1913–21) led the country through World War I and paved the way for the League of Nations.

John F. Kennedy (1961–3) was one of the most popular presidents. He sent the first astronaut into space, started the Peace Corps, and created the Arms Control and Disarmament Agency. His assassination rocked the nation.

Richard Nixon (1969–74) opened up China and sent the first men to the moon. He resigned after the Water-gate scandal *(see p111).*

Franklin D. Roosevelt (1933–45) started the New Deal, a reform and relief program, during the Great Depression. He was elected to four terms.

Jimmy Carter (1977–81)

George W. Bush (2000–)

George Bush (1989–93)

1900	1925	1950	1975	2000

1900	1925	1950	1975	2000

Dwight D. Eisenhower (1953–61)

William J. Clinton (1993–2000)

William H. Taft (1909–13)

Herbert Hoover (1929–33)

Calvin Coolidge (1923–9)

Warren Harding (1921–3)

Gerald Ford (1974–7)

Ronald Reagan (1981–9), a one-time movie actor and popular president, cut taxes, increased military spending, and reduced government programs.

Lyndon B. Johnson (1963–9) escalated the Vietnam conflict, resulting in widespread protests.

Theodore Roosevelt (1901–9) created many national parks and over-saw the construction of the Panama Canal.

cr eland –7)

THE ROLE OF THE FIRST LADY

In the 19th century, the First Lady acted primarily as hostess and "behind-the-scenes" adviser. Dolley Madison was known as the "Toast of Washington". Later, when Eleanor Roosevelt held her own press conferences, the role of First Lady changed greatly. Later, Jackie Kennedy gave unprecedented support to the arts, Rosalynn Carter attended Cabinet meetings, Nancy Reagan told the world to "Just Say No" to drugs, Barbara Bush promoted literacy, and Hillary Clinton ran her own political campaign.

Eleanor Roosevelt at a press conference in the 1930s

How the Federal Government Works

Great Seal of the United States

IN SEPTEMBER 1787, the Constitution of the United States of America was signed *(see p85)*. It was created as "the supreme Law of the Land", to ensure that it would take precedence over state laws. The powers of the federal government were separated into three distinct areas: the legislative branch to enact the laws, the executive branch to enforce them, and the judicial branch to interpret them. No one branch, however, was to exert too much authority, and the system of checks and balances was instituted. Provisions were made for amending the Constitution, and by December 1791 the first ten amendments, called the Bill of Rights, were ratified.

CHECKS AND BALANCES

The system of checks and balances means that no one branch of government can abuse its power.

The Executive Branch: The President can recommend and veto legislation and call a special session of Congress. The President appoints judges to the courts and can grant pardons for federal offenses.

The Judicial Branch: The Supreme Court interprets laws and treaties and can declare an act unconstitutional. The Chief Justice presides at an impeachment trial of the President.

The Legislative Branch: Congress can override a presidential veto of a bill with a two-thirds majority. Presidential appointments and treaties must be approved by the Senate. Congress also oversees the jurisdiction of the courts and can impeach and try the President and federal judges.

The Senate, sitting in session in the US Capitol.

THE EXECUTIVE BRANCH

The President, together with the Vice President, is elected for a four-year term. The President suggests, approves, and vetoes legislation. The Executive also develops foreign policy and directs relations with other countries, serves as Commander-in-Chief of the armed forces, and appoints ambassadors. Secretaries to the Cabinet, composed of various heads of departments, meet regularly to advise the President on policy issues. Several agencies and councils, such as the National Security Council and the Office of Management and Budget, help determine the executive agenda.

Seal of the President

Ulysses S. Grant served as the US President from 1869 to 1877.

Henry A. Wallace *served as Vice President under Franklin D. Roosevelt, from 1941 to 1945.*

EXECUTIVE BRANCH

PRESIDENT

VICE PRESIDENT

CABINET

The White House is the official residence of the US President.

Madeleine Albright, the first woman to serve as Secretary of State, was appointed in 1997.

THE JUDICIAL BRANCH

The Supreme Court and other federal courts determine the constitutionality of federal, state, and local laws. They hear cases relating to controversies between states and those affecting ambassadors or citizens of different states. They also try cases on appeal. The Supreme Court consists of nine justices appointed for life by the President.

The Supreme Court is the highest court in the United States and is the last stop in issues of constitutionality.

JUDICIAL BRANCH

9 SUPREME COURT JUSTICES

OF WHOM ONE IS **CHIEF SUPREME COURT JUSTICE**

***Thurgood Marshall** was the first African American to be a Supreme Court Justice. He held the position from 1967 to 1991.*

***Oliver Wendell Holmes**, Supreme Court Justice from 1902 to 1932, was a strong advocate of free speech.*

***Earl Warren** was Supreme Court Justice from 1953 to 1969. He wrote the unanimous opinion in Brown v. Board of Education (1954). (See p46).*

THE LEGISLATIVE BRANCH

The Congress of the United States consists of two bodies, the House of Representatives and the Senate. Representatives to the House are elected by the voters in each state for a two-year term. The number of Representatives for each state is determined by the state's population. The Senate is composed of two Senators from each state, elected for six-year terms. Congress regulates commerce and is empowered to levy taxes and declare war. This branch also makes the laws: bills discussed, written, and revised in legislative committees must be passed first by the House and by the Senate before being approved by the President.

***Daniel Webster** served both in the House of Representatives (1813–17) and in the Senate (1822–41).*

LEGISLATIVE BRANCH

HOUSE OF REPRESENTATIVES

SENATE

***Sam Rayburn** was a popular and distinguished Speaker of the House.*

***Edward Kennedy**, leader of the United States' most famous political family, has served in the Senate since 1962.*

The US Capitol is home to both the House of Representatives and the Senate.

WASHINGTON, DC AT A GLANCE

WASHINGTON IS more than just the political capital of the United States. It is also the home of the Smithsonian Institution, and as such is the cultural focus of America. Its many superb museums and galleries have something to offer everyone. Always one of the most popular sights, the president's official residence, the White House, attracts millions of visitors each year. Equally popular is the National Air and Space Museum, which draws vast numbers of visitors to its awe-inspiring displays of air and spacecraft. Also unique to Washington are its many monuments and memorials. The huge Washington Monument, honoring the first US president, dominates the city skyline. In contrast, the war memorials, dedicated to the thousands of soldiers who died in battle, are quietly poignant.

WASHINGTON'S TOP TEN ATTRACTIONS

The White House *See pp102–105*

National Air and Space Museum
See pp60–63

Vietnam Veterans Memorial
See p79

National Gallery of Art
See pp56–9

Kennedy Center
See pp112–3

National Cathedral
See pp136–7

Arlington National Cemetery
See pp124–5

Washington Monument
See p74

Lincoln Memorial
See p78

US Capitol
See pp48–9

◁ **View from the US Capitol looking down Pennsylvania Avenue**

Museums and Galleries in Washington, DC

FEW CITIES CAN CLAIM to have as many museums and galleries in such a concentrated area as Washington. The Mall forms the main focus because it is lined with museums, most of which are owned by the Smithsonian Institution *(see p68)*. They cover a wide range of exhibits, from great works of art to space shuttles to mementos of major events in American history. Admission to most of the museums and galleries is free.

National Museum of American History
This statue of a toga-clad George Washington is one of millions of artifacts in this museum of American history (see pp70–73).

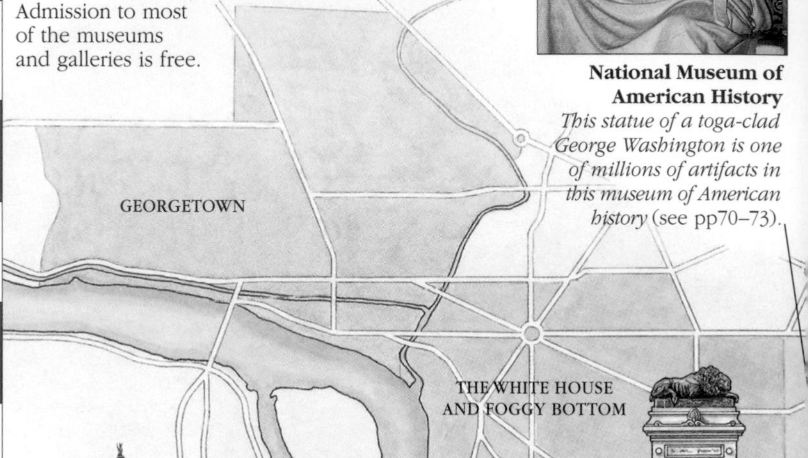

GEORGETOWN

THE WHITE HOUSE AND FOGGY BOTTOM

Tidal Basin

Potomac River

Corcoran Gallery of Art
This Beaux Arts building houses a collection of American and European art and sculpture, including some of the best works by US artists of the 19th and 20th centuries (see p107).

US Holocaust Memorial Museum
Photographs, videos, and re-created concentration camp barracks bring to life the brutality of the Holocaust and movingly illustrate the terrible fate of Jews in World War II Nazi Germany (see pp76–7).

National Museum of Natural History
A huge African elephant is the focal point of the building's main foyer. The museum's fascinating exhibits trace the evolution of animals and explain the creation of gems and minerals (see pp66–7).

National Portrait Gallery and Smithsonian American Art Museum
This Neoclassical building houses the world's largest collection of American paintings, sculpture, photographs, and crafts (see pp92–5).

0 meters 500

0 yards 500

OLD DOWNTOWN

CAPITOL HILL

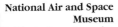

HE MALL

National Gallery of Art
The futuristic East Building houses the 20th-century art in this collection, while the 1930s West Building is home to older works (see pp56–9).

National Air and Space Museum
Washington's most popular museum has exhibits from aviation and space history, including the Wright Brothers' first airborne plane and the Apollo 14 space module (see pp60–63).

Monuments and Memorials in Washington, DC

As THE POLITICAL CENTER of the United States, and home of its president, Washington has a great number of monuments and memorials honoring America's key figures and historic events. The most well-known among these are the Washington Monument and the Lincoln Memorial – sights of great interest to all who visit the city. For those who wish to remember the countless men and women who lost their lives fighting for their nation, there are poignant monuments, set in tranquil parks, where visitors can reflect in peace.

Korean War Veterans Memorial
Created in 1995, the 19 stainless steel, life-size statues of this memorial recall the thousands who died in the Korean War of 1950–53 (see p78).

GEORGETOWN

Lincoln Memorial
This emotive and inspirational marble figure has often been the focus of civil rights protests (see p78).

Iwo Jima Memorial
This impressive memorial, situated near Arlington Cemetery, depicts US Marines capturing the Japanese island of Iwo Jima at the end of World War II (see p126).

Potomac River

Vietnam Veterans Memorial
Visitors to this dramatic memorial are confronted by a sobering list of names on the V-shaped granite walls (see p79).

Washington Monument
*One of the most enduring images of
Washington, this 555-ft (170-m) marble
obelisk can be seen from all over the city.
Built in two parts, the monument was
finally completed in 1884 (see p74).*

Jefferson Memorial
*This Neoclassical building
houses a bronze statue of
President Jefferson, the key
player in America's struggle
for independence (see p75).*

E WHITE
USE AND
OGGY
OTTOM

OLD
DOWNTOWN

THE MALL

CAPITOL HILL

0 meters 500

0 yards 500

Franklin D. Roosevelt Memorial
*This vast memorial, in the form of a 7-
acre park, includes statuary, waterfalls,
and ornamental gardens (see pp78–9).*

WASHINGTON, DC
THROUGH THE YEAR

A WIDE VARIETY of events takes place in Washington, DC all through the year. In early April, when the famous cherry blossoms bloom, the city really comes to life. Parades and outdoor festivals begin, and continue through the summer as more and more people come to explore the DC area in June, July, and August.

Patriotic member of the public celebrating Independence Day

The White House is the main focus for visitors, and it plays host to many annual events during all seasons – the Easter Egg Roll in the spring, concerts throughout the summer and fall, and a Candlelight tour at Christmas. Some of the more popular events are listed below; for further details contact the Washington, DC Convention and Visitors Association *(see p195)*.

SPRING

THE AIR IS clear in springtime in Washington, DC, with crisp mornings and warm, balmy days. The cherry tree blossoms surrounding the Tidal Basin are world famous and should not be missed, although the area does get very busy. Memorial Day is a big event in DC; it marks the official beginning of summer, and is celebrated in many ways.

MARCH

Washington Home and Garden Show, DC Convention Center, 900 9th St, NW. ☎ 789-1600. A vast array of garden items is displayed.
St. Patrick's Day *(Mar 17)*, Constitution Ave, NW. Parade celebrating Irish culture, with food, music, and dancing. There are also celebrations in Old Town Alexandria.

Smithsonian Kite Festival *(last Saturday)*, Washington Monument. ☎ 357-2700. Kite designers fly their best models and compete for prizes.

APRIL

National Cherry Blossom Festival *(early Apr)*, Constitution Ave, NW. ☎ 619-7222. Parade, concerts, and dancing to celebrate the blooming of Washington's famous trees.
White House Egg Roll *(Easter Mon)*, White House Lawn. ☎ 456-2200. Children from three to six, aided by an adult, roll eggs in a race across the lawn.
Imagination Celebration *(Sept–May)*, Kennedy Center. ☎ 467-4600. A series of plays aimed at young children.
Thomas Jefferson's Birthday *(Apr 13)*, Jefferson Memorial. ☎ 619-7222. Military drills, speeches, and wreath-laying.
Shakespeare's Birthday Celebration *(end of Apr)*, Folger Shakespeare Library,

Mother-and-daughter team in the Easter Egg Roll at the White House

201 E Capitol St. ☎ 544-7077. A day of music, plays, food, exhibits, and children's events in honor of the Bard's birthday.

MAY

Goodwill Embassy Tour, An annual tour that includes several embassies. Tickets go on sale in March. ☎ 636-4225, *extension 1211.*
Flower Mart *(first weekend)*, Washington National Cathedral. ☎ 537-2223. Flower booths, music, and demonstrations.
Memorial Day Weekend Concert *(last Sun)*, West Lawn of Capitol. ☎ 619-7222. National Symphony Orchestra performs.
Memorial Day *(last Mon)*, Arlington National Cemetery. ☎ *(703) 607-8052.* US Navy Memorial. ☎ 737-2300. Vietnam Veterans Memorial. ☎ 426-6841. Wreath-laying, speeches, and music to honor war veterans.
Memorial Day Jazz Festival *(last Mon)*, Old Town Alexandria. ☎ *(703) 883-4686.* Live, big-band jazz music.

Cherry tree blossoms surrounding Jefferson Memorial at the Tidal Basin

AVERAGE DAYS OF SUNSHINE PER MONTH

Days
25
20
15
10
5
0
Jan Feb Mar Apr May Jun Jul Aug Sep Oct Nov Dec

Sunshine Chart
The amount of sunshine per month in Washington does not vary greatly – even in winter months half the days will enjoy blue skies. In summer the sunshine is at its most persistent, although it is best to be prepared for the occasional rainstorm. The chart gives the number of days per month with little or no cloud.

SUMMER

IN JUNE, JULY, and August, visitors come to Washington, DC from far and wide. The streets and parks are packed with people enjoying the sunshine. Many attractions become overcrowded, so it is important to call ahead and make reservations at this time of year.

The summer months can also be extremely hot and humid; even so, parades and outdoor fairs are usually very popular. Independence Day on July 4 is particularly exciting, with a parade during the day and fireworks at night.

JUNE

Shakespeare Free for All
(throughout Jun), Carter Barron Amphitheater, Rock Creek Park. **C** *547-3230/619-7222.* Nightly performances by the Shakespeare Theater Company, free of charge.
Alexandria Waterfront Festival *(first or second weekend)*, Oronoco Bay Park, Alexandria. **C** *(703) 549-8300.* Tall ships, games, and music celebrating maritime history.
Smithsonian Festival of American Folklife *(late Jun early Jul)*, The Mall. **C** *357-2700.* A huge celebration of folk culture, including music, dance, games, and food.
Washington National Cathedral Summer Festival of Music *(mid-Jun mid-Jul)*, Washington National Cathedral. **C** *537-6200.* A varied program of modern and classical concerts.
Dance Africa *(mid-Jun)*, Dance Place, 3225 8th St, NE. **C** *269-1600.* African dance, street markets, and concerts.

Fireworks over Washington, DC on the Fourth of July

JULY

Independence Day *(Jul 4)*, Constitution Ave & US Capitol. A parade along Constitution Avenue, with fireworks from the steps of the US Capitol.
Bastille Day *(Jul 14)*, Les Halles Restaurant, 1201 Pennsylvania Ave, NW. Racing waiters and live entertainment.
Twilight Tattoo Military Pageant *(7pm every Wed, Apr–Aug)*, Ellipse south of the White House. **C** *685-2851.* Military parade presenting the history of the US Army.

Mary McLeod Bethune Celebration *(Jul 10)*, Bethune Statue, Lincoln Palk, E Capitol St, SE, between 11th St & 13th St. **C** *673-2402.* Memorial wreath-laying, gospel music, and speeches.
Caribbean Summer in the Park *(mid-Jul)*, RFK Stadium, 2400 E Capitol St, SE. **C** *547-9077.* Music, food, and dancing, Caribbean style.
Hispanic-Latino Festival *(late Jul)*, Washington Monument. **C** *426-6841.* Music, food, and celebration of 40 Latin American Nations.

AUGUST

Arlington County Fair *(mid-Aug)*, Thomas Jefferson Center, Arlington, VA. **C** *(703) 228-4747.* Food, crafts, music, and fairground rides.
Georgia Avenue Day *(end of Aug)*, Georgia Ave, NW. A parade plus food, stalls, rides, and music.
National Frisbee Festival *(late Aug)*, Washington Monument. **C** *426-6841.* A weekend celebrating the game of Frisbee, including a free Frisbee contest for champions and amateurs alike.

A frenzy of Frisbee throwing at Washington's National Frisbee Festival

AVERAGE MONTHLY RAINFALL

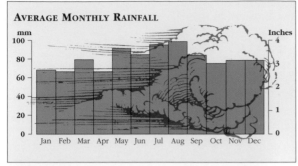

Rainfall Chart
It is impossible to escape the rain completely in Washington. The heaviest rainfall occurs during the summer months of May through August, when rain can come as a welcome break from the humidity. Rainfall tails off in the fall months of September and October and reaches its lowest ebb in late winter. Rain rarely lingers for long in the city.

A school band performing in Constitution Gardens

FALL

WITH THE AIR turning cooler, Labor Day (the first Monday in September) bids goodbye to the summer. The fall (autumn) season covers September, October, and November in Washington, when the temperatures steadily drop. A particularly enjoyable event at this time of year is Halloween, when children dress up as their favorite creatures or characters to go trick-or-treating.

Halloween Jack-O'-Lantern

SEPTEMBER

Labor Day Weekend Concert *(Sun before Labor Day)*, West Lawn of the US Capitol. **C** *619-7222.* National Symphony Orchestra performs a concert.
John F. Kennedy Center for the Performing Arts Open House *(early Sep).* **C** *416-8341.* A one-day celebration with performances of blues, rock, jazz, dance, drama, and film.

International Children's Festival, Wolf Trap Park, Vienna, VA. **C** *(703) 642-5000.* Performers come from around the world.
18th-century Fair, Mount Vernon, VA. **C** *(703) 780-2000.* Craft demonstrations and 18th-century entertainment.

OCTOBER

Taste of DC *(weekend before the second Mon)*, Pennsylvania Ave, NW. **C** *724-4093.* A food festival by street restaurants.
Columbus Day *(second Mon)*, Columbus Memorial, Union Station. **C** *289-1908.* Speeches and wreath-laying celebrate the man who discovered America.
White House Fall Garden Tours *(mid-Oct).* **C** *208-1631.* Opportunity to walk the grounds of the President's home, accompanied by military band concerts.
Halloween *(Oct 31).* Trick-or-treating is popular with young children. They appear on the

streets of Washington dressed as ghosts, clowns, witches, or favorite cartoon characters. Dupont Circle and Georgetown are popular areas.

NOVEMBER

Annual Seafaring Celebration *(date varies)*, Navy Museum. **C** *433-4882.* A maritime event for the whole family with food, music, and naval displays.
Veterans Day Ceremonies *(Nov 11)*, Arlington National Cemetery. **C** *(703) 607-8052.* Services, parades, and wreath-layings at various memorials around the city, commemorating United States military personnel who died in war. There are special Veterans Day ceremonies also at the Vietnam Veterans Memorial *(**C** 619-7222)* and at the US Navy Memorial *(**C** 737-2300).*
Kennedy Center Holiday Festival *(late Nov- New Year's Eve).* **C** *467-4600.* Free performances.

Military guard on Veterans Day in Arlington National Cemetery

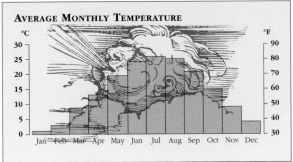

AVERAGE MONTHLY TEMPERATURE

°C / °F chart with months: Jan Feb Mar Apr May Jun Jul Aug Sep Oct Nov Dec

Temperature Chart
Washington's climate varies greatly. In winter the air is bitterly cold, with temperatures rising little above freezing. In July and August, however, it becomes very hot and extremely humid. The best time to visit the city is in the spring or fall, when the weather is pleasantly mild and the air is clear.

WINTER

TEMPERATURES can plummet below freezing during the winter months of December, January, and February. Hence the city is generally quieter at this time of year, making it a good time to see the most popular sights. Over the Christmas period, Washington becomes busy again with festive events to get people into the holiday spirit. Decorations are visible across the city, and many places, including the White House, offer Christmas tours.

Toward the end of winter, a number of famous birthdays are celebrated, including those of Martin Luther King Jr. and Presidents Abraham Lincoln and George Washington.

DECEMBER

National Christmas Tree Lighting *(mid-Dec)*, Ellipse south of the White House. **C** *208-1631.* The President turns on the lights on the National Christmas tree.

Washington National Cathedral Christmas Services *(throughout Dec).* **C** *537-2223.* Holiday celebrations with festive music.
White House Candlelight Tours *(after Christmas).* **C** *208-1631 or 456-7041.* The President's Christmas decorations on display to the public.

JANUARY

Robert E. Lee's Birthday *(mid-Jan)*, Arlington National Cemetery (**C** *(703) 235-1530)* and Old Town Alexandria, VA. **C** *(703) 548-1789.* Commemoration at Lee's house in Alexandria.
Martin Luther King Jr.'s Birthday *(third Mon)*, Lincoln Memorial. **C** *426-6841.* A recording of King's "I Have A Dream" speech is played.

FEBRUARY

Chinese New Year *(first two weeks)*, N St, Chinatown. **C** *789-7000.* Parades, dancing, and live music.
African American History Month *(throughout Feb).*

Various events across the city: contact the Smithsonian (**C** *357-2700)* and the National Park Service (**C** *426-6841).*
George Washington's Birthday Parade *(around Feb 15)*, Old Town Alexandria, VA. **C** *(703) 838-4200.*
Abraham Lincoln's Birthday, *(Feb 12)*, Lincoln Memorial. **C** *426-6841.* A wreath-laying ceremony and reading of the Gettysburg Address.

Girl Scouts watching George Washington's Birthday Parade

FEDERAL HOLIDAYS

New Year's Day (Jan 1)
Martin Luther King Jr.'s Birthday
(3rd Mon in Jan)
Presidents' Day
(3rd Mon in Feb)
Easter Monday
(Mar or Apr)
Memorial Day
(last Mon in May)
Independence Day
(Jul 4)
Labor Day
(1st Mon in Sep)
Columbus Day
(2nd Mon in Oct)
Veterans Day (Nov 11)
Thanksgiving
(4th Thu in Nov)
Christmas Day
(Dec 25)

The National Christmas tree outside a snow-covered White House

WASHINGTON, DC
AREA BY AREA

CAPITOL HILL

OON AFTER the Constitution was ratified in 1788, America's seat of government began to take root on Capitol Hill. The site was chosen in 1791 from 10 acres that were ceded by the state of Maryland. Pierre L'Enfant *(see p17)* chose a hill on the east side of the area as the foundation for the Capitol building and the center of the new city.

In more than 200 years, Capitol Hill has developed into a bustling microcosm of modern America.

Statue of Roman Legionnaire at Union Station

Symbols of the country's cultural development are everywhere, from its federal buildings to its centers of commerce, shops, and restaurants, as well as residential areas for a wide variety of people.

The Capitol Hill area is frequented by the most powerful people in the United States, yet at the same time, ordinary citizens are able to petition their congressional representatives here, or pose for a photograph with them on the steps of the Capitol building.

SIGHTS AT A GLANCE

Historic Buildings
Folger Shakespeare Library ❷
Library of Congress pp44–5 ❶
Sewall-Belmont House ❹
Union Station ⓮
US Capitol pp48–9 ❺
US Supreme Court ❸

Museums and Galleries
Capital Children's Museum ⓭
National Postal Museum ⓯

Market
Eastern Market ⓬

Monuments and Memorials
National Japanese American Memorial ❼

Robert A. Taft Memorial ❻
Ulysses S. Grant Memorial ❽

Parks and Gardens
Bartholdi Park and Fountain ❿
US Botanic Garden ❾

Church
Ebenezer United Methodist Church ⓫

KEY
▦	Street-by-street map *pp42–3*
Ⓜ	Metro station
ℹ	Tourist information
🚓	Police
P	Parking
⊠	Post office
🚆	Train station

0 meters	500
0 yards	500

GETTING THERE
The best way to get to Capitol Hill is by Metro. Take the red line to Union Station, or the blue or orange line to Capitol South, Eastern Market, or Federal Center SW. Metrobuses 30, 32, 34, 35, and 36 stop at various points on Capitol Hill.

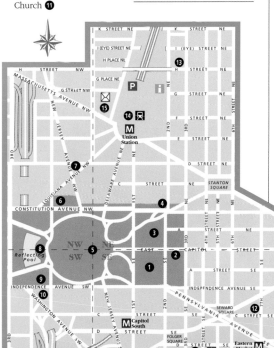

◁ **The stunning front doors of the Supreme Court surrounded by Corinthian columns**

Street-by-Street: Capitol Hill

THE CITYSCAPE EXTENDING from the Capitol is an impressive combination of grand classical architecture and stretches of grassy open spaces. There are no skyscrapers here, only the immense marble halls and columns that distinguish many of the government buildings. The bustle and excitement around the US Capitol and US Supreme Court contrast with the calm that can be found by a reflecting pool or in a quiet residential street. Many of the small touches that make the city special can be found in this area, such as the antique lighting fixtures on Second Street, the brilliant bursts of flowers along the sidewalks, or the brightly painted façades of houses on Third Street near the Folger Shakespeare Library.

★ **US Capitol**
The famous dome of the nation's seat of government is one of the largest in the world ❺

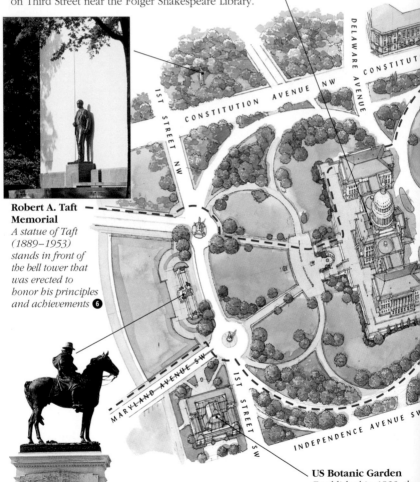

Robert A. Taft Memorial
A statue of Taft (1889–1953) stands in front of the bell tower that was erected to honor his principles and achievements ❻

Ulysses S. Grant Memorial
General Grant (1822–85), the Union leader in the American Civil War, is the central figure in a remarkable group of bronze equestrian statuary ❼

US Botanic Garden
Established in 1820, the Botanic Garden contain thousands of exotic and domestic plants ❽

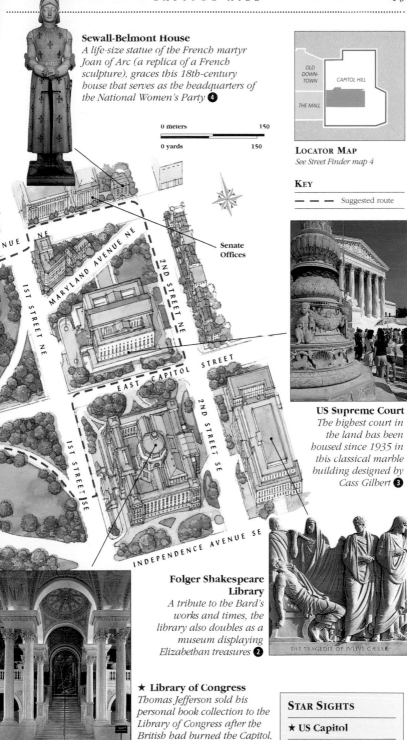

Sewall-Belmont House
A life-size statue of the French martyr Joan of Arc (a replica of a French sculpture), graces this 18th-century house that serves as the headquarters of the National Women's Party ❹

| 0 meters | 150 |
| 0 yards | 150 |

LOCATOR MAP
See Street Finder map 4

KEY

― ― ― Suggested route

Senate Offices

US Supreme Court
The highest court in the land has been housed since 1935 in this classical marble building designed by Cass Gilbert ❸

THE TRAGEDIE OF IVLIVS CÆSAR

Folger Shakespeare Library
A tribute to the Bard's works and times, the library also doubles as a museum displaying Elizabethan treasures ❷

★ Library of Congress
Thomas Jefferson sold his personal book collection to the Library of Congress after the British had burned the Capitol, which housed the Library, using the books as kindling ❶

STAR SIGHTS

★ US Capitol

★ Library of Congress

Library of Congress ❶

Thomas Jefferson (1743–1826)

Congress first established a reference library in the U.S. Capitol in 1800. When the Capitol was burned in 1814, Thomas Jefferson offered his own collection as a replacement, his belief in a universality of knowledge becoming the foundation for the Library's acquisition policy. In 1897 the Library of Congress moved to a new Italian Renaissance-style main building designed by John L. Smithmeyer and Paul J. Pelz. The main building, now known as the Thomas Jefferson Building, is a marvel of art and architecture, with its paintings and mosaics, and several exhibitions, including World Treasures and the Bob Hope Gallery of American Entertainment. The Library of Congress has the world's largest collection of books and special materials.

Front façade of the Jefferson Building

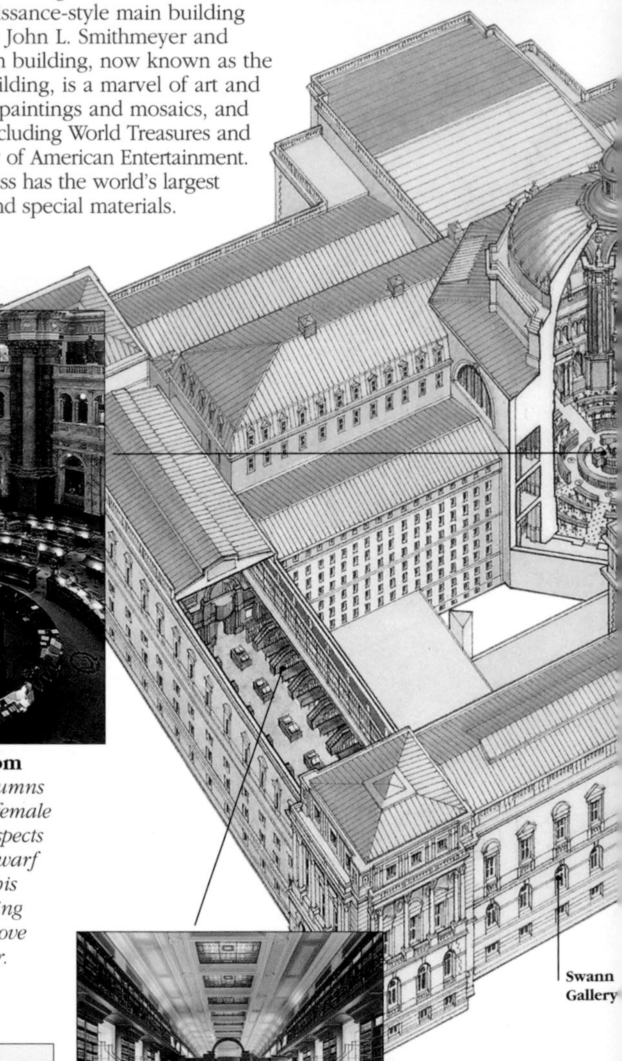

★ **Main Reading Room**
Eight huge marble columns and 10-ft (3-m) high female figures personifying aspects of human endeavor dwarf the reading desks in this room. The domed ceiling soars 160 ft (49 m) above the reading room floor.

Swann Gallery

African & Middle Eastern Reading Room
This is one of 10 reading rooms in the Jefferson Building where visitors can use books from the Library's collections.

STAR SIGHTS

★ **Great Hall**

★ **Gutenberg Bible**

★ **Main Reading Room**

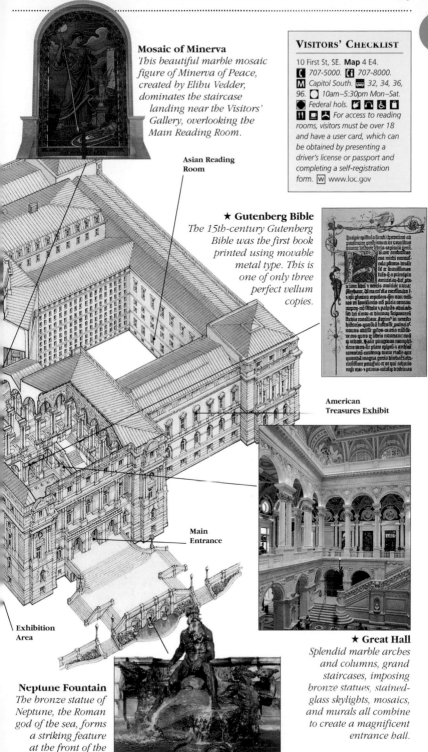

Mosaic of Minerva
This beautiful marble mosaic figure of Minerva of Peace, created by Elihu Vedder, dominates the staircase landing near the Visitors' Gallery, overlooking the Main Reading Room.

Asian Reading Room

★ Gutenberg Bible
The 15th-century Gutenberg Bible was the first book printed using movable metal type. This is one of only three perfect vellum copies.

American Treasures Exhibit

Main Entrance

Exhibition Area

Neptune Fountain
The bronze statue of Neptune, the Roman god of the sea, forms a striking feature at the front of the Jefferson Building.

★ Great Hall
Splendid marble arches and columns, grand staircases, imposing bronze statues, stained-glass skylights, mosaics, and murals all combine to create a magnificent entrance hall.

Folger Shakespeare Library **❷**

201 E Capitol St, SE. **Map** 4 F4.
[544-7077. **M** Capitol South.
○ 10am–4pm Mon–Sat. **●** federal
hols. **[✔] [&]** Tickets for plays, concerts,
and readings available from box office.
[W] www.folger.edu

INSPIRED BY Shakespeare's own era, this library and museum celebrate the works and times of the Elizabethan playwright.

The research library was a gift to the American people in 1932 from Henry Clay Folger who, as a student in 1874, began to collect Shakespeare's works. Folger also funded the construction of this edifice, built specifically to house his collection. It contains 310,000 Elizabethan books and manuscripts, as well as the world's largest collection of Shakespeare's writings, including a third of the surviving copies of the 1623 First Folio (first editions of Shakespeare's works). One of these first editions is displayed in the oak-paneled Great Hall, along with books and engravings.

The Shakespeare Gallery presents the Elizabethan Age through a multimedia exhibition based around "The Seven Ages of Man" from the comedy *As You Like It* (c. 1599).

The Folger hosts many cultural events. For example, There are regular performances of Shakespeare's plays in the library's 250-seat Elizabethan theater. There is

The Great Hall in the Folger Shakespeare Library

also an annual series of poetry readings, as well as numerous lectures and talks throughout the year. The acclaimed Folger Consort early music ensemble, performs concerts of 12th- to 20th-century music.

US Supreme Court **❸**

1st St between E Capitol St and
Maryland Ave. **Map** 4 E4.
[479-3000. **M** Capitol South.
○ 9am–4:30pm Mon–Fri.
● federal hols. **[▯] [▭] [&]** **Lectures.**

THE SUPREME COURT forms the judicial and third branch of the US government (see pp26–7). It was established in 1787 at the Philadelphia Constitutional Convention and provides the last stop in the disposition of the nation's legal disputes and issues of constitutionality. Groundbreaking cases settled here include *Brown v. Board of Education*, which abolished racial segregation in schools, and *Miranda v. Arizona*, which declared crime suspects were entitled to a lawyer before

The impressive Neoclassical façade of the US Supreme Court

being interrogated. The Court is charged to guarantee "Equal Justice Under Law," the motto emblazoned over the entrance.

As recently as 1929 the Supreme Court was still meeting in various sections of the US Capitol building. Then, at Chief Justice William Howard Taft's urging, Congress authorized a separate building to be constructed. The result was a magnificent Corinthian edifice, designed by Cass Gilbert, that opened in 1935. Sculptures depicting the allegorical figures of the Contemplation of Justice and the Guardian of the Law stand beside the steps while on the pediment above the entrance are figures of Taft (far left) and John Marshall, the fourth Chief Justice (far right).

Visitors are permitted to watch the court in session Monday to Wednesday from October through April. Admission is on a first-come, first-served basis. When court is not in session, public lectures on the Supreme Court are held every hour on the half-hour in the Courtroom (contact for confirmation).

Sewall-Belmont House **4**

144 Constitution Ave, NE. **Map** 4 E4.
(546-1210. **M** Capitol South,
Union Station. **◯** 11am–3pm
Tue–Fri, noon–4pm Sat. **●** federal
hols. **Donations welcome.** **☑** **☐**
W www.sewallbelmont.org

ROBERT SEWALL, the original
owner of this charming
18th-century house, rented it
out to Albert Gallatin, the
Treasury Secretary under
President Thomas Jefferson,
in the early 1800s. It was here
Gallatin entertained a number
of wealthy contributors whose
financial backing brought

**Hallway of the 18th-century
Sewall-Belmont House**

about the Louisiana Purchase
in 1803, which doubled the
size of the United States. During the British invasion in
1814, the house was the only
site in Washington to resist
the attack. While the US
Capitol was burning,
American soldiers took refuge
in the house from where they
fired upon the British.
   The National Women's Party,
who won the right to vote for
American women in 1920,
bought the house in 1929
with the help of feminist
divorcee Alva Vanderbilt
Belmont. Today, the house is
still the headquarters of the
Party, and visitors can admire
the period furnishings and
suffragist artifacts. The desk
on which the, as yet unratified,
Equal Rights Amendment of
1923 was written by Alice Paul,
leader of the Party, is here.

US Capitol **5**

See pp48–9.

Robert A. Taft Memorial **6**

Constitution Ave and 1st St,
NW. **Map** 4 E4. **M** Union
Station. **&**

THIS STATUE of Ohio
senator Robert A. Taft
(1889–1953) stands in a
park opposite the US
Capitol. The statue
itself, by sculptor
Wheeler Williams, is
dwarfed by a vast, white bell
tower that rises up behind the
figure of the politician. The
memorial, designed by
Douglas W. Orr, was erected
in 1959 as a "tribute to the
honesty, indomitable courage,
and high principles of free
government symbolized by his
life." The son of President
William Howard Taft, Robert
Taft was a Republican,
famous for sponsoring the
Taft-Hartley Act, the regulator
of collective bargaining
between labor and
management.

National Japanese American Memorial **7**

Louisiana and New Jersey Avenues at
D St, NW. **Map** 4 E3. **M** Union
Station.

THIS MEMORIAL, designed by
Davis Buckley, commem-
orates the story of the 120,000

Japanese Americans interned
during World War II and the
more than 800 Japanese
Americans who died in
military service. The
names of these service-
men are carved upon a
curving granite wall,
while etched on the
top are the names of
the ten detention camps
where Japanese American
civilians were confined.
An 18-foot long aluminum
bell may be rung by
visitors, serving as a
call to reflection and
remembrance.

**Statue of
Robert Taft**

Ulysses S. Grant Memorial **8**

Union Square, west side of US Capitol
in front of Reflecting Pool. **Map** 4 E4.
M Capitol South, Union Station. **&**

THIS DRAMATIC memorial was
sculpted by Henry Merwin
Shrady and dedicated in 1922.
With its 13 horses, it is one
of the world's most complex
equestrian statues. The bronze
groupings around General
Grant provide a graphic depiction of the suffering of
the Civil War. In the artillery
group, horses and soldiers
pulling a cannon are urged
on by their mounted leader,
the staff of his upraised flag
broken. The infantry group
storms into the heat of battle,
where a horse and rider have
already fallen under the charge.
   Shrady worked on the
sculpture for 20 years, using
soldiers in training for his
models. He died two weeks
before it was dedicated.

The artillery group in the Ulysses S. Grant Civil War Memorial

United States Capitol ❺

THE US CAPITOL IS ONE of the world's best-known symbols of democracy. The center of America's legislative process for 200 years, its Neoclassical architecture reflects the principles of ancient Greece and Rome that influenced the development of America's political system. The cornerstone was laid by George Washington in 1793, and by 1800 the Capitol was occupied, although it was unfinished. With more funding, construction resumed under architect Benjamin Latrobe, but the British burned the Capitol in the War of 1812. Restoration began in 1815. Many architectural and artistic features, such as the Statue of Freedom and Brumidi's murals, were added later.

The Dome
Originally a wood and copper construction, the dome was designed by Thomas U. Walter.

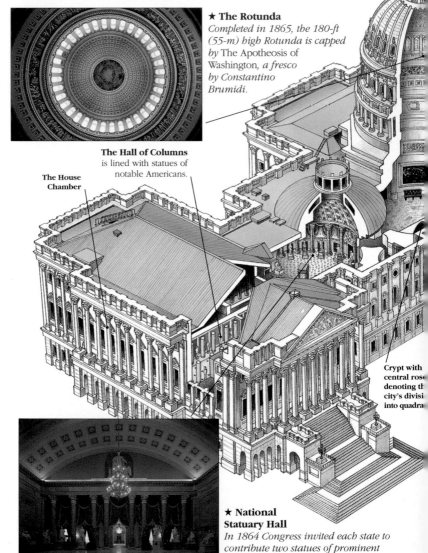

★ The Rotunda
Completed in 1865, the 180-ft (55-m) high Rotunda is capped by The Apotheosis of Washington, *a fresco by Constantino Brumidi.*

The Hall of Columns
is lined with statues of notable Americans.

The House Chamber

Crypt with central rose denoting the city's division into quadrants

★ National Statuary Hall
In 1864 Congress invited each state to contribute two statues of prominent citizens to stand in this hall.

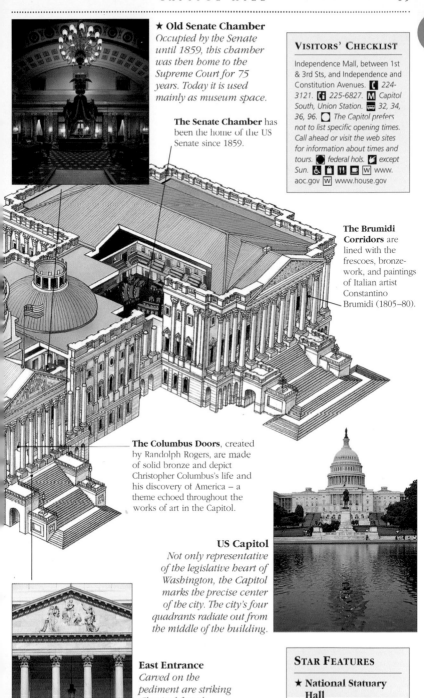

★ Old Senate Chamber
Occupied by the Senate until 1859, this chamber was then home to the Supreme Court for 75 years. Today it is used mainly as museum space.

The Senate Chamber has been the home of the US Senate since 1859.

The Brumidi Corridors are lined with the frescoes, bronze-work, and paintings of Italian artist Constantino Brumidi (1805–80).

The Columbus Doors, created by Randolph Rogers, are made of solid bronze and depict Christopher Columbus's life and his discovery of America – a theme echoed throughout the works of art in the Capitol.

US Capitol
Not only representative of the legislative heart of Washington, the Capitol marks the precise center of the city. The city's four quadrants radiate out from the middle of the building.

East Entrance
Carved on the pediment are striking Classical female representations of America. These are flanked by figures of Justice and Hope.

STAR FEATURES

★ **National Statuary Hall**

★ **Old Senate Chamber**

★ **The Rotunda**

US Botanic Garden ❾

1st St and Maryland Ave, SW. **Map** 4
D4. 📞 225-8333. Ⓜ *Federal Center
SW.* ◯ *call for details.* ◑ *Federal hols.*
🖼 🎫 ♿ 🆆 www.aoc.gov/usbg

A FTER A three-year renovation, the Botanic Garden
reopened with better exhibits
than ever, the 80-ft (24-m) tall
Palm House being the
centerpiece of the Conservatory. The appearance of the
1933 buildings has been preserved but modernized,
creating a spacious venue for
the collection of tropical and
subtropical plants, and the
comprehensive fern and orchid
collections. Other specialties
are plants native to deserts
in the Old and New Worlds,
plants of economic and
healing value, and endangered
plants rescued through an
international trade program.

The Botanic Garden was originally established by Congress
in 1820 to cultivate plants that
could be beneficial to the
American people. The garden
was revitalized in 1842, when
the Wilkes Expedition to the
South Seas brought back an
assortment of plants from
around the world, some of
which are still are on display.

A National Garden of plants
native to the mid-Atlantic
region was created on three
acres next to the Conservatory.
It includes a Showcase
Garden, a Water Garden, a
Rose Garden, and an Environ-
mental Learning Center.

Bartholdi Park and Fountain ❿

Independence Ave and 1st St, SW.
Map 4 D4. Ⓜ *Federal Center SW.* ♿
🆆 www.aco.gov/usbg/barthold.htm

T HE GRACEFUL fountain that
dominates this jewel of a
park was created by Frédéric
August Bartholdi (sculptor of
the Statue of Liberty) for the
1876 Centennial. Originally lit
by gas, it was converted to
electric lighting in 1881 and
became a nighttime attraction.

Made of cast iron, the sym-
metrical fountain is decorated
with figures of nymphs and

**The elegant Bartholdi Fountain,
surrounded by miniature gardens**

tritons. Surrounding the fountain are tiny model gardens,
planted to inspire the urban
gardener. They are themed,
and include Therapeutic,
Romantic, and Heritage plants,
such as Virginia sneezeweed,
sweet william, and wild oats.

Ebenezer United Methodist Church ⓫

4th St & D St, SE. 📞 544-9539.
Map 4 F5. Ⓜ *Eastern Market.* ◯
10am–3pm Tue–Fri. ◑ *Federal hols.*

E BENEZER CHURCH, established
in 1819, was the first black
church to serve Methodists in
Washington. Attendance grew
rapidly and a new church,
Little Ebenezer, was built to
take the overflow. After the

Emancipation Proclamation in
1863 *(see p19)*, Congress
decreed that black children
should receive public education. So in 1864, Little
Ebenezer became the home
for the District of Columbia's
first school for black children.
The number of members grew
and another church was built
in 1868, but this was badly
damaged by a storm in 1896.
The replacement church, built
in 1897 and still here today,
is Ebenezer United Methodist
Church. A model of Little
Ebenezer, now no longer in
existence, stands next to it.

Eastern Market ⓬

7th St and C St, SE. 📞 546-2698.
Map 4 F4. Ⓜ *Eastern Market.* ◯
7am–6pm Tue–Sat, 9am–4pm Sun.
◑ *Mon, Jan 1, Jul 4, Thanksgiving,
Dec 25 & 26.* ♿ *at West end.*

T HIS BLOCK-LONG market
hall has been a fixture in
Capitol Hill since 1871, and
the provisions sold today still
have an Old World flavor. Big
beefsteaks and fresh pigs' feet
are plentiful, along with gourmet sausages and cheeses
from all over the world. The
aroma of fresh bread, roasted
chicken, and flowers pervades
the hall. On Saturdays, the
covered stalls outside are
filled with crafts and farmers'
produce, while on Sundays
they host a flea market.

The redbrick, late 19th-century Ebenezer United Methodist Church

Decorative frieze on the sidewalk outside the Capital Children's Museum

Capital Children's Museum ⑬

800 3rd St, NE. **Map** 4 F2. 675-4120. Ⓜ *Union Station.* ◯ *10am–5pm daily.* ● *Jan 1, week after Labor Day, Thanksgiving, Dec 25.* ⚐ & Ⓦ www.ccm.org

Tʜᴇ ᴄʟᴀᴍᴏʀ of exuberant children echoes throughout this rambling complex, which is less museum and more an experience of art, culture, and science. A garden of fantasy characters created out of scrap materials by Indian artist Nek Chand sets the tone at the entrance. Inside, children can make crafts and tortillas in a re-created Mexican village, experiment with a giant bubble machine, and negotiate a maze.

An animation exhibit, featuring the work of Chuck Jones, shows how a cartoon is made. Children can "become" a cartoon character in the video studio. In the Chemical Science Center, a chemist dramatizes the mysteries of dry ice and other natural phenomena.

Two popular play areas are the fire station and the Ice Age cave. The newest exhibits are a real Metro train car and Japan through a child's eyes.

Union Station ⑭

50 Massachusetts Ave, NE. **Map** 4 E3. 371-9441. Ⓜ *Union Station.* ◯ *daily.* ⚑ ⑪ ⚐ *by appt.* & Ⓦ www.unionstationdc.com

Wʜᴇɴ ᴜɴɪᴏɴ sᴛᴀᴛɪᴏɴ opened in 1908, its fine Beaux Arts design set a standard that influenced architecture in Washington for 40 years. The elegantly proportioned white granite structure, its three main archways modeled on

the Arch of Constantine in Rome, was the largest train station in the world. For half a century, Union Station was a major transportation hub, but as air travel became increasingly popular, passenger trains went into decline.

By the late 1950s, the size of the station outweighed the number of passsengers it served. For two decades, the railroad authorities and Congress debated its fate. Finally, in 1981, a joint public and private venture set out to restore the building.

Union Station reopened in 1988, and today is the second most visited tourist attraction in Washington. Its 96-ft (29-m) barrel-vaulted ceiling has been covered with 22-carat gold leaf. There are around 100 specialty shops and a food court to visit, and the Main Hall hosts cultural and civic events throughout the year. The building still serves its original purpose as a station, however, and over 100 trains pass through daily.

Vintage stamp depicting Benjamin Franklin

National Postal Museum ⑮

1st St and Massachusetts Ave, NE. **Map** 4 E3. 357-2700. Ⓜ *Union Station.* ◯ *10am–5:30pm daily.* ● *Dec 25.* ⚑ ⚐ & Ⓦ www.si.edu/postal

Oᴘᴇɴᴇᴅ ʙʏ the Smithsonian in 1990, this fascinating museum is housed in the former City Post Office building. Exhibits include a stagecoach and a postal rail car, showing how mail traveled before modern airmail.

The "Art of Cards and Letters" exhibit highlights the personal and artistic nature of correspondence. "Stamps and Stories" displays some of the museum's vast stamp collection. Multimedia exhibits illustrate how the mail system works and how a stamp is created.

At postcard kiosks, visitors can address a postcard electronically, see the route it will take to its destination, and, for the price of a stamp, drop it in a mailbox on the spot.

Columbus Memorial, sculpted by Lorado Taft, in front of Union Station

THE MALL

N L'ENFANT'S ORIGINAL plan for the new capital of the United States, the Mall was conceived as a grand boulevard lined with diplomatic residences of elegant, Parisian architecture. L'Enfant's plan was never fully realized, but it is nevertheless a moving sight – this grand, tree-lined expanse is bordered on either side by the Smithsonian museums and features the Capitol at its eastern end and the Washington Monument at its western end. This dramatic formal version of the Mall did not materialize until after World War II. Until then the space was used for everything from a zoo to a railroad

Gold mirror back, Sackler Gallery

terminal to a wood yard. The Mall forms a vital part of the history of the United States. Innumerable demonstrators have gathered at the Washington Monument and marched to the US Capitol. The Pope said Mass here, African-American soprano Marian Anderson sang here at the request of first lady Eleanor Roosevelt, and Dr. Martin Luther King, Jr. delivered his famous "I have a dream" speech here. Every year on the Fourth of July (Independence Day), America's birthday party is held on the Mall, with a fireworks display. On summer evenings, teams of federal employees play softball on its fields.

SIGHTS AT A GLANCE

Museums and Galleries

Arthur M. Sackler Gallery **8**
Arts and Industries Building **4**
Freer Gallery of Art **9**
Hirshhorn Museum **3**
National Air and Space Museum pp60–63 **2**
National Gallery of Art pp56–9 **1**
National Museum of African Art **5**
National Museum of American History pp70–73 **10**
National Museum of Natural History pp66–7 **6**
Smithsonian Castle **7**
United States Holocaust Memorial Museum pp76–7 **12**

Monuments and Memorials

Franklin D. Roosevelt Memorial **16**
Jefferson Memorial **14**
Korean War Veterans Memorial **17**
Lincoln Memorial **18**
Vietnam Veterans Memorial **19**
Washington Monument **11**

Parks and Gardens

Tidal Basin **15**

Official Buildings

Bureau of Engraving and Printing **13**

GETTING THERE

Although visitors can park at the limited parking meters on the Mall, it is easier to get to the area by Metrobus (on routes 32, 34, 36, or 52) or by Metrorail. The nearest Metrorail stops are Smithsonian and Archives-Navy Memorial.

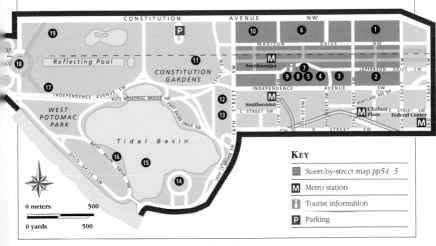

KEY

	Street-by-street map *pp54–5*
M	Metro station
i	Tourist information
P	Parking

◁ **Night-time view of the Washington Monument with the US Capitol in the background**

Street-by-Street: The Mall

T HIS 1-mile (1.5-km) boulevard between the Capitol and the Washington Monument is the city's cultural heart; the many different museums of the Smithsonian Institution can be found along this green strip. At the northeast corner of the Mall is the National Gallery of Art. Directly opposite is one of the most popular museums in the world – the National Air and Space Museum – a soaring construction of steel and glass. Both the National Museum of American History and the National Museum of Natural History, on the north side of the Mall, also draw huge numbers of visitors.

Smithsonian Castle
Now the main information center for all Smithsonian activities, this building once housed the basis of the collections found in numerous museums along the Mall **7**

★ **National Museum of Natural History**
The central Rotunda was designed in the Neoclassical style and opened to the public in 1910 **6**

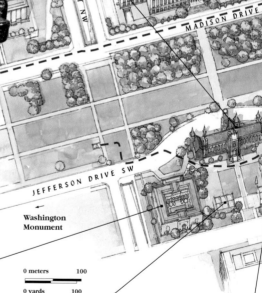

★ **National Museum of American History**
From George Washington's uniform to this 1940s Tucker Torpedo, US history is documented here **10**

Washington Monument

0 meters   100
0 yards   100

Freer Gallery of Art
The Freer displays both American and Asian art, including this 13th-century Chinese ink on silk painting **9**

Arthur M. Sackler Gallery
This extensive collection of Asian art was donated to the nation by New Yorker Arthur Sackler **8**

National Museum of African Art
Founded in 1965 and situated underground, this museum houses a comprehensive collection of ancient and modern African art **5**

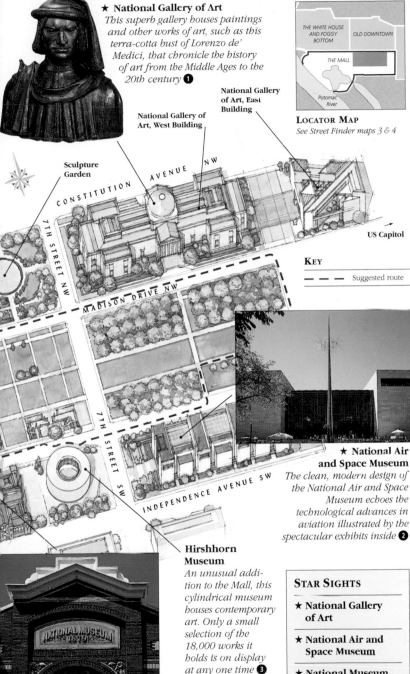

★ **National Gallery of Art**
This superb gallery houses paintings and other works of art, such as this terra-cotta bust of Lorenzo de' Medici, that chronicle the history of art from the Middle Ages to the 20th century ❶

National Gallery of Art, East Building

National Gallery of Art, West Building

Sculpture Garden

CONSTITUTION AVENUE NW

7TH STREET NW

MADISON DRIVE NW

7TH STREET SW

INDEPENDENCE AVENUE SW

US Capitol

LOCATOR MAP
See Street Finder maps 3 & 4

THE WHITE HOUSE AND FOGGY BOTTOM

OLD DOWNTOWN

THE MALL

Potomac River

KEY

– – – Suggested route

★ **National Air and Space Museum**
The clean, modern design of the National Air and Space Museum echoes the technological advances in aviation illustrated by the spectacular exhibits inside ❷

Hirshhorn Museum
An unusual addition to the Mall, this cylindrical museum houses contemporary art. Only a small selection of the 18,000 works it holds is on display at any one time ❸

Arts and Industries Building
This masterpiece of Victorian architecture was built to contain exhibits from the Centennial Exposition in Philadelphia ❹

NATIONAL MUSEUM 1879

STAR SIGHTS

★ **National Gallery of Art**

★ **National Air and Space Museum**

★ **National Museum of Natural History**

★ **National Museum of American History**

National Gallery of Art ❶

IN THE 1920s, American financier and statesman Andrew Mellon began collecting art with the intention of establishing a new art museum in Washington. In 1936 he offered his collection to the country and offered also to provide a building for the new National Gallery of Art. Designed by architect John Russell Pope, the Neoclassical building was opened in 1941. Other collectors followed Mellon's example and donated their collections to the Gallery, and by the 1960s it had outgrown the West Building. I.M. Pei designed the new East Building which was opened in 1978. It was hailed as the most innovative example of modern architecture in the city.

★ **Ginevra de' Benci**
This depiction of a thoughtful young Florentine girl is by Leonardo da Vinci. It was painted c.1474.

The Alba Madonna
Painted c.1510 by Raphael, this work is considered one of the major achievements of the Renaissance.

West Garden Court

A Young Man with His Tutor
This charming work by French artist Nicolas de Largilliere (1656–1746) was painted in 1685.

KEY TO FLOOR PLAN

- ☐ 13th-15th-century Italian
- ☐ 16th-century Italian
- ☐ 17th-century Dutch and Flemish
- ☐ 17th-18th-century Spanish, Italian, and French
- ☐ 18th-19th-century Spanish and French
- ☐ 19th-century French
- ☐ 20th-century
- ☐ American paintings
- ☐ British paintings
- ☐ Sculpture and Decorative Arts
- ☐ Special exhibitions
- ☐ Nonexhibition space

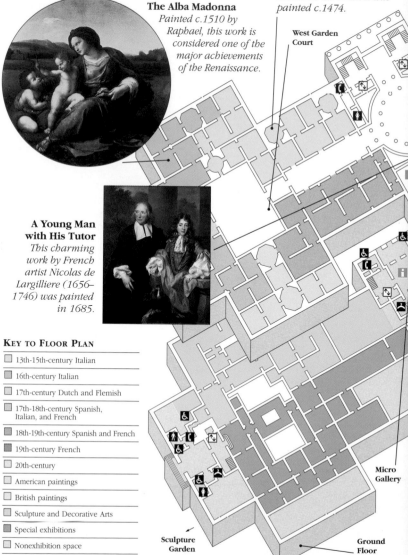

Micro Gallery

Sculpture Garden

Ground Floor

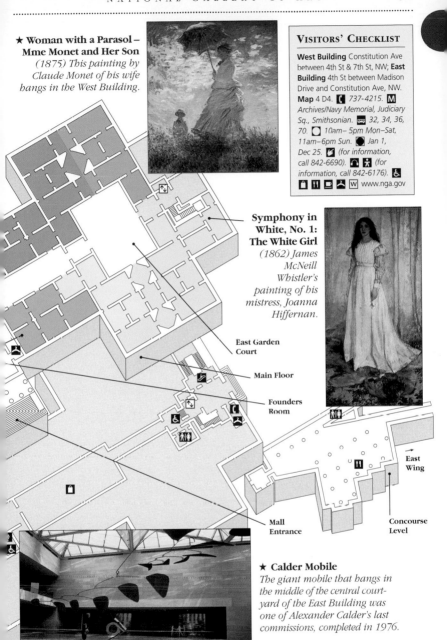

★ **Woman with a Parasol –
Mme Monet and Her Son**
*(1875) This painting by
Claude Monet of his wife
hangs in the West Building.*

**Symphony in
White, No. 1:
The White Girl**
*(1862) James
McNeill
Whistler's
painting of his
mistress, Joanna
Hiffernan.*

**East Garden
Court**

Main Floor

**Founders
Room**

**East
Wing**

**Mall
Entrance**

**Concourse
Level**

★ **Calder Mobile**
*The giant mobile that hangs in
the middle of the central courtyard of the East Building was
one of Alexander Calder's last
commissions, completed in 1976.*

GALLERY GUIDE
*The National Gallery of Art is divided into two main
buildings. The West Building features European
paintings and sculptures from the 13th to the 19th
centuries, including American works and a substantial
Impressionist collection. The East Building features
modern art. Both buildings have temporary exhibitions.
An underground concourse connects the two buildings.*

STAR EXHIBITS

★ **Calder Mobile**

★ **Ginevra de' Benci**

★ **Woman with a
Parasol**

Exploring the National Gallery of Art

The NATIONAL GALLERY'S West and East Buildings are an unusual pair. The West Building, designed by John Russell Pope, is stately and Classical, with matching wings flanking its rotunda. Built of Tennessee marble, it forms a majestic presence on the Mall. Its collection is devoted to Western art from the 13th through the 19th centuries. The East Building, completed in 1978, occupies a trapezoidal plot of land adjacent to the West Building. The triangular East Building is as audacious as the West one is conservative, but together they are harmonious. The interior of the East Building is a huge, fluid space, with galleries on either side housing works of modern art. The Sculpture Garden, adjacent to the West Building, has a fountain area that becomes an ice rink in winter.

Detail of *Christ Cleansing the Temple* (c.1570), by El Greco

Giotto's *Madonna and Child*, painted between 1320 and 1330

13TH- TO 15TH-CENTURY ITALIAN ART

The ITALIAN GALLERIES house paintings from the 13th to 15th centuries. The earlier pre-Renaissance works of primarily religious themes illustrate a decidedly Byzantine influence.

The Florentine artist Giotto's *Madonna and Child* (c.1330) shows the transition to the Classical painting of the Renaissance. *Adoration of the Magi*, painted in the early 1480s by Botticelli, portrays a serene Madonna and Child surrounded by worshipers in the Italian countryside. Around the same date Pietro Perugino painted *The Crucifixion with the Virgin, St. John, St. Jerome and St. Mary Magdalene*. Andrew Mellon bought the triptych from the Hermitage Gallery in Leningrad. Raphael's *The Alba Madonna* of 1510 was called

by one writer "the supreme compositional achievement of Renaissance painting." Leonardo da Vinci's *Ginevra de' Benci* (c.1474) is thought to be the first ever "psychological" portrait (depicting emotion) to be painted.

16TH-CENTURY ITALIAN ART

This COLLECTION includes works by Tintoretto, Titian, and Raphael. The 1500s were the height of Italian Classicism. Raphael's *St. George and the Dragon* (c.1506) typifies the perfection of technique for which this school of artists is known. Jacopo Tintoretto's *Christ at the Sea of Galilee* (c.1575/1580) portrays Christ standing on the shore while his disciples are on a storm-tossed fishing boat. The emotional intensity of the painting and the role of nature in it made Tintoretto one of the greatest of the Venetian artists.

17TH- TO 18TH-CENTURY SPANISH, ITALIAN, AND FRENCH ART

Among the 17th- and 18th-century European works are Jean-Honoré Fragonard's *Diana and Endymion* (c.1765), which was heavily influenced by Fragonard's mentor, François Boucher. El Greco's *Christ Cleansing the Temple* (pre-1570) demonstrates the influence of the 16th-century Italian schools. El Greco ("The Greek") signed his real name, Domenikos Theotokopoulos, to the panel.

17TH-CENTURY DUTCH AND FLEMISH ART

This COLLECTION holds a number of Old Masters including works by Rubens, Van Dyck, and Rembrandt. An example of Rembrandt's self-portraits is on display, which

Oil painting, *Diana and Endymion* (c.1753), by Jean-Honoré Fragonard

he painted in oils in 1659, ten years before his death.

Several paintings by Rubens in this section testify to his genius, among them *Daniel in the Lions' Den* (c.1615). This depicts the Old Testament prophet, Daniel, thanking God for his help during his night spent surrounded by lions. In 1617, Rubens exchanged this work for antique marbles owned by a British diplomat. Rubens also painted *Deborah Kip, Wife of Sir Balthasar Gerbier, and her Children* (1629–30). Not a conventional family portrait, the mother and her four children seem withdrawn and pensive, suggesting unhappiness and perhaps even foreboding tragedy. Van Dyck painted Rubens's first wife, *Isabella Brant* (c.1621) toward the end of her life. Although she is smiling, her eyes reveal an inner melancholy.

19TH-CENTURY FRENCH ART

THIS IS one of the best Impressionist collections outside Paris. Works on display include Paul Cézanne's *The Artist's Father* (1866), Edouard Manet's *Gare St Lazare* (1873), Auguste Renoir's *Girl with a Watering Can* (1876), *Four Dancers* (c.1899) by Edgar Degas, and Claude Monet's *Woman with a Parasol – Madame Monet and Her Son* (1875)

Miss Mary Ellison by Mary Cassatt (1880)

and *Palazzo da Mula, Venice* (1908). Post-Impressionist works include Seurat's pointillist *The Lighthouse at Honfleur* (c.1886), in which thousands of dots are used to create the image, and Van Gogh's *Self Portrait*. The latter was painted in St Rémy in 1889 when he was staying in an asylum and shows his mastery at capturing character and emotion. Toulouse-Lautrec's painting, *Quadrille at the Moulin Rouge* (1892), depicts a dancer provocatively raising her skirts above her ankles.

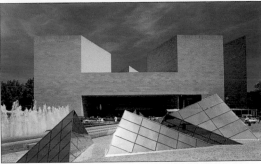

Geometric skylights in the plaza from the West Building to the East Building

AMERICAN PAINTING

THIS IMPORTANT collection of American artists shows evidence of European influence, but in themes that are resolutely American. James McNeill Whistler's *The White Girl* (1862) has a European sophistication. Mary Cassatt left America for exile in Europe and was heavily influenced by the Impressionists, especially Degas. *Boating Party* (1893–4) is an unsentimental example of one of her recurrent themes; mother and child. *Children Playing on a Beach* (1884) is also a good example of her child paintings, and *Miss Mary Eillson* of her portraiture. Winslow Homer's *Breezing Up* (1876) is a masterpiece by the pre-eminent American Realist. His painting is a charming depiction of three small boys and a fisherman enjoying sailing on a clear day.

MODERN AND CONTEMPORARY ART

THE ENORMOUS East Building houses modern and contemporary art. The building's vast courtyard is edged by four balconies and adjacent galleries. Architecturally, this space provides a dramatic focus and spatial orientation for visitors to the East Building. Centered in the courtyard is *Untitled*, a vast red, blue, and black creation by Alexander Calder. It was commissioned in 1972 for the opening of the museum in 1978. At the entrance to the East Building is Henry Moore's bronze sculpture *Knife Edge Mirror Two Piece* (1977–8). The courtyard also holds Joan Miró's 1977 tapestry *Woman.*

Also in the East Building are a research center for schools, offices for the curators, a library, and a large collection of drawings and prints.

Both the East and West buildings also host traveling exhibits. These are not limited to modern art, but have included the art of ancient Japan, American Impressionists, and the sketches of Leonardo da Vinci. The East Building's galleries are surprisingly intimate.

SCULPTURE GARDEN

Located adjacent to the West Building at 7th Street, the Sculpture Garden holds 17 sculptures. Late 20th-century works sit around the perimeter of the garden, offering a display of work by Isamu Noguchi, Louise Bourgeois, Roy Lichtenstein, and Joan Miró. Although all very different, the sculptures do not compete with each other because they are comfortably spread out. Transformed into an ice rink in winter, the garden functions both as an outdoor gallery and as a pleasant oasis within the city. The pavilion houses a year round café.

National Air and Space Museum ❷

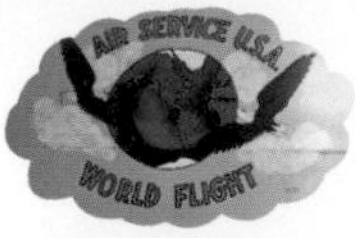

United States Air Force insignia

THE SMITHSONIAN'S National Air and Space Museum was opened on July 1, 1976, during the country's bicentennial. From 1964 to 1976 the National Air Museum was housed in the Washington Armory, a cramped 19th-century building on the site of the present National Museum of African Art and the Arthur M. Sackler Gallery. The soaring architecture of the new building, designed by Hellmuth, Obata, and Kassabaum, is better suited to the airplanes, rockets, balloons, and space capsules of aviation and space flight.

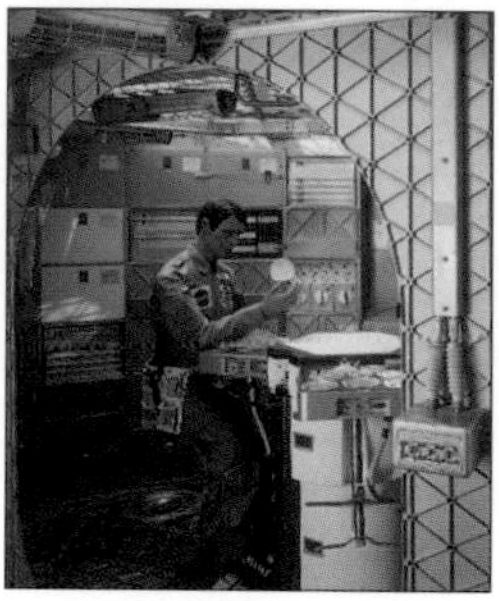

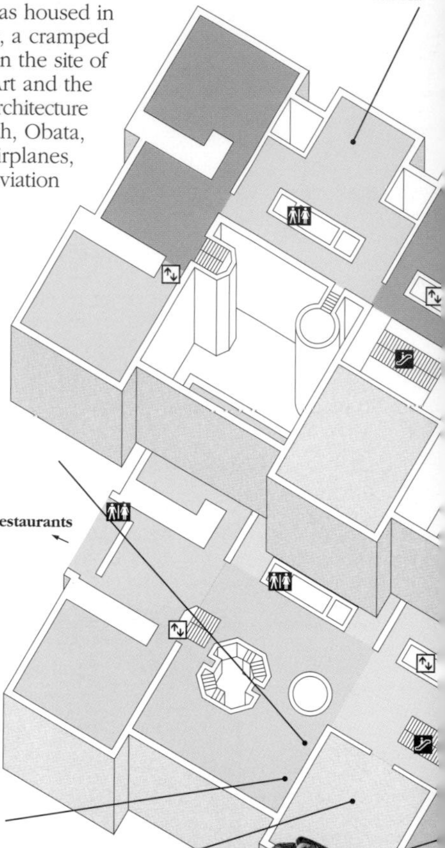

Apollo to the Moon
Full of artifacts, this exhibit tells the story of how the United States put a man on the moon.

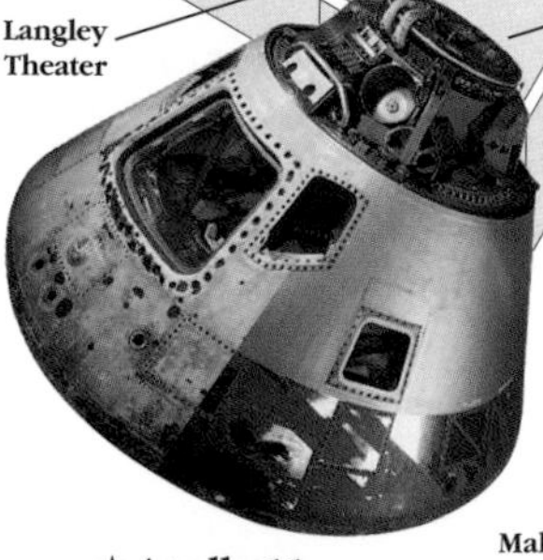

Skylab
This was an orbiting work-shop for sets of three-person crews, who conducted research experiments.

Restaurants

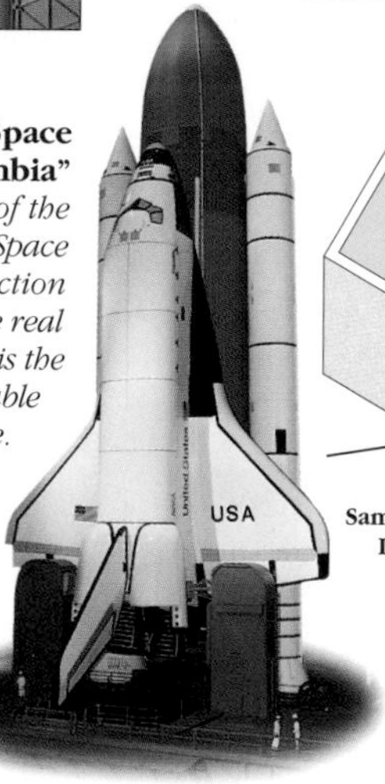

★ **Space Shuttle "Columbia"**
This model of the Columbia Space Shuttle is a fraction of the size of the real one. The shuttle is the world's first reusable space vehicle.

USA

Samuel P. Langley IMAX® Theater

STAR EXHIBITS

★ **Wright 1903 Flyer**

★ **Columbia Space Shuttle model**

★ **Apollo 11 Command Module**

★ **Spirit of St. Louis**

GALLERY GUIDE

The lofty first-floor ceilings of the National Air and Space Museum show the history of flight, from the early days to the space age. The Museum shop and the IMAX® theater are also on the first floor. The second level houses a variety of themed displays.

Mall Entrance

★ **Apollo 11 Command Module**
This module carried astronauts Buzz Aldrin, Neil Armstrong, and Michael Collins on their historic mission to the moon in July 1969, when Neil Armstrong took his famous first steps.

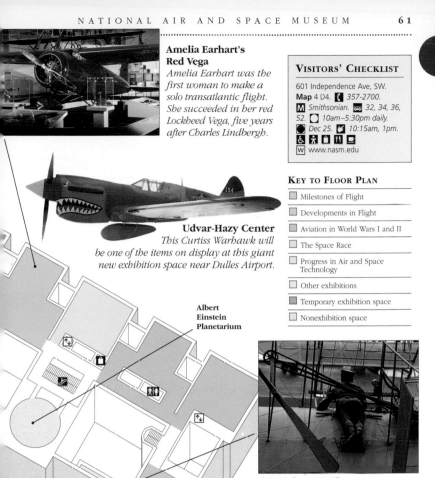

Amelia Earhart's Red Vega
Amelia Earhart was the first woman to make a solo transatlantic flight. She succeeded in her red Lockheed Vega, five years after Charles Lindbergh.

VISITORS' CHECKLIST

601 Independence Ave, SW.
Map 4 D4. 357-2700.
Smithsonian. 32, 34, 36, 52. 10am–5:30pm daily.
Dec 25. 10:15am, 1pm.
www.nasm.edu

KEY TO FLOOR PLAN

- Milestones of Flight
- Developments in Flight
- Aviation in World Wars I and II
- The Space Race
- Progress in Air and Space Technology
- Other exhibitions
- Temporary exhibition space
- Nonexhibition space

Udvar-Hazy Center
This Curtiss Warhawk will be one of the items on display at this giant new exhibition space near Dulles Airport.

Albert Einstein Planetarium

★ Wright 1903 Flyer
The first powered, heavier-than-air machine to achieve controlled, sustained flight.

Second Floor

★ Spirit of St. Louis
At the age of 25, pilot Charles Lindbergh made the first solo transatlantic flight in this plane, landing in France on May 21, 1927.

Milestones of Flight Exhibition
Many of the firsts in both aviation and space travel are on display in this gallery.

First Floor

Exploring the National Air and Space Museum

THE NATIONAL AIR AND SPACE MUSEUM has a massive 200,000 sq ft (18,500 sq m) of exhibition space. The most visited museum in the world, it has to cope not only with millions of visitors but also with the vast range and sheer size of its artifacts, which include hundreds of rockets, planes, and space capsules. A single airplane, including one as diminutive as the Wright brothers' 1903 *Flyer*, would dwarf a conventional gallery. Even this vast building needs a sister exhibition space: the Udvar-Hazy Center is due to open near Dulles Airport in December 2003 and will house items now in storage.

The Boeing F4B Navy fighter

The **Pioneers of Flight** gallery celebrates the men and women who have challenged the physical and psychological barriers faced when leaving the earth. Adventurer Cal Rogers was the first to fly across the United States, but it was not non-stop. In 1911 he flew from coast to coast in less than 30 days, with almost 70 landings. His early biplane is one of the exhibits. (Twelve years later, a Fokker T-2 made the trip in less than 27 hours.)

Amelia Earhart was the first woman to fly the Atlantic, just five years after Charles Lindbergh. Her red Lockheed Vega is displayed. Close by is *Tingmissartoq*, a Lockheed Sirius seaplane belonging to Charles Lindbergh. Its unusual name is Inuit for "one who flies like a bird." Some of the greatest strides in aviation were made in the period between World War I and World War II, celebrated in the **Golden Age of Flight** gallery. The public's intense interest in flight resulted in races, exhibitions, and adventurous exploration. Here a visitor can see planes equipped with skis for landing on snow, with short wings for racing, and a "staggerwing" plane on which the lower wing was placed ahead of the upper.

The F4B Navy fighter, used by US Marine Corps squadrons, was developed between the world wars and is on display in the **Sea-Air Operations** gallery. Flight then progressed from propeller propulsion to

MILESTONES OF FLIGHT

ENTERING THE National Air and Space Museum from the Mall entrance, first stop is the soaring **Milestones of Flight** gallery, which gives an overview of the history of flight. The exhibits in this room are some of the major firsts in aviation and space technology, as they helped to realize man's ambition to take to the air.

The gallery is vast, designed to accommodate the large aircraft – many of which are suspended from the ceiling – and space capsules. Some of these pioneering machines are surprisingly small, however. Charles Lindbergh's *Spirit of St. Louis*, the first aircraft to cross the Atlantic with a solo pilot, was designed with the fuel tanks ahead of the cockpit so Lindbergh had to use a periscope to look directly ahead. John Glenn's Mercury spacecraft, *Friendship 7*, in which he orbited the earth, is smaller than a sports car.

Near the entrance to the gallery is a moon rock – a symbol of man's exploration of space. Also in this gallery is the *Apollo 11* Command

Module, which carried the first men to walk on the moon. Overhead is the Wright brothers' *Flyer*, the first plane to be successfully airborne on December 17, 1903, at Kitty Hawk, North Carolina.

DEVELOPMENTS IN FLIGHT

TRAVELERS NOW take flying for granted – it is safe, fast, and for many people routine. The Air and Space Museum, however, displays machines and gadgets from an era when flight was new and daring.

Early mail and cargo planes in the Air Transportation Gallery

Rockets on display in the Space Race gallery

jets. The **Jet Aviation** gallery has the first jet warplane, the German Messerschmitt Me 262A. *Lulu Belle*, the first US jet, was used in the Korean War of 1950–53.

The **Air Transportation** Gallery has planes from the earliest days of air mail, when open-cockpit planes flew with mail in the front cockpit and the pilot in the rear. Early planes, like the Fairchild FC-2, consisted of fabric and wood.

AVIATION IN WORLD WARS I AND II

ONE OF THE MOST popular parts of the museum is the **World War II Aviation** gallery, which has planes from the Allied and the Axis air forces. Nearby is an example of the Japanese Mitsubishi A6M5 Zero Model 52, which was a light, highly maneuverable fighter plane.

The maneuverability of the Messerschmitt Bf 109 made it Germany's most successful fighter. It was matched, and in some areas surpassed, by the Supermarine Spitfire of the Royal Air Force, which helped to win control of the skies over Britain in 1940–41.

SPACE HALL

THE ANIMOSITY that grew between the United States and the Soviet Union after World War II manifested itself in the Space Race. America was taken by surprise when

the Soviets launched *Sputnik 1* on October 4, 1957. The US attempt to launch their first satellite proved a spectacular failure when the *Vanguard* exploded in December 1957. Pieces from the satellite are on display here.

In 1961, Soviet cosmonaut Yuri Gagarin became the first man to orbit the earth. The Americans countered with Alan Shepard's manned space flight in *Freedom 7* later the same year. The first space walk was from the *Gemini IV* capsule by American astronaut Edward H. White in 1965.

The history of man's desire to get into space is explored further in the **Rocketry and Space Flight** gallery, which examines concepts about space travel from the 13th century to the present. It also **Gemini IV capsule** houses "Earth Today," a video presentation of satellite data, and the space suits worn by the first astronauts.

Other artifacts from the Space Race include a full-size mock-up of a lunar module, a Lunar Roving Vehicle, *Skylab 4* command module, and *Gemini 7*, a two-person spacecraft that successfully orbited the earth in 1965.

The Space Hall gallery shows the result of the final détente between the superpowers with the Apollo-Soyuz Test Project. This involved the *Apollo* module docking alongside the Soviet *Soyuz* spacecraft – a project that marked the beginning of the end of the Space Race.

PROGRESS IN AIR AND SPACE TECHNOLOGY

MAN'S FASCINATION with flight is in part a desire to see earth from a great distance and to get closer to other planets. In the Independence Avenue lobby is artist Robert T. McCall's interpretation of the birth of the universe, the planets, and astronauts reaching the moon.

The Hubble Telescope, launched from the *Discovery* shuttle in April 1990, provides pictures of distant astronomical objects. The large observatory on *Skylab* enabled greater study of the sun. Lunar orbiters were equipped with photographic laboratories that sent back detailed maps of the moon. Launched in 1964, the *Ranger* lunar probe also took high-quality pictures of the moon, transmitting them to Cape Canaveral.

Beyond the Limits explains how computers have revolutionized flight technology and displays some of the recent achievements in aircraft design.

The spacesuit worn by Apollo astronauts in 1961

Hirshhorn Museum ❸

Independence Ave and 7th St, SW.
Map 3 C4. 🖪 *357-2700.*
Ⓜ *Smithsonian.* ⬜ *10am–5:30pm daily (Sculpture Garden 7:30am–dusk).* ⬤ *Dec 25.* 🖪 🖪
🖪 ⬛ Ⓦ www.si.edu/hirshhorn

WHEN THE Hirshhorn Museum was in its planning stages, S. Dillon Ripley, then Secretary of the Smithsonian Institution, told the planning board that the building should be "controversial in every way" so that it would be fit to house contemporary works of art.

The Hirshhorn fulfilled its architectural mission. It has been variously described as a doughnut or a flying saucer, but it is actually a four-story, not-quite-symmetrical cylinder. It is also home to one of the greatest collections of modern art in the United States.

The museum's benefactor, Joseph H. Hirshhorn, was an eccentric, flamboyant immigrant from Latvia who amassed a collection of 6,000 pieces of contemporary art. Since the museum opened in 1974, the Smithsonian has built on Hirshhorn's original donation, and the collection now consists of 3,000 pieces of sculpture, 4,000 drawings and photographs, and approximately 5,000 paintings. The works of art are arranged

Two Disks (1965) by Alexander Calder, in the Hirshhorn plaza

chronologically. The main floor and second floor house art from the 19th and 20th centuries, including works by Matisse and Degas; the third floor has contemporary works by artists such as Bacon, de Kooning, John Singer Sargent, and Cassatt. The outdoor sculpture garden, across the street from the museum, includes pieces by Auguste Rodin, Henry Moore, and many others.

In addition to the permanent collection, the Hirshhorn has at least three major temporary exhibitions every year. These are usually arranged thematically, or as tributes to individual artists,

Arts and Industries Building's fountain

such as Lucien Freud, Alberto Giacometti, or Francis Bacon. An outdoor café in the circular plaza at the center of the building provides light lunches during the summer.

Arts and Industries Building ❹

900 Jefferson Drive, SW. **Map** 3 C4.
🖪 *357-2700.* Ⓜ *Smithsonian.*
⬜ *10am–5:30pm daily.* ⬤ *Dec 25.*
🈚 *for Discovery Theater only.* 🖪 *by appt.* 🖪 🖪 Ⓦ www.si.edu/ai

THE ORNATE, vast galleries and rotunda of the Victorian Arts and Industries Building were designed by Montgomery Meigs, architect of the National Building Museum *(see p97).* The Arts and Industries Building is extraordinary because of its expanse of open space (17 uninterrupted exhibition areas) and abundance of natural light.

The museum has served many functions since its completion on March 4, 1881. In its opening year it was the site of President James Garfield's inaugural ball; it displayed artifacts from Philadelphia's 1876 Centennial Exposition, including a complete steam train; and it was home to a collection of the First Ladies' Gowns, as well as Lindbergh's

Fountain in the central plaza of the Hirshhorn Museum, surrounded by a garden of sculptures

Rotunda of the Arts and Industries Building

famous airplane the *Spirit of St. Louis*, before these exhibits were moved to other Smithsonian museums on the Mall.

The Arts and Industries Building hosts a series of temporary exhibitions, many of which focus on African-American and Native American culture. The Discovery Theater, a children's theater, has a program of performances by singers, dancers, and puppeteers from September through July. The rest of the Arts and Industries Building is now used as administrative offices for the Smithsonian Institution.

National Museum of African Art ❺

950 Independence Ave, SW.
Map 3 C4. 📞 357-2700.
Ⓜ *Smithsonian.* ⏰ 10am–5:30pm
daily. ⬤ *Dec 25.* 🎫 ♿ 🏛 🔼
Ⓦ www.si.edu/nmafa

THE NATIONAL MUSEUM of African Art is one of the quietest spots on the Mall. Perhaps because it is mostly underground, with a relatively low above-ground presence, it is often missed by visitors. The small entrance pavilion at ground level leads to three subterranean floors, where the museum shares space with the adjacent Ripley Center (housing Smithsonian administration offices) and

the Arthur M. Sackler Gallery *(see pp68–9).*

Founded in 1965 by Warren Robbins, a former officer in the American Foreign Service, the National Museum of African Art was first situated in the home of Frederick Douglass *(see p139),* on Capitol Hill. The Smithsonian acquired Robbins' collection in 1979, and the works were moved to their new home in 1987.

The 7,000-piece permanent collection includes both modern and ancient art from Africa, although the majority of pieces date from the 19th and 20th centuries. Traditional African art of bronze, ceramics, and gold is on display, along with an extensive collection of masks. There is also a display of *kente* cloth from Ghana – brightly colored and patterned

cloth used to adorn clothing as a symbol of African nationalism. The Eliot Elisofon Photographic Archives contain 300,000 prints and a large number of films concerning African art and culture.

There are special exhibits and workshops, some of which cater specifically to children. The museum's gift shop sells colorful clothes and materials, as well as books and postcards.

A Benin bronze head at the National Museum of African Art

HISTORY OF THE MALL

In September, 1789, French-born Pierre L'Enfant (1754–1825) asked George Washington for permission to design the capital of the new United States. While the rest of the city developed, the area planned by L'Enfant to be the Grand Avenue, running west from the Capitol, remained swampy and undeveloped. In 1850, landscape gardener Andrew Jackson Downing was employed to develop the land in accordance with L'Enfant's plans. However, the money ran out, and the work was abandoned. At the end of the Civil War in 1865, President Lincoln, eager that building in the the city should progress, instructed that work on the area should begin again, and the Mall began to take on the park-like appearance it has today. The addition of many museums and memorials in the latter half of the 20th century established the Mall as the cultural heart of Washington.

Aerial view, showing the Mall stretching down from the Capitol

National Museum of Natural History ❻

THE NATIONAL MUSEUM OF NATURAL HISTORY, which opened in 1911, preserves artifacts from the earth's diverse cultures and collects samples of fossils and living creatures from land and sea. Although only a fraction of its 124 million artifacts is displayed, visiting the museum is a vast undertaking. The trick is to sample the best of the exhibits and leave the rest for return visits. The Insect Zoo, with its giant hissing cockroaches and large leaf-cutter ant colony, is popular with children, while the Discovery Room allows visitors to hold objects like crocodile heads and elephant tusks. The newly renovated Dinosaur Hall delights young and old.

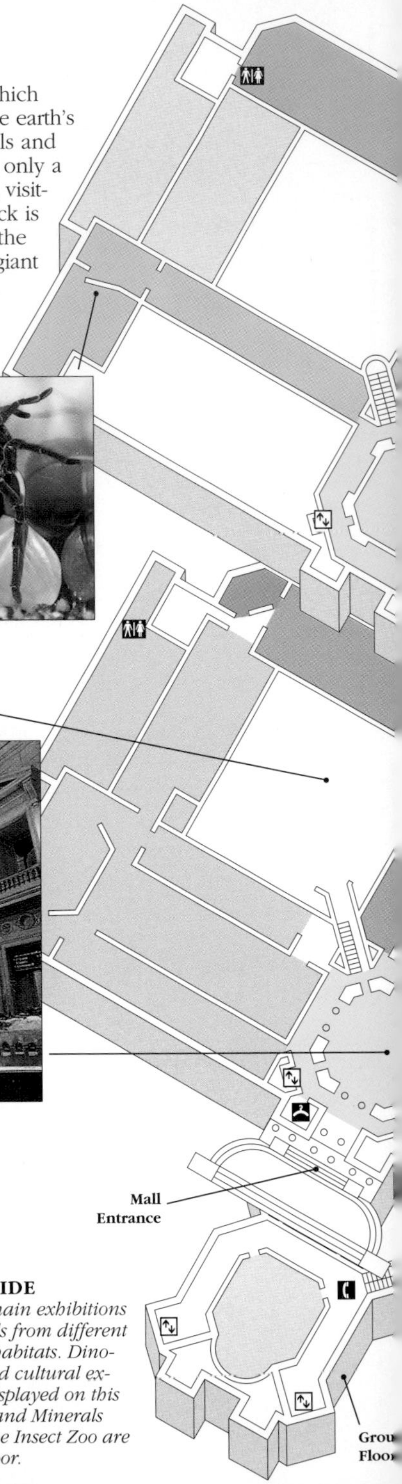

★ Insect Zoo
This popular exhibit explores the lives and habitats of the single largest animal group on earth and features many live specimens.

**The Samuel Johnson IMAX®
Theater** shows 2-D and 3-D films on a range of fascinating subjects.

African Elephant
The massive African Bush elephant is one of the highlights of the museum. It is the centerpiece of the Rotunda and creates an impressive sight as visitors enter the museum.

Mall
Entrance

STAR SIGHTS
★ Dinosaur Hall
★ Insect Zoo
★ Hope Diamond

GALLERY GUIDE
The first floor's main exhibitions feature mammals from different continents and habitats. Dinosaurs and myriad cultural exhibits are also displayed on this level. The Gems and Minerals collection and the Insect Zoo are on the second floor.

Ground
Floor

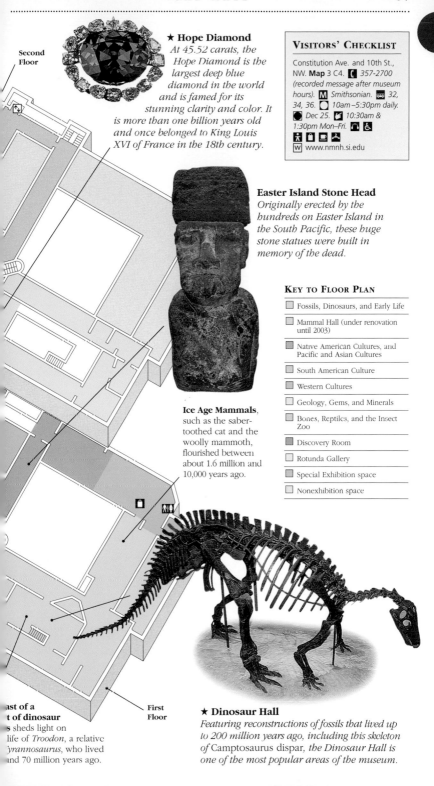

★ Hope Diamond
At 45.52 carats, the Hope Diamond is the largest deep blue diamond in the world and is famed for its stunning clarity and color. It is more than one billion years old and once belonged to King Louis XVI of France in the 18th century.

Second Floor

VISITORS' CHECKLIST

Constitution Ave. and 10th St., NW. **Map** 3 C4. ☎ *357-2700 (recorded message after museum hours).* Ⓜ *Smithsonian.* 🚌 *32, 34, 36.* ◯ *10am –5:30pm daily.* ⬤ *Dec 25.* 🎟 *10:30am & 1:30pm Mon–Fri.* 🔾 ♿
🚼 🎁 🍴 ⛺
Ⓦ www.nmnh.si.edu

Easter Island Stone Head
Originally erected by the hundreds on Easter Island in the South Pacific, these huge stone statues were built in memory of the dead.

KEY TO FLOOR PLAN

☐ Fossils, Dinosaurs, and Early Life

☐ Mammal Hall (under renovation until 2003)

☐ Native American Cultures, and Pacific and Asian Cultures

☐ South American Culture

☐ Western Cultures

☐ Geology, Gems, and Minerals

☐ Bones, Reptiles, and the Insect Zoo

☐ Discovery Room

☐ Rotunda Gallery

☐ Special Exhibition space

☐ Nonexhibition space

Ice Age Mammals, such as the saber-toothed cat and the woolly mammoth, flourished between about 1.6 million and 10,000 years ago.

ast of a t of dinosaur s sheds light on life of *Troodon,* a relative *yrannosaurus,* who lived and 70 million years ago.

First Floor

★ Dinosaur Hall
Featuring reconstructions of fossils that lived up to 200 million years ago, including this skeleton of Camptosaurus dispar, *the Dinosaur Hall is one of the most popular areas of the museum.*

The elegant Victorian façade of the Smithsonian Castle, viewed from the Mall

Smithsonian Castle ❼

1000 Jefferson Drive, SW. **Map** 3 C4.
📞 357-2700. Ⓜ *Smithsonian.*
🕐 9am–5:30pm daily. ⬤ Dec 25.
🅿 ♿ 🏠 Ⓦ www.si.edu

THIS ORNATE Victorian edifice served as the first home of the Smithsonian Institution, and was also home to the first Secretary of the Smithsonian, Joseph Henry, and his family. A statue of Henry stands in front of the building.

Constructed of red sandstone in 1855, the Castle was designed by James Renwick,

The tomb of James Smithson

architect of the Renwick Gallery *(see p107)* and St Patrick's Cathedral in New York. It is an outstanding example of the Gothic Revival style. Inspired also by 12th-century Norman architecture, the Castle has nine towers and an elaborate cornice.

Today it is the seat of the Smithsonian administration and houses its Information Center. Visitors can visit the Crypt Room and see the tomb of James Smithson, who bequeathed his fortune to the United States. The South Tower Room was the first children's room in a Washington museum. The ceiling and colorful wall

stencils that decorate the room were restored in 1987.

Outside the castle is the Smithsonian rose garden, filled with beautiful hybrid tea roses. The garden was a later addition that now connects the Castle to the equally ornate Arts and Industries Building *(see p64)*.

Arthur M. Sackler Gallery ❽

1050 Independence Ave, SW.
Map 3 C4. 📞 357-4880. Ⓜ *Smithsonian.* 🕐 10am–5:30pm daily.
⬤ Dec 25. 🕤 11:30am. ♿ 🏠 🔺
Ⓦ www.asia.si.edu

DR. ARTHUR M. SACKLER, a New York physician, started collecting Asian art in the 1950s. In 1982, he

JAMES SMITHSON (1765–1829)

Although he never once visited the United States, James Smithson, English scientist and philanthropist, and illegitimate son of the first Duke of Northumberland, left his entire fortune of half a million dollars to "found at Washington, under the name of the Smithsonian Institution, an establishment for the increase and diffusion of knowledge among men." However, this was only if his nephew and heir were to die childless. This did happen and hence, in 1836, Smithson's fortune passed to the government of the United States, which did not quite know what to do with such a vast bequest. For 11 years Congress debated various proposals, finally agreeing to set up a government-run foundation that would administer all national museums. The first Smithson-funded collection was shown at the Smithsonian Castle in 1855.

James Smithson

Sculpture of the goddess Uma in the Arthur M. Sackler Gallery

donated more than 1,000 artifacts, along with $4 million in funds, to the Smithsonian Institution to establish this museum. The Japanese and Korean governments also contributed $1 million each toward the cost of constructing the building, and the museum was completed in 1987.

The entrance to the gallery is a small pavilion at ground level that leads down to two subterranean floors of exhibits. Among its 3,000 works of Asian art, the Sackler has paintings from Iran and India, and Chinese ceramics from the 7th to the 10th centuries AD. There are also textiles and village crafts from South Asia, and stunning displays of Chinese bronzes and jades, some dating back to 4000 BC.

Over the years the gallery has built on Arthur Sackler's original collection. In 1987 it acquired the impressive Vever Collection from collector Henri Vever, which includes such items as Islamic books from the 11th to the 19th centuries, 19th- and 20th-century Japanese prints, Indian, Chinese, and Japanese paintings, and modern photography.

The Sackler is one of two underground museums in this area; the other is the National Museum of African Art *(see p65)*, which is part of the same complex. The Sackler is also connected by underground exhibition space to the Freer Gallery of Art. The two galleries share a director and administrative staff as well as the Meyer Auditorium, which hosts dance performances, films, and chamber music concerts. There is also a research library in the Sackler devoted to Asian art.

Freer Gallery of Art ❾

Jefferson Drive and 12th Street, SW.
Map 3 C4. 357-2700.
M *Smithsonian.* ◯ *10am–5:30pm daily.* ◯ *Dec 25.* 11:30am.
W www.asia.si.edu

THE FREER GALLERY of Art is named after Charles Lang Freer, a railroad magnate who donated his collection of 9,000 pieces of American and Asian art to the Smithsonian, and ordered the building of a museum to house the works. Freer died in 1919 before the building's completion. When the gallery opened in 1923 it became the first Smithsonian museum of art.

Detail of a screen by Thomas Wilmer Dewing

Constructed as a single-story building in the Italian Renaissance style, the Freer has an attractive courtyard with a fountain at its center. There are 19 galleries, most with skylights that illuminate a superb collection of Asian and American art. Since Freer's original donation, the museum has tripled its holdings. In the Asian Art collection are examples of Chinese, Japanese, and Korean art, including sculpture, ceramics, folding screens, and paintings. The gallery also has a fine selection of Buddhist sculpture, and painting and calligraphy from India.

There is a select collection of American art in the Freer as well, most of which shows Asian influences. Works by the artists Childe Hassam (1859–1935), John Singer Sargent (1865–1925), and Thomas Wilmer Dewing (1851–1938) are all on display.

The most astonishing room in the museum is James McNeill Whistler's "The Peacock Room." Whistler (1834–1903) was a friend of Freer's who encouraged his art collecting. Whistler painted a dining room for Frederick Leyland in London, but Leyland found that it was not to his taste. Freer purchased the room in 1904; it was later moved to Washington and installed here after his death. In contrast to the subtle elegance of the other rooms, this room is a riot of blues, greens, and golds. Whistler's painted peacocks cover the walls and ceiling.

The attractive courtyard of the Freer Gallery of Art

National Museum of American History ❿

THE NATIONAL MUSEUM of American History, often called "America's attic," is a collection of artifacts from the nation's past. Among the 3 million holdings are the first ladies' inaugural ball gowns, a mid-19th-century post office, computers, a 280-ton steam locomotive, and the ruby slippers from the *Wizard of Oz*. The original Star-Spangled Banner that flew over Fort McHenry in 1814 is currently being preserved. The museum's expanding, eclectic collection grew from the 1876 Philadelphia Centennial Exhibition and items held in the US Patent Office.

The Ruby Slippers, worn by Dorothy (Judy Garland) in the *Wizard of Oz*, are just one of the myriad exhibits from American popular culture.

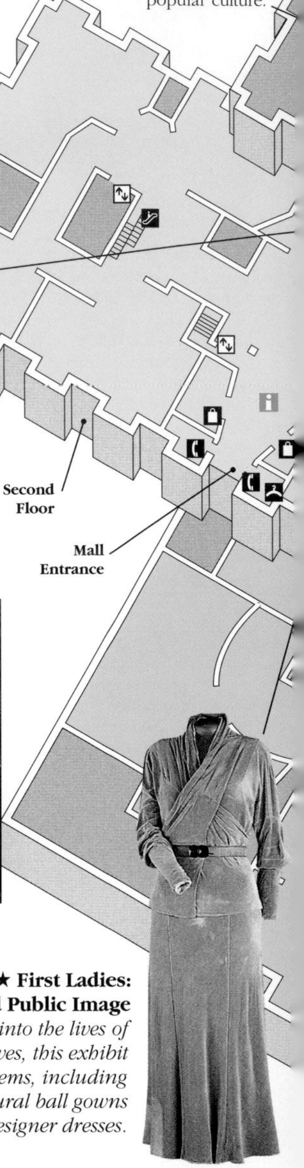

Redware and Blackware Pottery
These pots, by various Santa Clara artists, are decorated with serpent patterns. They can be seen in the American Encounters exhibit.

Second Floor

Mall Entrance

★ **Star-Spangled Banner**
Currently being preserved, the flag is the symbol of America. It inspired Francis Scott Key to write the poem that became the US national anthem.

KEY TO FLOOR PLAN

- ☐ First floor
- ☐ Second floor
- ☐ Third floor
- ☐ Temporary and non-exhibition space

STAR EXHIBITS

- ★ **Star-Spangled Banner**
- ★ **First Ladies**
- ★ **1913 *Model T***
- ★ **Headsville Post Office**

★ **First Ladies:**
Political Role and Public Image
Giving an insight into the lives of the presidents' wives, this exhibit contains over 800 items, including a collection of inaugural ball gowns and designer dresses.

GALLERY GUIDE
The first floor features the transportation and science exhibits and the Palm Court restaurant. The highlights of the second floor include the First Ladies exhibit and the Star-Spangled Banner. The third floor offers an eclectic selection including textiles, American Presidents, and military displays.

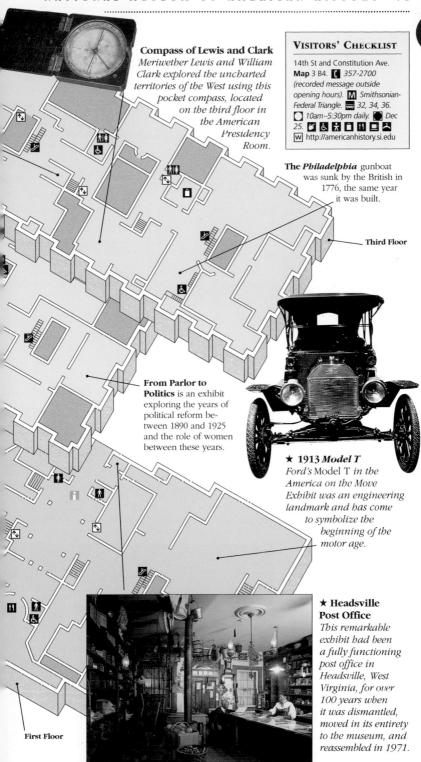

Compass of Lewis and Clark
Meriwether Lewis and William Clark explored the uncharted territories of the West using this pocket compass, located on the third floor in the American Presidency Room.

VISITORS' CHECKLIST

14th St and Constitution Ave.
Map 3 B4. 357-2700 (recorded message outside opening hours). Smithsonian-Federal Triangle. 32, 34, 36.
10am–5:30pm daily. Dec 25.
http://americanhistory.si.edu

The *Philadelphia* gunboat was sunk by the British in 1776, the same year it was built.

Third Floor

From Parlor to Politics is an exhibit exploring the years of political reform between 1890 and 1925 and the role of women between these years.

★ **1913 Model T**
Ford's Model T in the America on the Move Exhibit was an engineering landmark and has come to symbolize the beginning of the motor age.

★ **Headsville Post Office**
This remarkable exhibit had been a fully functioning post office in Headsville, West Virginia, for over 100 years when it was dismantled, moved in its entirety to the museum, and reassembled in 1971.

First Floor

Exploring the National Museum of American History

THE COLLECTION AT THE National Museum of American History is so diverse that a visitor could ricochet from exhibit to exhibit, running out of time and patience before seeing the entire collection. The best approach is to be selective; there is simply too much to take in during one visit. Whether you head straight for the first ladies' inaugural ball gowns or spend time viewing the collections of money, medals, or musical instruments, planning is the key to a successful visit.

The museum's modern façade on Madison Drive

FIRST FLOOR

FROM THE CONSTITUTION Avenue entrance, visitors to the museum first encounter the reassembled post office from Headsville, West Virginia. First established in 1861, the post office was transferred in its entirety to the Smithsonian in 1971. Visitors can mail letters from here with a special postmark.

Several of the galleries in the East Wing are devoted to artifacts of the Industrial Age. From agriculture to railroads, electricity to road transportation, heavy machinery and powerful engines feature widely in these exhibits. Some interesting vehicles on display are *Old Red*, the International Harvester cotton picker, and Ford's *Model T* of 1913.

In the West Wing, lovers of American popular culture will enjoy seeing the items from vintage television shows, including the leather jacket worn by the Fonz in *Happy Days*, displayed in the small exhibition near the escalators.

The West Wing also contains exhibits of a scientific nature. **The Information Age** deals with the history of telecommunications, from the telegraphs of the 1840s and

the invention of the telephone (1876) to the rise of the Internet and computer and information technology.

The **Science in American Life** exhibition explores the impact of scientific discovery on everyday life. The Hands-On-Science-Center allows visitors to explore everything from DNA fingerprinting to phenomena such as global warming and radioactivity.

Also on this floor are the Palm Court, containing a 1900 candy store, and an authentic ice-cream parlor from the early 20th century, which serves food and ice-cream to visitors.

SECOND FLOOR

DOMINATING THE EAST WING of the second floor is one of the museum's most popular exhibits, **First Ladies: Political Role and Public Image**. This display includes gowns worn to the presidents' inaugural balls. Candidates for the most elegant dress are those worn by Nancy Reagan and Jackie Kennedy, but Rosalynn Carter's dress is noteworthy as she bought it "off the rack." Next to the gowns is a re-creation of Cross Hall, the ceremonial front entrance to the White House. Furniture and accessories that were once used in the White House are exhibited here. Adjacent to the First Ladies' gowns is a delightful collection of teddy bears. The name of the bear was inspired by President Theodore "Teddy" Roosevelt, who, while out hunting one day, refused to shoot a bear cub that had been captured for him. A cartoon appeared in the *Washington Post* the next day, which inspired the production of a range of bears, named Teddy Bears.

Staying in the East Wing, visitors can discover the role played by women in early 20th-century reform in **From Parlor to Politics**. Symbols of philanthropy, such as pamphlets on education and banners demanding the end of child labor, are on display. Nannie

Interior of a Spanish home from Taos, New Mexico, on the second floor

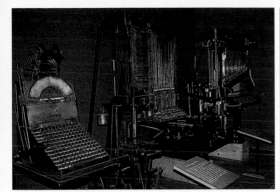

Early examples of printing equipment, on display on the third floor

Helen Burroughs founded the National Training School for Women and Girls in 1909 to provide African-American women with vocational skills and an education in the liberal arts. Her ground-breaking work is remembered here.

The exhibit **After the Revolution** can also be found in the East Wing. It features re-created interiors of ordinary American homes between 1780 and 1800, at the dawn of the new nation.

The Star-Spangled Banner that flew over Fort McHenry in 1814 and inspired Francis Scott Key to write the poem that was later to become the national anthem is undergoing an exensive program of conservation and stabilization that will last several years; visitors can learn about the preservation process in a laboratory and adjacent exhibit in the West Wing.

The **Communities in a Changing Nation** exhibit, also in the West Wing, includes the pocket compass that belonged to the explorers of the Western Frontier, Meriwether Lewis and William Clark.

The **American Encounters** exhibit examines how Anglo-Americans, American Indians, and Hispanics struggled to live alongside one another in the American Southwest. The display includes such exhibits as photographs, textiles, jewelry, and religious items, all of which illustrate how the

communities learned to co-exist in the new united nation.

One of the main draws on this floor is the **Hands-on History Room**. Popular with all ages, this is particularly enjoyed by young children. Everything can be touched, examined, and tried out. More than 30 activities give visitors a sense of what life was like in America's past. They can climb in a highwheeler (the precursor to the bicycle) or even send a real message by telegraph. They can test appliances that were invented to simplify housework in the 1800s and judge for themselves if they really did save labor. Other exhibits allow visitors to explore and learn what life was like for a slave, an itinerant peddler, or a Zuni Indian.

The activities in the Hands-on History Room correlate to exhibits in the rest of the museum. Children must be accompanied by an adult, and no children under five are allowed. Tickets are required on weekends and at other busy times. It is open from noon to 3pm daily.

Teddy Bear, dating from 1903

THIRD FLOOR

THE LARGEST EXHIBITIION on this floor is the **American Presidency: A Glorious Burden**. It displays objects that represent the lives and times of the 42 presidents in 11 themed sections. Artifacts include the lap desk on which Thomas Jefferson wrote the Declaration of Independence, George Washington's sword, and the top hat worn by Lincoln the night he was shot.

The West Wing offers a more eclectic range of exhibits, from ceramics, textiles, and musical instruments to money, medals, and printing. Some fine examples of presses and typesetting and papermaking equipment are on display in the **Printing and Graphic Arts Hall**.

Among the third floor's other highlights is the **Hall of Textiles**, which houses colorful pieces including the Pocahontas Quilt, depicting the life of the famous American Indian.

The **Hall of Musical Instruments** includes a violoncello made by Stradivari in 1701.

Two small exhibits will delight children: an elaborate dollhouse, and artifacts from popular culture, including the ruby slippers worn by Judy Garland in the *Wizard of Oz*.

Detail of the Pocahontas Quilt

Washington Monument ⓫

CONSTRUCTED OF 36,000 pieces of marble and granite, the Washington Monument remains one of the most recognizable monuments in the capital. Funds for this tribute to the first president of the United States initially came from individual citizens. A design by Robert Mills was chosen and construction began in 1848. When the money ran out the building work stopped for over 20 years. Then, in 1876, public interest revived the cause of completing the project. (A slight change in the color of stone marks the point where construction resumed.) The Monument has recently undergone a massive renovation; it has been thoroughly cleaned, cracks have been sealed, chipped stone patched, and the 192 commemorative stones repaired.

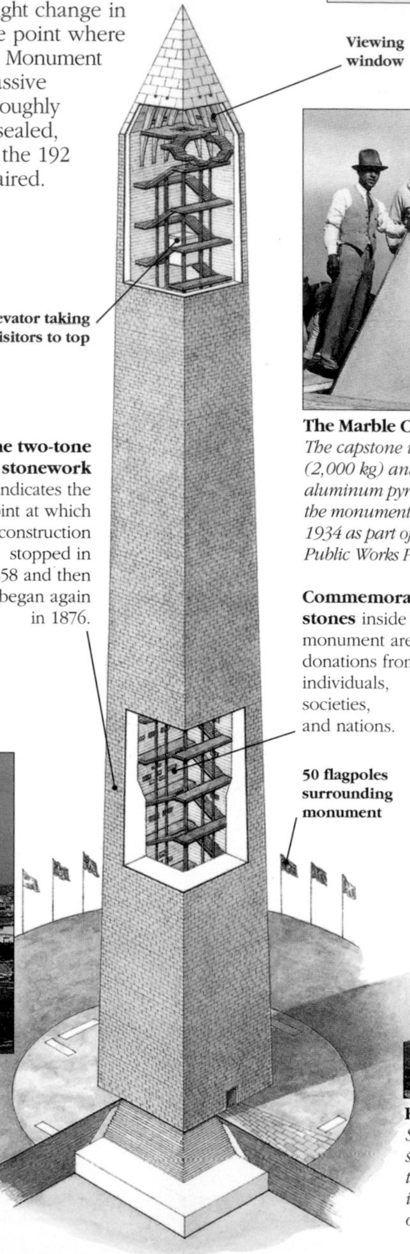

VISITORS' CHECKLIST

Independence Ave at 17th St, SW. **Map** 2 F5 & 3 B4. 426-6841. Smithsonian. 13, 52. early Sep–early Apr: 9am– 4:30pm; early Apr–early Sep: 8am–11:30pm. Dec 25. *Interpretive talks.* www.nps.gov/wamo

Viewing window

The Marble Capstone
The capstone weighs 3,300 pounds (2,000 kg) and is topped by an aluminum pyramid. Restoration of the monument was carried out in 1934 as part of President Roosevelt's Public Works Project (see p21).

Elevator taking visitors to top

The two-tone stonework indicates the point at which construction stopped in 1858 and then began again in 1876.

The Original Design
Although the original design included a circular colonnade around the monument, lack of funds prohibited its construction.

Commemorative stones inside the monument are donations from individuals, societies, and nations.

50 flagpoles surrounding monument

View of the Monument
The gleaming white stone of the newly restored monument makes it clearly visible from almost all over the city. The views from the top of the monument across Washington are stunning.

Restoration
Specially designed scaffolding encased the monument during its two year program of repair and cleaning.

The colonnaded domed Jefferson Memorial, housing the bronze statue

Critics at the time gave the Memorial the derisive nickname of "Jefferson's Muffin," and it was dismissed as being far too "feminine" for such a bold and greatly influential a man. Etched on the walls of the memorial are Jefferson's words from the Declaration of Independence as well as other writings.

United States Holocaust Memorial Museum ⑫

See pp76–7.

Bureau of Engraving and Printing ⑬

14th St, SW, between Maine Ave & Independence Ave. **Map** 3 B5. 874-3188 or 2330. Ⓜ Smithsonian. 9am–1:40pm Mon–Fri (Jun–Aug: 5– 6:40pm additional tours). ● Sat & Sun, week after Christmas, federal hols. 🕭 🛈 Ⓦ www.moneyfactory.com

UNTIL 1863, individual banks were responsible for printing American money. A shortage of coins and the need to finance the Civil War led to the production of standardized bank notes, and the Bureau of Engraving and Printing was founded. Initially housed in the basement of the Treasury Building (see p106), the bureau was moved to its present location in 1914. It prints over $140 billion a year, as well as stamps, federal documents, and White House invitations. Coins are not minted here, but in a federal facility in Philadelphia.

The 40-minute tour includes a short film, and a walk through the building to view the printing processes and checks for defects. Also on display are bills that are out of circulation, counterfeit money, and a special $100,000 bill. The Visitor Center has a gift shop, videos, and exhibits.

Jefferson Memorial ⑭

South bank of the Tidal Basin. **Map** 3 B5. 426-6841. Ⓜ Smithsonian. 8am–midnight. ● Dec 25. **Interpretive talks.** 🕭 🛈 Ⓦ www.nps.gov/thje/index2.htm

THOMAS JEFFERSON (see p154) was the third American president, from 1801 to 1809. He also played a significant part in drafting the Declaration of Independence in 1776.

Designed by John Russell Pope, this Neo Classical Memorial stands at the center of the Tidal Basin. However, when it was dedicated in 1943, metal was being rationed and so the standing statue of Jefferson was cast in plaster, not bronze. After the end of World War II, the statue was recast in metal and the plaster version was moved permanently to the basement of the building.

Majestic, 19-ft (6 m) statue of Jefferson

Tidal Basin ⑮

Boathouse: 1501 Maine Ave, SW. **Map** 2 F5 & 3 A5. 484-0206. Ⓜ Smithsonian. Apr–Oct: 10am–6pm. 🕭

THE TIDAL BASIN was built in 1897 to catch the overflow from the Potomac River and prevent flooding. In the 1920s, hundreds of cherry trees, given by the Japanese government, were planted along the shores of the manmade lake. The sight of the trees in bloom is one of the most photographed in the city. However, during the two weeks when the cherry trees bloom (sometime between mid-March and mid-April) chaos reigns around the Tidal Basin. The area is filled with cars and tour buses, which bring traffic to a standstill. The only way to avoid this gridlock is to see the blossoms on foot at dawn.

The Tidal Basin reverts to a relatively quiet park after the blossoms have fallen and the hordes depart. Blue paddleboats can be rented from the boathouse on Maine Avenue.

The banks of the Tidal Basin, with Jefferson Memorial in the distance

United States Holocaust Memorial Museum ⑫

THE US HOLOCAUST MEMORIAL MUSEUM, opened in 1993, bears witness to the systematic persecution and murder in Europe of six million Jews and others deemed undesirable by the Third Reich, including homosexuals and the disabled. The exhibition space ranges from the intentionally claustrophobic to the soaringly majestic. The museum contains 2,500 photographs, 1,000 artifacts, 53 video monitors, and 30 interactive stations that contain graphic and emotionally disturbing images of violence, forcing visitors to confront the horror of the Holocaust. While Daniel's Story is suitable for children of eight years and up, the Permanent Exhibition is recommended for children over 12.

★ Hall of Remembrance
The Hall of Remembrance houses an eternal flame that pays homage to the victims of the Holocaust.

Second Floor

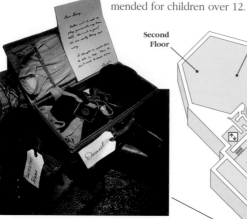

★ Daniel's Story
This exhibit, aimed at children between the ages of eight and 12, tells the history of the Holocaust from the point of view of an eight-year-old Jewish boy in 1930s Germany.

KEY TO FLOOR PLAN

☐ Concourse Level
☐ First Floor
☐ Second Floor
☐ Third Floor
☐ Fourth Floor

GALLERY GUIDE

The Holocaust Museum is meant to be experienced, not just seen. Starting from the top, footage, artifacts, photographs, and testimonies of survivors can be seen from the fourth to the second floors. The first floor has an interactive display, and the Concourse Level houses the Children's Tile Wall.

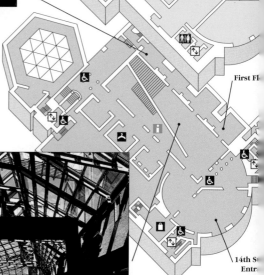

First Fl

14th S
Entr

★ Hall of Witness
The soaring central atrium features the Hall of Witness. The Museum aims to preser the memory of those who die

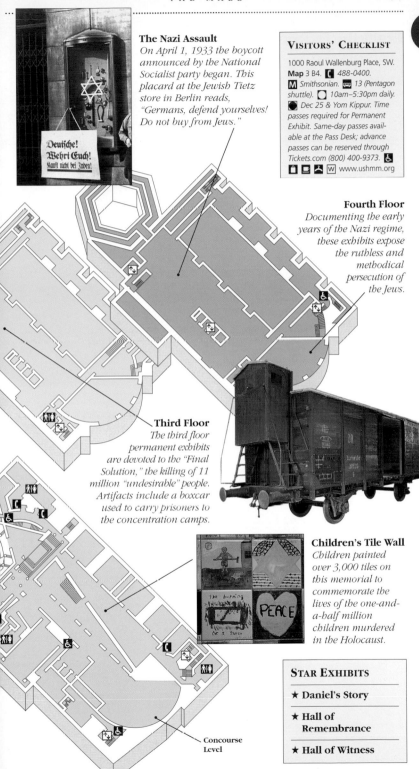

The Nazi Assault
On April 1, 1933 the boycott announced by the National Socialist party began. This placard at the Jewish Tietz store in Berlin reads, "Germans, defend yourselves! Do not buy from Jews."

VISITORS' CHECKLIST

1000 Raoul Wallenburg Place, SW. Map 3 B4. ☎ 488-0400. Ⓜ *Smithsonian.* 🚌 13 *(Pentagon shuttle).* ⭕ *10am–5:30pm daily.* ⬤ *Dec 25 & Yom Kippur. Time passes required for Permanent Exhibit. Same-day passes available at the Pass Desk; advance passes can be reserved through Tickets.com (800) 400-9373.* ♿ 🛗 ◻ ⛰ Ⓦ www.ushmm.org

Fourth Floor
Documenting the early years of the Nazi regime, these exhibits expose the ruthless and methodical persecution of the Jews.

Third Floor
The third floor permanent exhibits are devoted to the "Final Solution," the killing of 11 million "undesirable" people. Artifacts include a boxcar used to carry prisoners to the concentration camps.

Children's Tile Wall
Children painted over 3,000 tiles on this memorial to commemorate the lives of the one-and-a-half million children murdered in the Holocaust.

Concourse Level

STAR EXHIBITS

★ Daniel's Story

★ Hall of Remembrance

★ Hall of Witness

Franklin D. Roosevelt Memorial ⑯

The fourth room honors Roosevelt's fourth term in office. A statue of his wife, Eleanor, stands in this room.

Franklin Roosevelt once told Supreme Court Justice Felix Frankfurter, "If they are to put up any memorial to me, I should like it to be placed in the center of that green plot in front of the Archives Building. I should like it to consist of a block about the size of this," pointing to his desk. It took more than 50 years for a fitting monument to be erected, but Roosevelt's request for modesty was not heeded. Opened in 1997, this memorial is a mammoth park of four granite open-air rooms, one for each of Roosevelt's terms, with statuary and waterfalls. The president, a polio victim, is portrayed in a chair, with his dog Fala by his side.

A relief of Roosevelt's funeral cortège was carved into the granite wall by artist Leonard Baskin. It depicts the coffin on a horse-drawn cart, followed by the crowds of mourners walking behind.

Dramatic waterfalls cascade into a series of pools in the fourth room. The water reflects the peace that Roosevelt was so keen to achieve before his death.

The poignant statues of the Korean War Veterans Memorial

Korean War Veterans Memorial ⑰

21st St & Independence Ave, SW. **Map** 2 E5. ℂ 426-6841. Ⓜ Smithsonian. ◯ 8am–midnight daily. ● Dec 25. ☑ on request. ♿ Ⓦ www.nps. gov/kwvm

The Korean War Veterans Memorial is a controversial memorial to a controversial war. Although 1.5 million Americans served in the con-

flict, war was never officially declared. It is often known as "The Forgotten War." Intense debate preceded the selection of the memorial's design. On July 27, 1995, the 42nd anniversary of the armistice that ended the war, the Memorial was dedicated. Nineteen larger-than-life stainless steel statues, a squad on patrol, are depicted moving across the field of battle. On the south side is a polished black granite wall etched with the images of more than 2,400 veterans.

Lincoln Memorial ⑱

Constitution Ave, between French & Bacon Drives. **Map** 2 E5. ℂ 426-6841. Ⓜ Smithsonian. ◯ 8am–midnight daily. ● Dec 25. ☑ on request. ♿ Ⓓ Ⓦ www.nps.gov/linc

Many proposals were made for a memorial to President Abraham Lincoln. One of the least promising was for a monument on a swampy piece of land to the west of the Washington Monument. Yet this was to become one of the most awe-inspiring sights in Washington. Looming over the Reflecting Pool is the seated figure of Lincoln in his Neoclassical "temple."

Before the monument could be built in 1914, the site had to be drained. Solid concrete piers were poured for the foundation so that the building could be anchored in bedrock. Work continued through World War I, but as the memorial neared completion, architect Henry Bacon realized that the statue of Lincoln would be

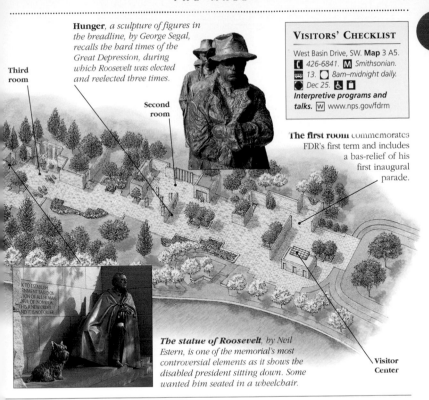

Hunger, *a sculpture of figures in the breadline, by George Segal, recalls the hard times of the Great Depression, during which Roosevelt was elected and reelected three times.*

Third room

Second room

The first room commemorates FDR's first term and includes a bas-relief of his first inaugural parade.

VISITORS' CHECKLIST

West Basin Drive, SW. **Map** 3 A5.
426-6841. M Smithsonian.
13. 8am–midnight daily.
Dec 25.
Interpretive programs and talks. www.nps.gov/fdrm

The statue of Roosevelt, *by Neil Estern, is one of the memorial's most controversial elements as it shows the disabled president sitting down. Some wanted him seated in a wheelchair.*

Visitor Center

---

dwarfed inside the huge edifice. The original 10-ft (3-m) statue by Daniel Chester French was doubled in size. As a result, it was carved from 28 blocks of white marble joined together, because no single block was big enough.

Engraved on the walls are Lincoln's Gettysburg Address *(see p151)* and Second Inaugural Address. This was the site of Dr. Martin Luther King, Jr.'s famous address, "I Have a Dream" *(see p91)*.

Vietnam Veterans Memorial ⑲

21st St & Constitution Ave, NW. **Map** 2 E4. 426-6841. M Smithsonian. 8am–midnight daily. Dec 25. on request. www.nps.gov/vive

MAYA LIN, A 21-year-old student at Yale University, submitted a design for the proposed Vietnam Veterans Memorial as part of her architecture course.

One of 1,421 entries, Maya Lin's design was simple – two triangular black walls sinking into the earth at an angle of 125 degrees, one end pointing to the Lincoln Memorial, the other to the Washington Monument. On the walls would be inscribed the names of the Americans who died in the Vietnam war, in chronological order, from the first casualty in 1959 to the last in 1975.

Lin received only a B grade on the course, but she won the competition. Her design, called by some a scar on the earth, has become one of the most moving monuments on the Mall. Veterans and their families leave tokens of remembrance – soft toys, poems, pictures, and flowers – at the site of the fallen soldier's name.

To mollify those opposed to the abstract memorial, a statue of three soldiers, sculpted by Frederick Hart, was added in 1984, two years after the memorial was dedicated. Further lobbying led to the Vietnam Women's Memorial, erected close by in 1993.

The majestic Lincoln Memorial, reflected in the still waters of the pool

OLD DOWNTOWN

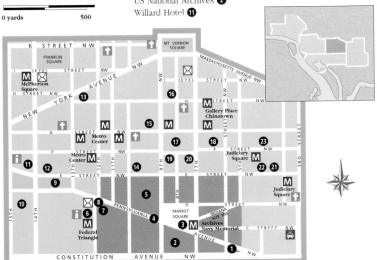

BORDERED BY the Capitol to the east and the White House to the west, Washington's Downtown was the heart of the city one hundred years ago. F Street, the city's first paved road, bustled with shops, newspaper offices, bars, and churches, as well as horses and carriages. Downtown was also an important residential neighborhood. The upper classes maintained elegant

Sculpture outside the National Museum of American Art

homes, while middle-class merchants lived above their shops. But by the 1950s suburbia had lured people away from the area, and in the 1980s Downtown had become a mixture of boarded-up buildings and discount shops. However, the 1990s saw a dramatic change in the area and the beginnings of regeneration, as the MCI Center attracted new restaurants and stores.

SIGHTS AT A GLANCE

Museums and Galleries
International Spy Museum **19**
National Building Museum **23**
National Museum of American Art and National Portrait Gallery pp92–5 **17**
National Museum of Women in the Arts **13**

Statues and Fountains
Benjamin Franklin Statue **8**
Mellon Fountain **1**

0 meters   500

0 yards   500

Aquarium
National Aquarium **10**

Historic and Official Buildings
FBI Building **5**
Ford's Theatre **14**
Martin Luther King Memorial Library **15**
MCI Center **18**
National Theater **12**
Old Post Office **7**
Ronald Reagan Building **6**
US National Archives **2**
Willard Hotel **11**

Districts, Streets, and Squares
7th Street **20**
Chinatown **16**
Freedom Plaza **9**
Judiciary Square **21**
Pennsylvania Avenue **4**

Memorials
National Law Enforcement Officers' Memorial **22**
US Navy Memorial **3**

GETTING THERE

Old Downtown is well served by several Metrorail stops: McPherson Square, Gallery Place-Chinatown, Metro Center, Judiciary Square, Archives-Navy Memorial, and Federal Triangle. The 32, 34, and 36 bus lines run along Pennsylvania Avenue.

KEY

▦ Street-by-street map *pp82–3*	🚔 Police station
Ⓜ Metro station	⊠ Post office
ℹ Tourist information	✚ Church

◁ **Statue of Benjamin Franklin outside the flag-festooned Old Post Office**

Street-by-Street: Old Downtown

IN THE MID-20TH CENTURY, Pennsylvania Avenue, the main route for presidential inaugural parades, was tawdry and run down. It is now a grand boulevard worthy of L'Enfant's original vision. The FBI Building, a concrete structure built in a challenging, modern style, is one of its most prominent features. Opposite the nearby US Navy Memorial is the US National Archives, housing original copies of the Constitution and the Declaration of Independence. To the east are the Mellon Fountain and the National Gallery of Art. The Ronald Reagan Building was the site of the 1999 NATO summit, and the Old Post Office has been wonderfully restored.

★ FBI Building
The headquarters of the Federal Bureau of Investigation was built in the austere Brutalist style between 1967 and 1972 to resemble a "central core of files" ❺

Pennsylvania Avenue
Part of L'Enfant's original plan for the city, Pennsylvania Avenue was the first main street to be laid out in Washington. It joins the US Capitol to the White House ❹

Benjamin Franklin Statue
This inventor, statesman, writer, publisher, and man of genius is remembered simply as "printer" ❽

Ronald Reagan Building
Built in 1997, this impressive edifice echoes the Classical Revival architecture of other buildings in the Federal Triangle ❻

CONSTITUTION AVENUE NW

Interstate Commerce Commission

★ Old Post Office
This majestic granite building was completed in 1899. It now houses shops and a food court. The elegant clock tower measures 315 ft (96 m) in height ❼

US Navy Memorial
The memorial at Market Square contains a huge etching of the world surrounded by low granite walls ❸

LOCATOR MAP
See Street Finder Maps 3 & 4

Commission on the Arts

6TH STREET NW

7TH STREET NW

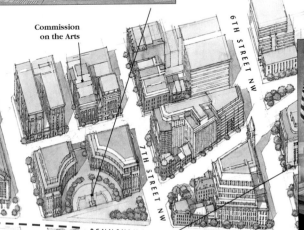

PENNSYLVANIA   AVENUE NW

9TH STREET NW

★ **US National Archives**
The Rotunda houses the National Archives' most precious documents, known as the "Charters of Freedom," including the Bill of Rights. A copy of England's Magna Carta is also on display ❷

CONSTITUTION   AVENUE NW

Federal Trade Commission

Justice Department

Mellon Fountain
Located by the National Gallery of Art's West Building, this fountain is named after Andrew Mellon, an industrialist and art collector who founded the gallery in the 1930s ❶

| 0 meters | 100 |
| 0 yards | 100 |

KEY

– – – Suggested route

STAR SIGHTS
★ FBI Building
★ Old Post Office
★ US National Archives

The cascading water of the Classical-style Mellon Fountain

Mellon Fountain **1**

Constitution Ave & Pennsylvania Ave, NW. **Map** 4 D4. **M** *Archives-Navy Memorial.*

Sʜᴜᴀᴛᴇᴅ ᴏᴘᴘᴏꜱɪᴛᴇ the National Gallery of Art *(see pp56–9),* this fountain commemorates the man who endowed the gallery with its collection. Andrew Mellon was Secretary of the Treasury and a financier and industrialist. At his death, his friends donated $300,000 to build the fountain, which was dedicated on May 9, 1952.

The three bronze basins with their cascades of water were inspired by a fountain seen in a public square in Genoa, Italy. On the bottom of the largest basin, the signs of the Zodiac are engraved in bas-relief. The Classical lines of the fountain echo the architectural style of the National Gallery of Art West Building.

US National Archives **2**

Constitution Ave, between 7th St & 9th St, NW. **Map** 3 D3. **C** *501-5000.* **M** *Archives-Navy Memorial.* **O** *Apr 1–Labor Day: 10am–9pm daily; Sep–Mar: 10am–5:30pm daily.* ● *Dec 25.* **Z** **&** **W** www.nara.gov

Iɴ ᴛʜᴇ 1930ꜱ, Congress recognized the need to preserve the country's paper records before they deteriorated, were lost or were destroyed. The National Archives building, created for this purpose, was designed by John Russell Pope, architect of the National Gallery of Art and the Jefferson Memorial; it opened in 1934. This impressive library is home to the most important historical and legal documents in the United States.

On display in the Archives' majestic Rotunda are the *Declaration of Independence,* the *Constitution of the United States,* and a 1297 copy of the

Statue outside the US National Archives

Magna Carta, which is on indefinite loan from Ross Perot. The documents are sealed in helium to help preserve them, and for additional security are lowered into underground vaults at night.

Also housed in the National Archives are millions of documents, photographs, motion picture film, and sound recordings going back over two centuries. There is enough material, in fact, to fill around 250,000 filing cabinets. The National Archives and Records Administration (NARA) is the body responsible for cataloging, managing, and conserving all this material. Much of the Archives' information is now stored on computer.

The National Archives is of great importance as a research center. The Central Research Room is reserved for scholars, who can order reproductions of rare documents for study purposes. Copies of military records, immigration papers, slave transit documents, death certificates, and tax information are also available, making the National Archives a useful source of information for people researching their family histories. The Archives also have an extensive database that can be accessed from its website.

The impressive Neoclassical façade of the National Archives Building

The Constitution of the United States

IN 1787, DELEGATES from the 13 original American states convened in the city of Philadelphia to redraft the Articles of Confederation (see p16). It soon became clear that an entirely new document was required, rather than a revised one. Weeks of debate grew into months, as delegates drafted the framework for a new country. Cooperation and compromise finally led to the creation of the Constitution, a document that outlines the powers of the central

Original flag of the 13 US states

government and the makeup of Congress. One of the main issues, how to elect the representatives, was finally determined to be by direct voting by the people. Once signed, the new Constitution was sent to the states for review. Federalists and anti-Federalists debated fervently over its content in pamphlets, speeches, and articles. In the end, the majority of states ratified the Constitution, giving up some of their power in "order to form a more perfect union."

The Preamble of the Constitution of the United States

Signatures on the US Constitution

SIGNING OF THE CONSTITUTION

After many months of debate by the delegates to the Federal Convention, the Constitution was completed and signed by 39 of the 55 state delegates on September 17, 1787, at Assembly Hall in Philadelphia. The oldest delegate was 81-year-old Benjamin Franklin. James Madison, another signatory, played a major role in achieving the ratification of the new Constitution during the two years after it was signed.

James Madison

THE CONSTITUTION TODAY

The seven articles of the Constitution (of which the first three lay out the principles of government; see pp26–7) still determine the laws of the United States today. In addition there are Amendments. The first ten form the Bill of Rights, which includes such famous issues as the right to bear arms and the freedom of religion and of speech.

Swearing Allegiance
The pledge of allegiance to the flag was written in 1892 to mark the 400th anniversary of Columbus's discovery of America. Today it is recited daily by schoolchildren and by immigrants taking up American citizenship.

Public Demonstration
Citizens demonstrate their right to free speech by protesting against the Persian Gulf War.

A view down tree-lined Pennsylvania Avenue toward the US Capitol

US Navy Memorial ❸

Market Square, Pennsylvania Ave between 7th St & 9th St, NW. **Map** 3 C3. **M** *Archives-Navy Memorial*. **♿ Naval Heritage Center** 701 Pennsylvania Ave, NW. **☎** *737-2300.* **◯** *9:30am–5pm Mon–Sat.* **◯** *Nov 1–Mar 1: Mon.* **♿**

THE MEMORIAL to the US Navy in Market Square centers on the statue of a single sailor. Sculpted in bronze by Stanley Bleifeld in 1990, the figure provides a poignant tribute to the men and women who have served in the US Navy.

The sculpture stands on a vast map of the world – the outlines of the countries are laid into the ground and protected by low walls. Four waterfalls and a group of flagpoles complete the memorial. During the summer, there is a series of free concerts by military bands in the square.

Behind the memorial is the **Naval Heritage Center**, with exhibits on the history of the navy as well as portraits of famous naval personnel, including John F. Kennedy.

The lone sailor of the US Navy Memorial

Pennsylvania Avenue ❹

Pennsylvania Ave. **Map** 3 A2 to 4 D4. **M** *Federal Triangle, Archives-Navy Memorial.*

WHEN PIERRE L'ENFANT drew up his plans in 1789 for the capital city of the new United States, he imagined a grand boulevard running through the center of the city, from the presidential palace to the legislative building.

For the first 200 years of its history, Pennsylvania Avenue fell sadly short of L'Enfant's dreams. In the early 19th century it was simply a muddy footpath through the woods. Paved in 1833, it became part of a neighborhood of boarding houses, shops, and hotels.

During the Civil War, the area deteriorated quickly into "saloons, gambling dens, lodging houses, quick-lunch rooms, cheap-jack shops, and catch penny amusement places" according to the *Works Progress Administration Guide to Washington.* When President John F. Kennedy's inaugural parade processed down Pennsylvania Avenue in 1961, Kennedy took one look at "America's Main Street" with its shambles of peep shows, pawn shops, and liquor stores and said, "It's a disgrace – fix it." This command by Kennedy provided the impetus to reevaluate the future of Pennsylvania Avenue.

Almost 15 years later, Congress established the Pennsylvania Avenue Development Corporation – a public and private partnership that developed a comprehensive plan of revitalization. Today, Pennsylvania Avenue is a

PRESIDENTIAL INAUGURAL PARADES

The tradition of inaugural parades to mark the occasion of a new president's coming-to-office started in 1809 when the military accompanied President James Madison from his Virginia home to Washington, DC. Military bands have been a part of the inaugural parades ever since, and the Army Band traditionally leads the procession down Pennsylvania Avenue from the US Capitol to the White House. The first parade to include floats was held in 1841 for President William Henry Harrison. In 1985, the freezing January weather forced Ronald Reagan's inaugural ceremony indoors to the Capitol Rotunda.

President Franklin D. Roosevelt's third inaugural parade in 1941

The authoritative exterior of the FBI Building on Pennsylvania Avenue

clean, tree-lined street. Parks, memorials, shops, theaters, hotels, museums, and assorted government buildings border the street on either side, providing a suitably grand and formal setting for all future presidential inaugural parades.

FBI Building ❺

935 Pennsylvania Ave, NW. **Map** 3 C3.
📞 324-3000 Ⓜ Archives-Navy Memorial, Gallery Place. ⏰ 8:45am–4:15pm Mon–Fri. ● Federal hols. ✉ call ahead for details. ♿ 🚻 W www.fbi.gov

THE HEADQUARTERS of the Federal Bureau of Investigation was started in 1964 and dedicated in 1975. The official name of the building is the J. Edgar Hoover FBI Building, in honor of the Bureau's longtime head.

Established in 1908 with the motto Fidelity, Bravery, and Integrity, the FBI has jurisdiction over federal crime. The Bureau, as it is commonly known, made its name in the 1920s and 1930s when it enforced Prohibition – the federal law that made the sale of alcohol a criminal offence.

The tour of the FBI building is one of the most popular in Washington, made even more so by the success of the cult TV show *The X Files*, starring two fictional FBI agents. Once inside, visitors are led through the exhibits by a tour guide. Criminal artifacts on display include pipe bombs, assault rifles, and handguns, some of which were owned by famous criminals such as Pretty Boy Floyd and John Dillinger. Visitors learn about the history of the FBI and the "Ten Most Wanted" list of fugitives. The future of crime detection is highlighted with a look at DNA analysis and advanced fingerprinting techniques. The tour ends with a display of FBI firearms, though these are rarely used on duty.

Sculpture from the Oscar Straus Memorial Fountain

Ronald Reagan Building ❻

1300 Pennsylvania Ave, NW. **Map** 3 B3.
📞 312-1300. Ⓜ Federal Triangle. ⏰ 7am–2am daily. ● Federal hols. ✉ call 312-1470. 🍴 🛍 ♿
W www.itcdc.com www.dcvisit.com

THE RONALD REAGAN building filled the last empty plot of land in the Federal Triangle area of Washington, DC's Old Downtown. Yet it has failed to fulfill its promise to provide a magnificent base for both a cultural center and an international trade center.

The Reagan Building looks as though it was designed by a committee that tried to please everyone, and ended by pleasing no one. Classical in appearance on the outside and modern on the inside, the huge complex is only slightly smaller than Vatican City in Rome. Completed in 1997, it was the most expensive federal building project ever undertaken. The doubtful architectural success of the Reagan Building is surprising considering its designer, James Inigo Freed, was also responsible for the design of the US Holocaust Memorial Museum *(see pp76–7)*. In fairness to Freed, his original design underwent many changes before it became this huge glass and steel hall.

The Washington DC Visitor Information Center is located in the building. It provides tour information and tickets to shows and events, and is open 8am to 6pm, Monday through Saturday.

Outside the building is the Oscar Straus Memorial Fountain, with sculpture by Adolph Alexander Weinman.

Mock-Classical entrance to the immense Ronald Reagan Building

Food court in the spectacular galleried hall of the Old Post Office

Old Post Office ⓻

1100 Pennsylvania Ave, NW. **Map** 3 C3.
⦗ 289-4224. Ⓜ *Federal Triangle.*
◯ *Mar–Aug: 10am–9pm Mon–Sat;*
Sep–Feb: 10am–7pm Mon–Sat,
noon–6pm Sun all year. ⏺ *Jan 1,*
Thanksgiving, Dec 25. ⧉ *tower only*
(call 606-8691). ⛐ ▣ ▯
ⓦ www.oldpostofficedc.com

Bᵁᴵᴸᵀ ᴵᴺ 1899, the Old Post
Office was Washington's
first skyscraper. Soaring 12
stories above the city, it was
a fireproof model of modern
engineering with a steel frame
covered in granite. The huge
interior had 3,900 electric lights
and its own generator, the
first one to be used in the city.
Its fanciful Romanesque architecture was fashionable at
the time it was built, and the
breathtaking hall, with its glass
roof and balconies, remains
a spectacular mixture of light,
color, and gleaming metal.

In the 15 years following its
construction, the Post Office
became an object of contro-
versy. Its turrets and arches,
once praised by critics, were
derided. The *New York Times*
newspaper said the building
looked like "a cross between
a cathedral and a cotton mill."
Government planners thought
the Post Office building
clashed with the Neoclassical
architecture that dominated
the rest of Washington. When
the postal system moved its
offices in 1934, there seemed

to be no reason to keep the
architectural relic. Only a lack
of funds during the Great
Depression of the 1930s (*see
p21*) prevented the Old Post
Office from being torn down.

The building was occupied
intermittently by various
government agencies until the
mid-1960s, when its decrepit
condition again drew a
chorus in favor of demolition.
A Washington preservation
group, Don't Tear It Down,
promoted the historical significance of the Old Post Office,
and it was spared once more.

The renovated building,
commonly known as the
Pavilion, is now home to a
broad range of shops and
restaurants. The Post Office
tower has an observation
deck rising 270 ft (82 m)
above the city, giving one of
the best views of Washington.

Benjamin Franklin Statue ⓼

Pennsylvania Ave & 10th St, NW.
Map 3 C3. Ⓜ *Federal Triangle.*

Dᴼᴺᴬᵀᴱᴰ ʙʏ publisher Stilson
Hutchins (1839–1912),
it was unveiled by Benjamin
Franklin's great-granddaughter
in 1889. The words "Printer,
Philosopher, Patriot, Philanthropist" are inscribed on
the four sides of the statue's
pedestal in tribute to this
man of diverse talents.

Postmaster general,
writer, and scientist,
Benjamin Franklin
was also a key member
of the committee that
drafted the 1776
Declaration of Inde-
pendence. As a diplo-
mat to the court
of Louis XVI of
France, he went to
Versailles in 1777 to
gain support for the
American cause of
independence from
Britain. Franklin returned to
France in 1783 to negotiate the
Treaty of Paris that ended the
American Revolution (*see p16*).

**Stately fig
of Benjam
Frankli**

Freedom Plaza ⓽

Pennsylvania Ave between 13th St &
14th St, NW. **Map** 3 B3. Ⓜ *Federal
Triangle, Metro Center.*

Fᴿᴱᴱᴰᴼᴹ ᴾᴸᴬᶻᴬ was conceived
as part of a Pennsylvania
Avenue redevelopment plan
in the mid-1970s. Designed
by Robert Venturi and Denise
Scott Brown, and completed in
1980, the plaza displays Pierre
L'Enfant's original plan for
Washington in black and white
stone embedded in the ground.
Around the edge are engraved
quotations about the new city
from Walt Whitman and President Wilson, among others.

Freedom Plaza provides a
dramatic entry to Pennsylvania
Avenue (*see pp86–7*). On the

The large-scale reproduction of
L'Enfant's city plans, Freedom Plaza

north side of the plaza, where Pennsylvania Avenue leads into E Street, are the **Warner Theatre** and the **National Theatre**. South of the plaza is the Beaux Arts **District Building** (housing government employees). Throughout the year, Freedom Plaza hosts festivals and open-air concerts.

National Aquarium ⓾

Commerce Building, 14th St & Constitution Ave, NW. **Map** 3 B3. 482-2825. Federal Triangle. 9am–5pm daily. Dec 25. www.nationalaquarium.com

ORIGINALLY LOCATED in 1873 at Woods Hole, Massachusetts (a major center for marine biology), the National Aquarium was moved to Washington in 1888 in order to make it accessible to more people. Since 1932 it has been located in the US Department of Commerce Building, and today the aquarium is home to around 1,200 specimens and 200 different species.

Green Turtle at the National Aquarium

The Aquarium has a wide range of freshwater and saltwater fish on display, such as nurse sharks, piranhas, and moray eels, and also a number of reptiles and various species of amphibians, for example, alligators and sea turtles, all displayed in simulated "natural environments."

There is a touch tank that allows visitors to handle some of the creatures.

Willard Hotel ⓫

1401 Pennsylvania Ave, NW. **Map** 3 B3. 628-9100, (800) 327-0200. Metro Center. www.washington@interconti.com

THERE HAS BEEN a hotel on this site since 1818. Originally called Tennison's, the hotel was housed in six adjacent two-story buildings. Refurbished in 1847, it was managed by hotel keeper

Henry Willard, who gave his name to the hotel in 1850. Many famous people stayed here during the Civil War (1861–65), including the writer Nathaniel Hawthorne, who was covering the conflict for a magazine, and Julia Ward Howe who wrote the popular Civil War standard *The Battle Hymn of the Republic*. The word "lobbyist" is said to have been coined because it was known by those seeking favors that President Ulysses S. Grant went to the hotel's lobby to smoke his after-dinner cigar.

The present 340-room building, designed by the architect of New York's Plaza Hotel, Henry Hardenbergh, was completed in 1904. It was the most fashionable place to stay in the city until the end of World War II, when the surrounding neighborhood fell into decline. For 20 years it was boarded up and faced demolition. A coalition, formed of preservationists and the Pennsylvania Avenue Development Corporation, worked to restore the Beaux Arts building, and it finally reopened in renewed splendor in 1986.

No other hotel can rival the Willard's grand lobby, with its 35 different kinds of marble, polished wood, and petal-shaped concierge station. There is a style café, a bar, and a restaurant called The Willard Room.

Façade of the National Theatre on E Street

National Theatre ⓬

1321 Pennsylvania Ave, NW. **Map** 3 B3. 628-6161. Metro Center, Federal Triangle. www.nationaltheatre.org

THE PRESENT National Theatre is the sixth theater to occupy this Pennsylvania Avenue site. The first four theaters burned down, and the fifth one was replaced by the current building in 1922. Extensively renovated in 1984, it hosts Broadway-bound productions and touring groups, which have included such major shows as "Mamma Mia" and "Les Miserables."

The National is known as an "actor's theater" because of its excellent acoustics (even a whisper on stage can be heard in the top tier of the balcony). The theater is haunted by the ghost of 19th-century actor John McCullough, who was murdered by a fellow actor and buried hastily under the stage.

Peacock Alley, one of the Willard Hotel's luxuriously decorated corridors

National Museum of Women in the Arts ⑬

1250 New York Ave, NW. **Map** 3 C3.
[783-5000. **M** *Metro Center.*
◯ *10am–5pm Mon–Sat, noon–5pm
Sun.* **●** *Thanksgiving, Dec 25, Jan 1.*
⬚ *for groups (call 783-7996).* **⬤ ⬜**
⬚ w www.nmwa.org

THIS MUSEUM of women's
art houses works that
span five centuries, from the
Renaissance to the present day.
The collection was started in
the 1960s by Wilhelmina
Holladay and her husband,
who gathered paintings,
sculpture, and photography
from all over the world.

The museum operated out
of the Holladays' private residence for several years, until
it acquired a more permanent
home in this Renaissance
Revival landmark building,
formerly a Masonic Lodge.
The collection has as its highlights masterpieces by female
American artists. Some of the
outstanding works on display
from the 19th century include
The Bath (1891) by Mary
Cassatt and *The Cage* (1885)
by Berthe Morisot. Among the
works by 20th-century artists
are *Bacchus 3* (1978) by Elaine
de Kooning and *Self-Portrait
Between the Curtains, Dedication to Trotsky* (1937) by
Mexican artist Frida Kahlo. The
museum shop sells a range of
gifts, all created by women.

Assassination of President Lincoln

On April 14, 1865, Good Friday evening, Abraham Lincoln
went to Ford's Theatre to see the play *Our American Cousin*.
From the rear of the presidential box John Wilkes Booth, a
Confederate sympathizer and an actor who often appeared

at the theater, shot Lincoln
in the head and then fled.
The wounded president
was carried across the
street to a boarding house
where, in the early morn-
ing of April 15, he died.
The assassin escaped on
horseback to Maryland
and then to Virginia,
where he was captured
by federal troops. Booth
was shot and killed on
the spot. Four others,
who were convicted for
conspiracy in the murder,
were later hanged.

**Painting of John Wilkes Booth
poised to shoot Abraham Lincoln**

Ford's Theatre ⑭

511 10th St between E St & F St, NW.
Map 3 C3. **[** 426-6924. **M** *Gallery
Place-Chinatown, Metro Center.*
◯ *9am–5pm daily (except matinee
or rehearsal days - call ahead).*
● *Dec 25.* **Petersen House**
◯ *9am–5pm daily.* **●** *Dec 25.* **⬤**
⬚ w www.fordstheatre.org

JOHN T. FORD, a theatrical pro-
ducer, built this small jewel
of a theater in 1863. Washington was a Civil War boomtown,
and the theater, located in the
thriving business district, enjoyed great popularity.

The fate of the theater was
sealed, however, on April 14,

**Exterior of Ford's Theatre, site of
the shooting of President Lincoln**

1865, when President Abraham
Lincoln was shot here by John
Wilkes Booth while watching
a performance. **Petersen
House**, where Lincoln died,
across the road from the
theater, has been preserved as
a museum where people can
see the bedroom in which the
president passed away.

After the tragedy, people
stopped patronizing the
theater, and Ford was forced
to sell the building to the federal government a year later.
It was left to spiral into decay
for nearly a century until the
government decided to restore
it to its original splendor.

Maintained by the National
Park Service, the theater now
stages small productions. The
Presidential Box is permanently
decorated in Lincoln's honor.

Impressive exterior of the National Museum of Women in the Arts

Martin Luther King Memorial Library ⑮

901 G St at 9th St, NW. **Map** 3 C3.
📞 727-1111. Ⓜ️ Gallery Place–
Chinatown, Metro Center. ⏲ 10am–
9pm Mon–Thu, 10am–5:30pm Fri &
Sat, call for Sun hours. ⬤ Federal
hols. 🚻 🅆 www.dclibrary.org/mlk

WASHINGTON's Martin Luther
King Memorial Library is
the only example of the architecture of Ludwig Mies van
der Rohe in the city. A prominent figure in 20th-century
design, van der Rohe finalized
his plans for the library short-
ly before his death in 1969. It
was named in honor of Dr.
Martin Luther King Jr. at the
request of the library's trustees
when it opened in 1972,
replacing the small and out-
dated Carnegie Library as the
city's central public library.

Architecturally, the building
is a classic example of van der
Rohe's theory of "less is more."
It is an austere, simple box
shape with a recessed entrance
lobby. Inside, there is a mural
depicting the life of Dr. Martin
Luther King Jr., the leader
of the Civil Rights Movement,
painted by artist Don Miller.

The library sponsors concerts
and readings, as well as a program of children's events.

The "Friendship Archway" spanning H Street in the heart of Chinatown

Chinatown ⑯

6th St to 8th St & G St to H St, NW.
Map 3 C3 & 4 D3. Ⓜ️ Gallery Place-
Chinatown.

THE SMALL AREA in Washington
known as Chinatown
covers just six square blocks.
Formed around 1930, it has
never been very large and
today houses about 500
Chinese residents. The area
has been reinvigorated by
the arrival of the adjacent
MCI Center (see p96) in 1997.
Although rents are up, and a
few well-established restaurants
have been forced to close, the
increased number of visitors

has brought new prosperity.
H Street is particularly lively,
with many shops and a
selection of good restaurants.

The "Friendship Archway,"
a dramatic gateway over H
Street at the junction with 7th
Street, marks the center of the
Chinatown area. Built in 1986,
it was paid for by Washington's
sister city, Beijing, as a token
of esteem, and is based on
the architecture of the Qing
Dynasty (1649–1911). Its seven
roofs, topped by 300 painted
dragons, are balanced on
a steel and concrete base,
making it the largest single-
span Chinese arch in the
world. It is lit up at night.

DR. MARTIN LUTHER KING, JR.

A charismatic speaker and proponent of
Mahatma Gandhi's theories of non-violence,
Dr. Martin Luther King, Jr. was a black Baptist
minister and leader of the the civil rights
movement in the United States.

Born in Atlanta, Georgia in 1929, King's
career in civil rights began with the 1955
Montgomery, Alabama bus boycott – a protest
of the city's segregated transit system. The
movement escalated to protests at schools,
restaurants, and hotels that did not admit
blacks. King's methods of non-violence were
often met with police dogs and brutal tactics.

The culmination of the movement was the
March on Washington on August 28, 1963,
when 200,000 people gathered at the Lincoln
Memorial in support of civil rights. The high-
light of this event was King's "I Have a
Dream" speech, calling for support of the
movement. A direct result was the passing by
Congress of the civil rights legislation in 1964,
and King was awarded the Nobel Peace Prize
the same year. In 1968 he was assassinated in
Memphis, Tennessee, triggering riots in 100
American cities, including Washington.

Dr. King speaking at the Lincoln Memorial

Smithsonian American Art Museum and National Portrait Gallery ⓱

THE NATIONAL PORTRAIT GALLERY and the Smithsonian American Art Museum, opened in 1968, are housed in the former US Patent Office, a wonderfully ornate building designed in 1836. Currently closed for renovation, these galleries reveal more about the nation's history than almost anywhere else. The National Portrait Gallery is America's family album, featuring paintings, photographs, and sculptures of thousands of famous Americans. The National Museum of American Art contains a wealth of works by American artists reflecting the history and culture of the country. Many of the paintings are regularly loaned out to other galleries.

Façade of the former US Patent Office, now home to the galleries

★ ACHELOUS AND HERCULES

This painting (1947) by Thomas Hart Benton (1889–1975) is a mythological analogy of early American life. Interpreted in many ways, it is widely accepted that Hercules is man taming the wild, then enjoying the results of his labors.

Hercules tries to capture the bull.

Achelous, the river god, appears as a bull being wrestled by Hercules, representing the struggle of the American people.

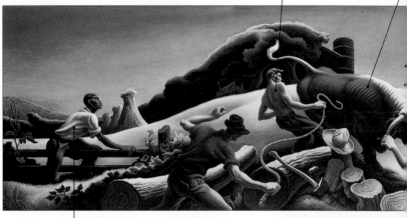

An African American is depicted climbing over a fence to the idealized equality of America.

★ Cliffs of the Upper Colorado River

This dramatic work, created in 1882, captures the vastness of the American West. It is just one of several landscapes in the museum by artist Thomas Moran.

Old Bear, a Medicine Man
This vibrant painting by George Caitlin dates from 1832. Native Americans were a popular choice of subject matter for this artist.

Mary Cassatt
This portrait by Edgar Degas, painted c.1882, depicts his fellow artist Mary Cassatt playing cards.

John Singleton Copley
This self-portrait of the artist, who was largely known for his depictions of others, was painted c.1780.

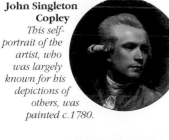

"Casey" Stengel
This bronze sculpture of the baseball great was created by Rhoda Sherbell in 1981 from a 1965 cast.

VISITORS' CHECKLIST

Smithsonian American Art Museum: 8th St & G St, NW. 357-2700. **Map** 3 C3. For foreign language tours or tours for the blind or hearing impaired. www.americanart.si.edu
National Portrait Gallery: 8th St & F St, NW. 357-2700. For pre-arranged tours, call 357-2920. www.npg.si.edu 10am–5:30pm daily. Dec 25. Gallery Place-Chinatown.

The man working in the field represents the people of America, enjoying the fruits of the land after laboring.

Hercules is about to break off the bull's horn.

The horn is transformed into a cornucopia, or horn of plenty, symbolizing America as a land of abundance and opportunity.

★ Game Fish
This amazing piece of art was created by Larry Fuente in 1988. The artist covered a mounted sailfish trophy with toys and objects from games, such as dominoes, Scrabble tiles, ping-pong balls, and yo-yos.

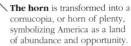

In the Garden
This charming depiction of the poet Celia Thaxter is by the artist Childe Hassam and was painted in 1892.

STAR SIGHTS

★ **Achelous and Hercules**

★ **Game Fish**

★ **Cliffs of the Upper Colorado River**

Exploring the Smithsonian American Art Museum

NOWHERE IN Washington is the city's penchant to copy Greek and Roman architecture more obvious than in the former US Patent Office building, now the home of the Smithsonian American Art Museum and the National Portrait Gallery. The Patent Office building was converted into the twin museums in 1968. Considering its office origins, the classical space provides a complementary backdrop to these collections.

A bottlecap giraffe

AMERICAN FOLK ART

THE COLLECTION of American folk art includes some truly amazing pieces of work, created from a wide range of materials. James Hampton's *Throne of the Third Heaven of the Nations' Millennium General Assembly* (c. 1950–1964) is one of the star pieces in the collection. Hampton, a janitor in Washington, created this wonderful piece of visionary art in his garage. His media were gold and tin foil, old furniture, and light bulbs. Over the course of many years he fashioned a throne, pulpits, crowns, and other devotional objects, all of which are included in this unusual yet beautiful work.

19TH- AND EARLY 20TH-CENTURY ART

SOME OF the highlights in this collection from the last two centuries are the Thomas Moran Western landscapes. Moran's paintings are monumental; he was one

of the few artists who captured the scale of the Grand Canyon and the Colorado River. Especially moving is *Cliffs of the Upper Colorado River, Wyoming Territory* (1882).

Many of the American artists on this floor, such as Albert Pinkham Ryder, Winslow Homer, and John Singer Sargent, were contemporaries to the Impressionist artists. Homer's *High Cliffs, Coast of Maine* (1894) is a dramatic meeting of land and sea. Seascapes were also a popular subject for Ryder. *Jonah*, painted c.1885, illustrates the Bible story of Jonah and the whale, depicting Jonah floundering in the sea during a storm, overlooked by God. Frederick Remington's *Fired On*, an impressive oil painting, is another highlight. The artist was best known as a sculptor, rather than a painter, of cowboys and horses.

The museum holds hundreds of paintings of Native Americans, many of them works by anthropologist George Caitlin. This was also a popular subject for Charles Bird King and John Mix Stanley.

American Impressionists are also well represented in the gallery, including Mary Cassatt, William Merritt Chase, John Henry Twachtman, and Childe Hassam. Hassam's paintings, inspired by the French Impressionists, are refreshing yet tranquil. The calm seascape of *The South Ledges, Appledore* (1913) is typical of his style.

Robert Rauschenberg's *Reservoir* (1961), mixed media on canvas

AMERICAN MODERNISTS

THE ENORMOUS canvases of the Modernists provide a dramatic contrast to the landscapes and portraits of the 19th and 20th centuries. Franz Kline's black slashes on a white canvas in *Merce C* (1961), which was inspired by his involvement with dancer Merce Cunningham, are the antithesis of the delicacy of the Impressionists. Kenneth Noland's geometrical compositions resemble firing targets. Other Modernists here include Robert Rauschenberg, Jasper Johns, Andy Warhol, Hans Hofman, and David Hockney.

THE GREAT HALL

THE THIRD FLOOR Great Hall is a crazy quilt of tiles and ceiling medallions. A frieze showing the evolution of technology in America also runs around the room. Once a display area for new inventions, it is a reminder of the building's past as the Patent Office.

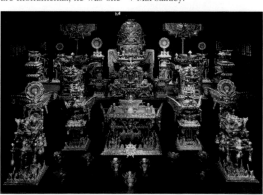

Throne of the Third Heaven of the Nations' Millennium General Assembly

Exploring the National Portrait Gallery

CURRENTLY CLOSED, along with the National Museum of American Art, for a massive renovation, the National Portrait Gallery is taking full advantage of this period to reorganize its impressive collection of paintings, sculpture, and photographs of famous Americans. Around 1,000 images from the gallery's collection are presently on loan to galleries around the world, including Japan and Europe, as well as other galleries in the United States. Contact the gallery directly for detailed information on where the collections can be seen during this time. The gallery is expected to reopen in 2005.

Ronald Reagan, painted in oils by Henry C. Casselli, Jr. in 1989

OVERVIEW OF THE COLLECTION

THE NATIONAL Portrait Gallery illuminates America's family album. The portraits not only reveal their subjects but also the times in which they were produced. There are thousands of images in the permanent collection – portraits, photographs, sculptures, etchings, drawings – and both heroes and villains are represented. The collection is limited to subjects who have been dead ten years or more, although special exceptions are made for the Presidents. Portraits taken from life sittings are favored by the gallery.

Portrait of Pocahontas by an unidentified artist

Cagney. There are also bronze busts of the poet T.S. Eliot and the humorist Will Rogers. Religious leaders, business magnates, pioneers in women's rights and civil rights (such as Dr. Martin Luther King Jr.), explorers, and scientists are portrayed in a whole range of media, including oils, clay, and bronze. There are also many photographic portraits, including some recent acquired pictures of Marilyn Monroe, which were taken during a morale-boosting visit the actress made to soldiers during the Korean War.

THE HALL OF PRESIDENTS

THE CHRONOLOGICALLY ordered portrayal of all of the country's leaders remains the heart of the National Portrait Gallery's collections. In 1857, Congress commissioned

George Peter Alexander Healy to paint portraits of the presidents. The likenesses were to be installed in the White House as an artistic chronicle of its occupants. A large number of paintings remain in the White House. The portraits of George and Martha Washington are featured prominently in the Portrait Gallery.

The most famous painting is Gilbert Stuart's portrait of George Washington, painted from life in 1796. The likeness is the basis for the image of the President on the one-dollar bill. Abraham Lincoln posed for photographer Alexander Gardener several months before he was assassinated (see p90). He looks careworn and weary. President Clinton's image is represented in a sculptured bust and a photograph. A painter has been selected and a portrait is in the process of being painted.

NOTABLE AMERICANS

THE NATIONAL Portrait Gallery's collection is not limited to the political history of the country. There is also a large collection of portraits of American people, notable for their achievements in the arts, sports, or in the country's religious or cultural history. Athletes honored include the famous baseball player Babe Ruth and baseball manager Casey Stengel. Among figures from the world of entertainment are portraits of actresses Judy Garland, Tallulah Bankhead, and Mary Pickford. John Wayne also features among the Hollywood stars, as does Buster Keaton, Clark Gable, and James

Diana Ross and The Supremes, photographed by Bruce Davidson in 1965

The 6th Street façade of the modern MCI Center sports complex

recognition. Many restaurants and shops have opened to cater to the increased flow of visitors to this part of the city. To conform to the height of older buildings in this historic neighborhood, Pollin built half of the arena's seats below ground level. The result is a vast but harmonious structure. In addition to sports events, the arena also hosts rock concerts and sports exhibitions. The center has only 500 parking spaces so it is best to travel by Metrorail.

MCI Center ⑱

601 F St, NW. **Map** 4 D3. ☎ 628-3200. M *Gallery Place-Chinatown.* ○ *11am–6pm daily (open later for games.)* ▨ *for National Sports Gallery.* ▨ *for National Sports Gallery.* ♿ 🚻 🏛 W www.mcicenter.com

O PENED IN 1997, the MCI Center is a sports complex that houses a number of shops and restaurants.

The 20,000-seat MCI stadium is the brainchild of Abe Pollin, owner of Washington's basketball teams, The Wizards (men's team) and The Mystics (women's), as well as the hockey team, The Capitals. The complex has been extremely successful, and its presence has revived the surrounding area beyond

Spy Museum ⑲

800 F St, NW. **Map** 3 C3. ☎ 393-7798, EYE-SPY-U. M *Gallery Place-Chinatown, National Archives-Navy Memorial.* ○ *10am–8pm.* ▨ ▨ *group tours by reservation.* W *www.spymuseum.org*

T HE SPY MUSEUM is the first museum in the world dedicated to the subject of international espionage. It has the largest collection of espionage artifacts to be put on public display, such as the German Enigma cipher machine from World War II and a Soviet shoe transmitter. Themed exhibits include "School for Spies", how spies are recruited and trained, and "War of the Spies" which covers the Cold War period.

7th Street ⑳

7th St, NW. **Map** 3 C2 & 3 C3. M *Gallery Place-Chinatown, Archives-Navy Memorial.*

T HE VICTORIAN buildings that border the southern stretch of 7th Street, where it meets Pennsylvania Avenue, are vestiges of Washington's past. Behind the historic façades, however, trendy new restaurants are changing the area. The stretch of 7th Street from Pennsylvania Avenue to Massachusetts Avenue is lined with art galleries.

Around G Street is an assortment of Asian shops and restaurants that form part of the city's Chinatown area *(see p91)*.

Judiciary Square ㉑

4th St & E St, NW. **Map** 4 D3. M *Judiciary Square.*

C ENTER OF LAW for the District of Columbia since 1800, Judiciary Square is a collection of municipal buildings and law courts. The most notable of these, architecturally, is the **United States Tax Court**, on 2nd Street between D Street and E Street. Built in 1973, and designed by Victor A. Lundy, it is an example of the International style of architecture.

The 19th-century **Old City Hall** building, on D Street, now houses law courts, as does the **Federal Courthouse**.

OLD DOWNTOWN RENAISSANCE

During the 1990s, Washington's Old Downtown was transformed from a derelict historic area to prime real estate. The construction of the MCI Center and renewed appreciation for the restoration of dilapidated Victorian buildings helped to accelerate this process. As a result of losing its shabby image, Old Downtown also lost many of the artists who carved studios out of the high-ceilinged, low-rent spaces, but their influence can still be seen in the large number of art galleries and exhibitions in the area. Some of the non-profit organizations and small businesses that leased offices in the big, aging buildings were forced to relocate due to an increase in rent. Soaring prices also closed a number of traditional Chinese restaurants around the MCI Center, which have been replaced by upscale eateries. Today Old Downtown is a safer area for those on foot, with a buzzing selection of nightly activities available, including sports events, theater shows, concerts, and lively restaurants.

A contemporary office building linking two Victorian façades on 7th Street

Majestic lion statue alongside a marble wall at the police memorial

National Law Enforcement Officers Memorial ㉒

E St between 4th St & 5th St, NW. **Map** 4 D3. ▐ 737-3400. Ⓜ *Judiciary Square.* **Visitor Center** ◯ *9am–5pm Mon–Fri, 10am–5pm Sat, noon–5pm Sun.* ● *Thanksgiving, Dec 25, Jan 1.* ▐ ⚲ ▐ W *www.nleomf.com*

Dedicated by President George Bush in 1991, the National Law Enforcement Officers Memorial honors the 15,000 police officers who have been killed since the founding of the United States. Spread over three acres in the center of Judiciary Square, the memorial's flower-lined pathways are spectacular in springtime. The names of the fallen officers are inscribed on marble walls. Each path is guarded by a statue of an adult lion shielding its cubs, symbolic of the US police force's protective role.

National Building Museum ㉓

401 F St at 4th St, NW. **Map** 4 D3. ▐ 272-2448. Ⓜ *Judiciary Square, Gallery Place-Chinatown.* ◯ *10am–5pm Mon–Sat, 11am–5pm Sun.* ● *Jan 1, Thanksgiving, Dec 25.* ▐ ⚲ ▐ ▐ W *www.nbm.org*

It is fitting that the National Building Museum, dedicated to the building trade, should be housed in the architecturally audacious former Pension Bureau building. Civil War General, Montgomery C. Meigs, saw Michelangelo's Palazzo Farnese on a trip to Rome and decided to duplicate it as a Washington office building, albeit twice as big and in red brick as opposed to the stone masonry of the Rome original.

Completed in 1887, the building is topped by a dramatic terra-cotta frieze measuring 3 ft (1 m) in height. The daring exterior of the building is matched by its flamboyant interior. The vast concourse, measuring 316 ft by 116 ft (96 m by 35 m), is lined with balconies containing exhibitions. The roof is supported by huge columns, constructed of brick, plastered, and faux-painted to give the appearance of marble. The Great Hall has been the impressive venue for many presidential inaugural balls.

In 1926 the Pension Bureau relocated to different offices, and there was a move to demolish Miegs' building.

Ornamental plinth in the grounds of the museum

Instead it was occupied by various government agencies for a time and was even used as a courthouse for a while.

The building was eventually restored, and in 1985 opened in renewed splendor as the National Building Museum. A privately owned collection, the museum has a display on the architectural history of the city – "Washington: Symbol and City." It includes an excellent illustration of Pierre L'Enfant's original plans for the capital, as well as other photographs, models, and interactive exhibits demonstrating how the city grew and changed. The temporary exhibits in the museum often highlight controversial issues in the field of design and architecture, and facets of the building trade. There is a small café in the courtyard, and a well-stocked gift shop. Free tours offer access to the restricted areas of the building.

The splendid, colonnaded Great Hall in the National Building Museum

THE WHITE HOUSE AND FOGGY BOTTOM

THE OFFICIAL RESIDENCE of the President, the White House is one of the most distinguished buildings in DC and was first inhabited in 1800. Although burned by the British during the War of 1812, most of today's building remains as it was planned. Other buildings surrounding the White House are worth a visit,

Second Division Memorial

such as the Daughters of the American Revolution building and the Corcoran Gallery. East of the White House is the Foggy Bottom area, which was built on swampland. Notable edifices here include the Kennedy Center, the State Department building, and the notorious Watergate Complex, focus of the 1970s Nixon scandal.

SIGHTS AT A GLANCE

Galleries
Corcoran Gallery of Art **7**
Renwick Gallery **5**

Squares
Lafayette Square **3**
Washington Circle **17**

Historic Buildings
Daughters of the American Revolution **9**
George Washington University **15**

Hay-Adams Hotel **4**
Octagon **8**
Old Executive Office Building **6**
Watergate Complex **18**

Official Buildings
Department of the Interior **11**
Federal Reserve Building **12**
National Academy of Sciences **13**
Organization of the American States **10**

State Department **14**
Treasury Building **2**
The White House pp102–105 **1**

Performing Arts Center
Kennedy Center pp112–3 **19**

Church
St. Mary's Episcopal Church **16**

0 meters   500

0 yards   500

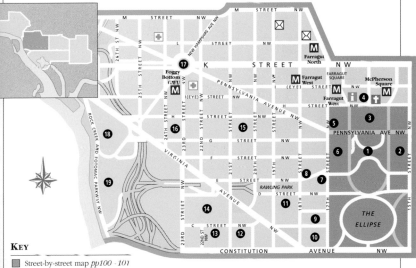

KEY

■	Street-by-street map *pp100 - 101*
M	Metro station
ℹ	Tourist information
✚	Hospital emergency room
⊠	Post office
✝	Church

GETTING THERE

The closest Metrorail stations to the White House and Foggy Bottom area are Metro Center, McPherson Square, and Foggy Bottom-GWU station. Also, Metrobuses 32, 34, and 36 travel east to west and will take you to most of the major sights within the area.

◁ **The First Division Monument in front of the Old Executive Office Building**

Street-by-Street: Around The White House

THE AREA SURROUNDING the White House is filled with grand architecture and political history, and the vistas from the Ellipse lawn are breathtaking. It is worth spending a day exploring the area and visiting some of its buildings (by appointment only), such as the Treasury Building with its statue of Alexander Hamilton (the first Secretary of the Treasury) and the Old Executive Office Building. The buildings of the Daughters of the American Revolution and the Organization of American States both offer the visitor an insight into the pride the nation takes in its past.

Old Execut
Office Build
Although it was poorly received
its completion in 1888,
attractive building has been ho
to many state departments

Renwick Gallery of the Smithsonian American Art Museum
The inscription above the entrance of this 19th-century building reads "Dedicated to Art." ❺

Octagon
At one time James Madison's home, this building has had a varied history functioning as a hospital and a school, among other things ❽

★ Corcoran Gallery of Art
A treasure trove of fine art, the Corcoran Gallery counts works by Rembrandt, Monet, Picasso, and de Kooning among its many exhibits ❼

0 meters 100
0 yards 100

DAR Building
This beautiful Neoclassical building is one of three founded by the historical organization, the Daughters of the American Revolution ❾

KEY

— — — Suggested route

OAS Building
The central statue of Queen Isabella of Spain stands in front of this Spanish Col-onial-style mansion. Built in 1910, it houses the Organization of American States ❿

Hay-Adams Hotel
Formed by the joining of two town houses, this luxurious hotel has been the scene of political activity since it opened in the 1920s ❹

LOCATOR MAP
See Street Finder map 3

Lafayette Square
Named after the Marquis de Lafayette, a Revolutionary War hero, this leafy square has at its center this statue of Andrew Jackson, the seventh president, sculpted by Clark Mills ❸

★ Treasury Building
Widely regarded as the most impressive Neoclassical structure in the city, this building took over 60 years to complete ❷

★ The White House
The most famous sight in Washington, DC, the White House has been the President's official residence since the 1820s ❶

STAR SIGHTS

★ Corcoran Gallery of Art

★ Treasury Building

★ The White House

The White House ❶

IN 1791 GEORGE WASHINGTON chose this site as the location for the new President's House. Irish-born architect James Hoban was selected to design the building, known as the Executive House. In 1800, President and Mrs. John Adams became the first occupants, even though the building was not yet completed. Burned by the British in 1814, the partially rebuilt edifice was occupied again in 1817, by James Monroe. In 1901, President Theodore Roosevelt changed the name of the building to the White House and in 1902 ordered the West Wing to be built. The East Wing was added in 1942 on the instruction of President Franklin D. Roosevelt, completing the building as it is today.

The White House
The official residence of the US president for 200 years, the White House façade is familiar to millions of people around the world.

★ State Dining Room
Able to seat as many as 140 people, the State Dining Room was enlarged in 1902. A portrait of President Abraham Lincoln, by George P.A. Healy, hangs above the mantel.

The West Terrace
leads to the West Wing and the Oval Office, the President's official office.

The stonewor has been pain over and over maintain the b ing's white faç

★ Red Room
One of four reception rooms, the Red Room is furnished in red in the Empire Style (1810–30). The fabrics were woven in the US from French designs.

STAR ROOMS

★ Red Room

★ State Dining Room

★ Vermeil Room

Lincoln Bedroom
*President Lincoln
_sed this room as his
_abinet Room, then
_urned it into a bed-
room, furnishing it
_h Lincoln-era decor.
Today it is used as
a guest room.*

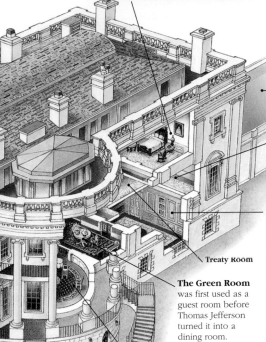

VISITOR'S CHECKLIST

1600 Pennsylvania Ave, NW.
Map 3 B3. ◯ *Tue–Sat:
10am–noon. Contact Visitor
Center for information.* ◓
federal hols and official functions
✔ *obligatory.* W *www.nps.gov*
White House Visitor Center
1450 Pennsylvania Ave, NW.
◖ *208 1631.* Ⓜ *Federal
Triangle.* ◯ *daily 7:30am–4pm.*
◉ *Jan 1, Thanksgiving, Dec 25.
See White House Visitor Center
(pp104–5) for information on
obtaining advance tickets.* ◫ ♿
✔ W *www.nps.gov/whho*

The East Terrace leads
to the East Wing.

The East Room is used
for large gatherings, such
as dances and concerts.

Treaty Room

The Green Room
was first used as a
guest room before
Thomas Jefferson
turned it into a
dining room.

★ **The Vermeil Room**
*This yellow room houses seven
paintings of first ladies, including this portrait of Eleanor
Roosevelt by Douglas Chandor.*

Blue Room

Diplomatic Reception
*This room is used to
welcome friends and
ambassadors. It is
elegantly furnished
in the Federal Period
style (1790–1820).*

WHITE HOUSE ARCHITECTS

After selecting the site, George Washington held
a design competition to find an architect to build
the residence where the US president would
live. In 1792 James Hoban, an Irish-born architect, was chosen for the task. It is from Hoban's
original drawings that the White House was
initially built and all subsequent changes grew.
In 1902 President Teddy Roosevelt hired the
New York architectural firm of McKim, Mead,
and White to check the structural condition of
the building and refurbish areas as necessary.
The White House underwent further
renovations and refurbishments during the
administrations of Truman and Kennedy.

**James Hoban, architect
of the White House**

Exploring the White House

MORE THAN a million and a half visitors each year wander through the home of the President of the United States on the free tour. The White House rooms are beautifully decorated in period styles and are filled with valuable antique furniture, china, and silverware. Hanging on its walls are some of America's most treasured paintings, including many portraits of past presidents and first ladies.

THE LIBRARY

ORIGINALLY USED as a laundry area, this room was turned into a "gentleman's ante-room" at the request of President Theodore Roosevelt in 1902. In 1935 it was re-modeled into a library. Furnished in the style of the late Federal period (1800–1820) the library was redecorated in 1962, and then again in 1976. Today, its soft gray and rose-colored tones make it a perfect room for informal gatherings, such as afternoon teas.

Portraits of four native-American chiefs, painted by Charles Bird King, are displayed in the library. The chandelier was crafted in the early 1800s and was originally owned by the family of James Fenimore Cooper, author of *The Last of the Mohicans*.

THE VERMEIL ROOM

OFTEN CALLED the Gold Room, the Vermeil Room was redecorated in 1991. It is named after the collection of vermeil, or gilded silver, that is on display in the cabinets. On show are 18th-, 19th-, and 20th-century tableware crafted by English Regency silver-smith Paul Storr (1771–1836) and French Empire silver-smith Jean-Baptist Claude Odiot (1763–1850). The collection was bequeathed to the White House in 1956.

Seven portraits of first ladies hang on the walls: Elizabeth Shoumatoff's painting of Claudia (Lady Bird) Johnson, Aaron Shikler's portraits of Nancy Reagan and of Jackie Kennedy in her New York apartment, and an unusual portrait of Eleanor Roosevelt, caught in various moods, by Douglas Chador. Also on display are portraits of Ellen Wilson, Patricia Ryan Nixon and Lou Henry Hoover.

THE CHINA ROOM

USED BY Mrs. Woodrow Wilson in 1917 to display the White House China, this room was redecorated in 1970. Today it is used as a reception room. The rich red color scheme is suggested by the stunning portrait of Mrs. Calvin Coolidge, painted in 1924 by Howard Chandler Christy. The Indo-Isfahan rug dates from the early 20th century.

The red and cream color scheme of the China Room

THE BLUE ROOM

PRESIDENT James Monroe chose the French Empire-style decor for this magnificent, oval-shaped room in 1817. The Classically inspired furniture and accompanying motifs, such as urns, acanthus leaves, and imperial eagles, typify the style. The settee and seven chairs were created by Parisian cabinetmaker, Pierre- Antoine Bellangé.

A portrait of Thomas Jefferson by Rembrandt Peale, dating from 1800, hangs in this elegant room, along with a portrait of President John Adams, painted in 1793 by artist John Trumball. The Blue Room has always been used as a reception room, except for a brief period during the John Adams administration.

THE RED ROOM

THIS ROOM was decorated in the Empire style by Jackie Kennedy in 1962 and was refurbished in 1971 and again in 2000. Much of the wooden furniture in the room, including the beautiful inlaid round table, was created by cabinetmaker Charles-Honoré Lannuier in his New York workshop. Above the mantel hangs a portrait of Angelica Singleton Van Buren, the daughter-in-law of President Martin Van Buren, which was painted by Henry Inman in 1842. The room was used as a parlor or sitting room; in recent times it has been used for small dinner parties.

THE STATE DINING ROOM

AS A RESULT of the growing nation and its international standing, the size of official dinners in the White House increased. Finally in 1902 the architects McKim, Mead, and White were called in to enlarge the State Dining Room. The plaster and paneling was modeled on the style of 18th-century Neoclassical English houses. The mahogany dining table was created in 1997. The pieces of French giltware on the table were bought by President Monroe in 1817.

The dining room was re-decorated in 1998. The Queen Anne-style chairs date from 1902 and were reuphol-stered in 1998.

THE LINCOLN BEDROOM

Used today as the guest room for the friends and family of the President, the Lincoln Bedroom is decorated in the American Victorian style, dating from 1850–70. Used by Lincoln as an office and cabinet room, this room became the Lincoln Bedroom when President Truman decid-ed to fill it with furniture from Lincoln's era. In the center is a 6 ft- (1.8 m-) wide rosewood bed with an 8 ft- (2.5 m-) high headboard. The portrait of General Andrew Jackson next to the bed is said to have been one of President Lincoln's favorites. A painting of Lincoln's wife, Mary Todd Lincoln, also hangs here.

THE TREATY ROOM

Beginning with Andrew Johnson's presidency in 1865, the Treaty Room served as the Cabinet Room for 10 presidential Administrations. The room contains many Victorian pieces bought by President Ulysses S. Grant, including the original table used by the Cabinet. The cut-glass chandelier that hangs here was made in Birmingham, England around 1850. The chandelier has 20 arms, each one fitted with a frosted-glass globe.

THE WHITE HOUSE VISITOR CENTER

The White House Visitor Center has free, same-day tickets for tours conducted around the presidential official resi-dence by the National Park Service. However, the number

of tickets available varies, and they are on a first-come, first-served basis. Lines for tickets can start forming as early as 3am in summer, and tickets are often gone by 9am. Tours are not given on days when there are state visits or other important events. The Visitor Center also has exhibits about the history of the White House and an extensive gift shop.

To reserve tickets for an 8am guided tour, American visitors can contact their state senator or congressman three to six months in advance. Non-US citizens should contact the White House Visitors Center.

Façade of the White House Visitor Center

THE EAST WING

The east wing houses offices rather than ceremonial rooms and was built in 1942. The walls of the Lobby are adorned with portraits of presidents. Both the Garden Room and the East Colonnade, which fronts the East Terrace, look out onto the Jacqueline Kennedy Garden. The Terrace, which links the East Wing to the Residence, houses the White House Movie Theater.

THE WEST WING

In 1902, the West Wing, including the Oval Office, was built by the architectural firm McKim, Mead, and White for a total cost of $65,196. In

The interior of the Oval Office, located in the West Wing

this wing, the former Fish Room was renamed the Roosevelt Room by President Nixon, in honor of presidents Theodore and Franklin Roosevelt who created this wing. Their portraits still hang in the room today.

Also in the West Wing are the Cabinet Room, where government officials meet with the president, and the Oval Office, where the presi-dent meets with visiting heads of state. Many presidents have personalized this room in some way; President George W. Bush uses a desk given to President Rutherford B. Hayes by Queen Victoria in 1880.

Detail of _The Peacemakers_ by George Healy, located in the Treaty Room

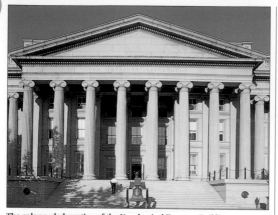

The colonnaded portico of the Neoclassical Treasury Building

Treasury Building ②

15th St & Pennsylvania Ave, NW. **Map** 3 B3. 🄲 622-0896. Ⓜ McPherson Square. 🄶 Sat only – call in advance, giving name, date of birth, and social security number or passport number. 🄳 🅆 www.ustreas.gov

THE SITE OF this massive, four-story Greek Revival building, home to the Department of the Treasury, was chosen by President Andrew Jackson. The grand, sandstone-and-granite edifice was designed by architect Robert Mills, who also designed the Washington Monument *(see p74)*. A statue of Alexander Hamilton, the first Secretary of the Treasury, stands in front of the southern entrance to the building.

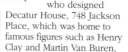

Liberty Bell in front of the Treasury

On the official guided tour, visitors are shown the restored historic rooms, including the 1864 burglar-proof vault, the Andrew Johnson suite (Johnson's temporary office after the assassination of President Lincoln in 1865), and the marble Cash Room.

Between 1863 and 1880, US currency was printed in the basement, and during the Civil War it was used as storage space for food and arms. Today, the building is home to the Department of the Treasury, which manages the government's finances and protects US financial systems.

Lafayette Square ③

Map 2 F3 & 3 B3. Ⓜ Farragut West, McPherson Square.

SET BEHIND the White House is Lafayette Square, named after the Marquis de Lafayette (1757–1834), a hero of the American Revolutionary War *(see p17)*. Due to its proximity to the White House, this public park is often the scene of peaceful demonstrations. It is home to 19th-century mansions and the historic church of St. John's (the "Church of the Presidents"), built in 1816 by Benjamin Latrobe, who designed Decatur House, 748 Jackson Place, which was home to famous figures such as Henry Clay and Martin Van Buren,

Federal-style 19th-century houses overlooking tranquil Lafayette Square

and is open to the public. In the center of the Square is a huge statue of President Andrew Jackson (1767–1845) seated on a horse. Cast in bronze by Clark Mills, it was the first equestrian statue of its size to be built in the US and was dedicated in 1853.

At each of the square's four corners stand statues of men who took part in America's struggle for liberty. The southeast corner has the bronze figure of French compatriot Lafayette. In the southwest corner is a statue of another Frenchman, Jean-Baptiste Donatien de Vimeur, Comte de Rochambeau (1725–1807). This was a gift from France to the American people and accepted by Theodore Roosevelt in 1902. A statue of Polish general, Thaddeus Kosciuszko (1746–1817), who fought with the American colonists in the Revolutionary War, stands in the northeast corner. Baron von Steuben (1730–94), a German officer and George Washington's aide at the Battle of Valley Forge, is honored at the northwest end.

Hay-Adams Hotel ④

1 Lafayette Square, NW. **Map** 2 F3 & 3 B3. 🄲 638-6600, 1-800-424-5054. Ⓜ Farragut North, Farragut West. 🅆 www.hayadams.com

SITUATED CLOSE to the White House, the historic Hay-Adams Hotel is an Italian Renaissance landmark in Washington. Its plush interior is adorned with European and Oriental antiques.

It was originally two adjacent houses, built by Henry Hobson Richardson in 1885, belonging to statesman and author John Hay and diplomat and historian Henry Adams. A popular hotel since its conversion in 1927 by developer Harry Wardman, the exclusive Hay-Adams remains one of Washington's top establishments *(see p163)*, well situated for all the major sights. Afternoon tea and drinks are available in the Lafayette Restaurant.

Renwick Gallery ❺

Pennsylvania Ave at 17th St, NW. **Map** 2 F3 & 3 A3. **C** 357-2531. **M** Farragut West. ◯ 10am–5:30pm daily. ⬤ Dec 25. 📷 noon Mon–Fri. ♿ 🛍 Ⓦ www.americanart.si.edu

Forming part of the Smithsonian American Art Museum *(see pp92–5)*, this red-brick building was designed and constructed by James Renwick in 1858. It originally housed the art collection of William Wilson Corcoran until this was moved to the current Corcoran Gallery of Art in 1897.

The building was bought by the Smithsonian. Refurbished and renamed, the Renwick Gallery opened in 1972. It is dedicated primarily to 20th-century American crafts, and houses some impressive exhibits in every medium including metal, clay, and glass. *Game Fish* (1988) by Larry Fuente is a stunning example of mixed media art.

Old Executive Office Building ❻

17th St at Pennsylvania Ave, NW. **Map** 2 F4 & 3 A3. **C** 395-5895. **M** Farragut West. 🗓 Sat by appt. ♿ Ⓦ www.whitehouse.gov

Recently renamed the Dwight D. Eisenhower Executive Office Building, this building stands on the West side of the White House. It was once the home of the War, Navy, and State Departments. Built between 1871 and 1888 by

The magnificent Renwick Gallery, a fine example of French Empire style

Alfred B. Mullett, its French Second Empire design, which was inspired by the 1852 expansion of the Louvre in Paris, generated much criticism at the time.

The building has long been the site of historic events, such as the meeting between Secretary of State Cordell Hull and the Japanese after the bombing of Pearl Harbor in 1941.

Today the building houses government agencies, including the White House Office, the Office of the Vice President, the National Security Council, and the Office of Management and Budget.

Lion statue guarding the Corcoran Gallery

The tour takes in many of the beautifully restored rooms, with their curved staircases and stained-glass rotundas, though it would be best to call to confirm details.

Corcoran Gallery of Art ❼

500 17th St, NW. **Map** 2 F4 & 3 A3. **C** 639-1700. **M** Farragut West, Farragut North. ◯ 10am–5pm daily. ⬤ Thanksgiving, Dec 25, Jan 1. 📷 🚻 ♿ 🖥 🛍 🏪 🛍 Ⓦ www.corcoran.org

One of the first fine art museums in the country, the Corcoran Gallery of Art opened in 1874. It outgrew its original home (what is now

the Renwick Gallery building) and moved to this massive edifice designed in 1897 by Ernest Flagg. A privately funded art collection, the Corcoran was founded by William Wilson Corcoran – a banker whose main interest was American art. Many of the European works in the collection were added in 1925 by art collector and US senator William A. Clark.

The Corcoran Gallery of Art is filled with works by European and American masters that span the centuries. These include 16th-century paintings by Titian, 17th-century works by Rembrandt, and 19th-century French Impressionist paintings by Monet and Renoir. The gallery also contains the largest collection of paintings by Jean-Baptiste Camille Corot outside France. There is a fine collection of modern and African-American art, which includes sculpture, paintings, textiles, and photographs. Paintings from the 20th century include a selection by Picasso, Singer Sargent, and de Kooning.

Within the building is the only accredited art school in Washington. A gospel brunch takes place every Sunday in the beautiful atrium, with live music and singing. The Corcoran also has a shop selling an excellent selection of books and postcards.

The imposing façade of the Old Executive Office Building

Octagon ❽

1799 New York Ave, NW. **Map** 2 F4
& 3 A3. 🎫 638-3221. Ⓜ *Farragut
West.* ⏲ *10am–4pm Tue–Sun.*
⬤ *Federal holidays.* 💷 ✔
♿ *(first floor only).*
🌐 www.amerarchfoundation.com

Aᴄᴛᴜᴀʟʟʏ hexagonal in shape,
the Octagon is a three-
story red-brick building,
designed in the late-Federal
style by Dr. William Thornton
(1759–1828), first architect of
the US Capitol. The Octagon
was completed in 1801 for
Colonel John Tayloe III, a rich
plantation owner from Richmond County, Virginia, and a
friend of George Washington.

When the White House was
burned in the War of 1812
against Britain *(see p17)*, President James Madison and his
wife, Dolley, lived here from
1814 to 1815. The Treaty of
Ghent that ended the war was
signed by Madison on the
second floor of the house
on February 17, 1815.

In the early 1900s, the
building was taken over by
the American Institute of Architects, which is now head-
quartered in the large
building behind the Octagon.
The American Architectural
Foundation, established in
1970, set up a museum of
architecture in the Octagon.
Following major renovation in
1996, the building has been
restored to its historically accu-
rate 1815 appearance, and has
some original furnishings and
fine architectural features,
such as a circular entrance hall.

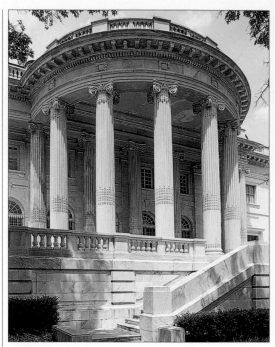

South portico of the DAR Memorial Continental Hall

Daughters of the American Revolution ❾

1776 D St, NW. **Map** 2 F4 & 3 A3.
🎫 879-3241. Ⓜ *Farragut West.*
⏲ *8:30am–4pm Mon–Fri, 1–5pm
Sun.* ⬤ *2 weeks in April, Federal hols.*
📷 *10am–2:30pm Mon–Fri, 1pm–
5pm Sat (book in advance).* ♿ 🚹
🌐 www.dar.org

Fᴏᴜɴᴅᴇᴅ ɪɴ 1890 as a non-
profit organization, the
Daughters of the American
Revolution (DAR) is dedicated
to historic preservation and
promoting education and
patriotism. In order to become a member, you must
be a woman with blood
relations to any person, male
or female, who fought in or
aided the Revolution. There
are currently over 170,000
members in 3,000 regional
branches throughout the USA
and in nine other countries.

The DAR museum is located
in the Memorial Continental
Hall, designed for the organi-
zation by Edward Pearce
Casey and completed in 1910.
The 13 columns in the south

portico symbolize the 13 original states of the Union.
Entrance to the museum is
through the gallery, which
displays an eclectic range of
pieces from quilts to glassware and china.

The 33 period rooms that
form the State Rooms in the
museum house a collection
of over 50,000 items, from
silver to porcelain, ceramics,
stoneware, and furniture. Each
room is decorated in a unique
style particular to an American
state from different periods
during the 18th and 19th
centuries. An attic room filled
with 18th- and 19th-century
toys will delight children. Also,
there is a huge genealogical
library, consisting of approximately 125,000 publications.

**The circular main entrance to the
attractive Octagon building**

**DAR Museum banners proclaiming
Preservation, Patriotism, Education**

Fountain in the courtyard of the OAS building

Organization of American States ⑩

17th St & Constitution Ave, NW. **Map** 2 F4 & 3 A4. ☎ 458-3000. ◑ 9am–5:30pm Mon–Fri. ⬤ Sat–Sun, Federal hols. **Art Museum of the Americas** 201 18th St NW. ◑ 10am–5pm Tue–Sun. ⬤ Good Friday, Federal hols. Ⓜ Farragut West. ☎ call 458-6301. Ⓦ www.oas.org

Dating back to the First International Conference of the American States, held from October 1889 to April 1890 in Washington, the Organization of American States (OAS) is the oldest alliance of nations dedicated to reinforcing the peace and security of the continent, and maintaining democracy. The Charter of the OAS was signed in Bogotá, Colombia, in 1948 by the United States and 20 Latin American republics. Today there are 35 members. The building dates from 1910 and houses the Columbus Memorial Library and the **Art Museum of the Americas**, which exhibits 20th-century Latin American and Caribbean art.

Department of the Interior Building ⑪

1849 C St, between 18th St & 19th St, NW. **Map** 2 F4 & 3 A3. ☎ 208-4743. Ⓜ Farragut West. ◑ 8:30am–4:30pm Mon–Fri. ⬤ Federal hols. ☑ call ahead. To enter the building you need a photo ID. ♿ Ⓦ www.doi.gov/museum

Designed by architect Waddy Butler Wood and built in 1935, this huge limestone building is the headquarters of the Department of the Interior. The building has a long central section, with six wings that extend off each side. In total it covers more than 16 acres of floor space, and has 2 miles (3 km) of corridors.

The Department of the Interior was originally formed of only the Departments of Agriculture, Labor, Education, and Energy, but it expanded to oversee all federally owned land across the United States. Visible inside, but only when taking the official guided tour, are 36 murals painted by Native American artists in the 1930s, including one of the singer Marian Anderson performing at the Lincoln Memorial in 1939 *(see p78–9)*.

The small **Department of the Interior Museum**, located on the first floor, opened in 1938. The displays include an overview of the Department's history, dioramas of American wildlife and important historical events as well as paintings by 19th-century surveyors, and crafts by Native Americans. There is a visitor shop selling a selection of gifts including Native American crafts.

The south façade of the immense Department of the Interior Building

---

THE TAYLOE FAMILY

Portrait, in crayon, by Saint Memin of Colonel John Tayloe III

John Tayloe III (1771–1828), a colonel in the War of 1812, was responsible for the construction of the unusual Octagon building. He and his wife Ann, the daughter of Benjamin Ogle (the governor of Maryland), had their primary residence at Mount Airy, an estate and tobacco plantation in Richmond County, Virginia. The Tayloes decided they wanted to build a second house where they could spend the inclement winter seasons. President George Washington, a close friend of Tayloe and his father, was at the time overseeing the building of the US Capitol and was eager for people to move into the new city. The president encouraged Tayloe and his family to choose a plot in Washington rather than in the more popular Philadelphia. The family heeded his advice and the triangular-shaped corner plot for the Octagon was chosen. Tayloe's vast wealth enabled him to employ the services of William Thornton, the original designer of the US Capitol building, and spend a total of $35,000 on the construction of the house.

Federal Reserve Building ⑫

C St between 20th St & 21st St. **Map**
2 E4 & 3 A4. 452-3686, for art
exhibitions. Foggy Bottom.
11am–2pm Mon–Fri. federal hols.
by appointment, call 452-3149 for
details. www.federalreserve.gov

KNOWN TO MOST people as
"the Fed," this building is
home to the Federal Reserve
System. This is the US banking
system under which 12 Federal
Reserve banks in 12 districts
across the country regulate
and hold reserves for member
banks in their districts. Dollar
bills are not printed here,
however, but at the
Bureau of Engraving
and Printing (see p75).

The four-story,
white marble edifice
was designed by Paul
P. Cret, architect for
the Organization of
American States
building (see p109)
and the Folger
Shakespeare Library (see p46).
The building opened in 1937.

Visitors can take a brief tour
of the Board Room and watch
a film about the history of the
building and the institution.
Small art exhibitions are also
held throughout the year.

The gleaming, white marble exterior of the Federal Reserve Building

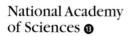

Marble eagle above the entrance to "the Fed"

National Academy of Sciences ⑬

2101 Constitution Ave, NW. **Map** 2 E4.
334-2000. Foggy Bottom.
8:30am–5pm Mon–Fri.
federal hols. www.nas.edu

ESTABLISHED IN 1863, the
National Academy
of Sciences is a non-
profit organization
that conducts over
200 studies a
year on sub-
jects such as
health,
science,

and technology, and educates
the nation by providing news
of scientific discoveries. Among
the past and present Members
of the Academy are
more than 120
Nobel Prize winners,
most notably Albert
Einstein – made a
member in 1942.

The three-story
white marble build-
ing, designed by
Bertram Grosvenor
Goodhue, was
completed in 1924. Inside is a
gold dome adorned with portraits of Greek philosophers
and panels illustrating various
scientists. A 700-seat auditorium hosts a series of free
chamber recitals throughout
the year, and there are also
occasional, temporary science
exhibitions. On the building's
upper floors are the offices
of the National Research
Council, the National Academy
of Sciences, and the National
Academy of Engineering.

Nestled among the trees in
front of the Academy is the
much-admired bronze statue
of Albert Einstein, sculpted
by Robert Berks. The same
artist created the bust of
President John F. Ken-
nedy, which can be seen
in the Grand Foyer of the
Kennedy Center
(see pp112–3).
The huge
statue of

Sculpture of Albert Einstein outside the National Academy of Sciences

Albert Einstein reaches 21 ft
(6 m) in height and weighs
7,000 pounds (3,175 kg). It
was erected in 1979.

State Department ⑭

23rd St & C St, NW. **Map** 2 E4 & 3
A3. 647-3241. Foggy
Bottom-GWU. 9:30am, 10:30am,
2:45pm Mon–Fri; must show photo
ID; call 4–6 weeks in advance to
reserve a place. Federal hols.
www.state.gov

AS THE OLDEST executive
department of the United
States government, established
in 1781, the State Department
handles all foreign policy.

Covering an expanse of 2.5
million sq ft (232,250 sq m)
over four city blocks, the
State Department building
rises eight stories high. Work-
place of the Secretary of State,
the State Department, and the
United States Diplomatic
Corps, the building is host
to 80,000 guests and 60,000
visitors every year. The State
Department's Diplomatic
Reception Rooms were lavishly
refurbished in the late 1960s,
and now contain antiques
worth over $90 million dollars.

George Washington University ⑮

2121 I (Eye) St, NW. **Map** 2 E3.
994-1000. Foggy Bottom-
GWU. **Lisner and Betts Auditoriums**
994-6800. www.gwu.edu

FOUNDED IN 1821, George
Washington University,
known as "GW" to many
people, is named after the
first president of the United

States. George Washington is the largest university in Washington, DC. There are nine schools offering both undergraduate and graduate studies. Strong subjects on offer include International Affairs, Business Administration, Medicine, Law, and Political Science.

As a result of its location, the university has many famous alumni, including Colin Powell (US Secretary of State in George W. Bush's administration) and Jacqueline Bouvier (who married John Kennedy) as well as a number of children of past presidents, including Linda Johnson, Margaret Truman, and D. Jeffrey Carter.

The on-campus Lisner, Morton and Betts auditoriums host a series of plays, dances, lectures, and concerts.

St. Mary's Episcopal Church, built for freed slaves

St. Mary's Episcopal Church ⑯

730 23rd St, NW. **Map** 2 E3.
(333-3985. **M** Foggy Bottom-GWU. **◯** 9am–4:30pm Mon–Fri. **✝** 8am, 11am Sun. **⌂**

OPENED ON January 20, 1887, the red-brick, Gothic St. Mary's Episcopal Church was the first church in Washington to be built specifically for freed slaves.

St Mary's was designed by James Renwick, who was the architect of the Renwick Gallery (see p107), the Smithsonian Castle (see p68), and St. Patrick's Cathedral in

New York City. The church was placed on the city's register of protected historic buildings in 1972.

Washington Circle ⑰

Map 2 E3. **M** Foggy Bottom-GWU.

ONE OF SEVERAL CIRCLES and squares created by Pierre L'Enfant's original design of the city (see p17), Washington Circle lies at the northern edge of Foggy Bottom. It forms the point where Pennsylvania Avenue and New Hampshire Avenue meet K Street and 23rd Street. The circle boasts an imposing bronze statue of George Washington astride his horse, designed by artist Clark Mills and unveiled in 1860. The statue faces east, looking toward the White House and the US Capitol.

The distinctive curved walls of the infamous Watergate Complex

Watergate Complex ⑱

Virginia Ave between Rock Creek Parkway and New Hampshire Ave, NW. **Map** 2 D3. **M** Foggy Bottom-GWU. **⌂**

LOCATED NEXT to the Kennedy Center (see pp112–3), on the bank of the Potomac River, the impressive, Italian-designed Watergate Complex was completed in 1971. The four rounded buildings that make up the complex were designed to contain shops, offices, apartments, hotels, and diplomatic missions.

In the summer of 1972 the complex found itself at the center of international news. Burglars, linked to President Nixon, broke into the offices of the Democratic National Committee, sparking off the Watergate scandal that led to the president's resignation.

THE WATERGATE SCANDAL

On June 17, 1972, during the US presidential campaign, five men were arrested for breaking into the Democratic Party headquarters in the Watergate Complex. The burglars were employed by the re-election organization of President Richard

Nixon, a Republican. Found guilty of burglary and attempting to bug telephones, the men were not initially linked to the White House. However, further investigation, led by Washington Post reporters Woodward and Bernstein, uncovered the extent of the president's involvement, including the possession of incriminating tapes and proven bribery. This led to an impeachment hearing, but before Nixon could be impeached, he resigned. Vice-President Gerald Ford succeeded him.

President Nixon addressing the nation while still in office

The Kennedy Center ⑲

IN 1958, PRESIDENT DWIGHT D. EISENHOWER signed an act to begin fund-raising for a national cultural center that would attract the world's best orchestras, opera, and dance companies to the US capital. President John F. Kennedy was an ardent supporter of the arts, taking the lead in fund-raising for it. He never saw the completion of the center, which was named in his honor. Designed by Edward Durrell Stone, it was opened on September 8, 1971. This vast complex houses three huge theaters; the Opera House, the Eisenhower Theater, and the Concert Hall, and on the roof is the Terrace Theater, the Theater Lab, and the American Film Institute.

African sculpture

Don Quixote Statue
This bronze and stone statue by Aurelio Teno was a gift to the center from Spain.

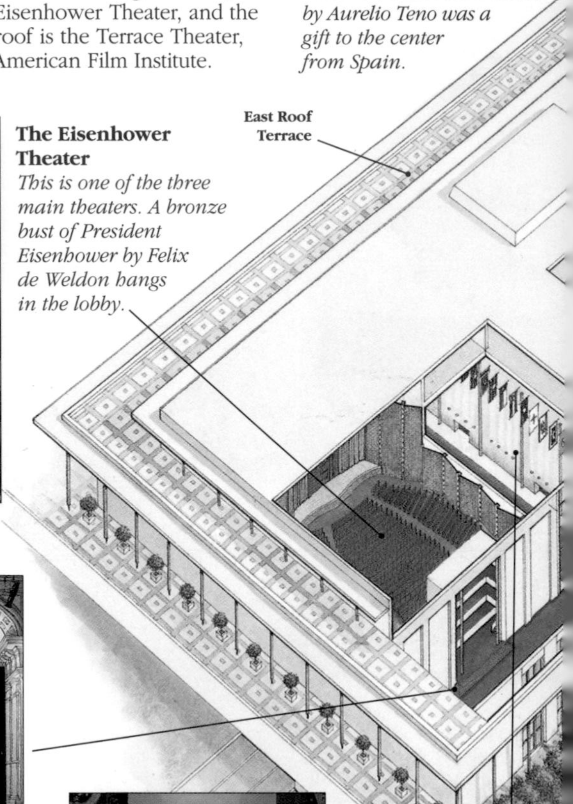

The Eisenhower Theater
This is one of the three main theaters. A bronze bust of President Eisenhower by Felix de Weldon hangs in the lobby.

East Roof Terrace

Millennium Stage
The Millennium Stage provides free performances put on in the Grand Foyer every afternoon at 6 pm.

STAR FEATURES

★ Bust of JFK

★ The Grand Foyer

★ The Opera House

The Hall of States
The flags of each of the 50 American states hang here. The sculpture by Jacques Douchez above the stairwell was a gift from Brazil.

The Hall of Nations houses the flag of every country with which the US has diplomatic relations.

★ **The Opera House**
The Opera House seats 2,318 people. The vast chandelier is made of Lobmeyr crystal and was a gift from Austria.

The Concert Hall is the largest auditorium, seating 2,500 people. It is the home of the National Symphony Orchestra.

★ **Bust of JFK**
Created by sculptor Robert Berks, this bronze bust stands in the Grand Foyer. Berks began the masterpiece the night Kennedy was assassinated.

★ **The Grand Foyer**
This enormous room stretches 630 feet (192 m) and provides an impressive entrance into the Opera House, the Concert Hall, and the Eisenhower Theater.

The JFK Terrace
This stretches the length of the Center and over- looks the Potomac and has glorious views up and down the river. Quotes by John F. Kennedy are engraved into the marble walls.

GEORGETOWN

GEORGETOWN developed well before Washington, DC. Native Americans had a settlement here, and in 1703 a land grant was given to Ninian Beall, who named the area the Rock of Dumbarton. By the mid-18th century immigrants from Scotland had swelled the population, and in 1751 the town was renamed George. It grew rapidly into a wealthy tobacco and flour port and finally, in 1789, the city of Georgetown was formed. The harbor and the Chesapeake and Ohio

John Carroll, University founder

Canal were built in 1828, and the streets were lined with town-houses. The birth of the railroad undercut Georgetown's economy, which by the mid-1800s was in decline. But by the 1950s it had improved; the cobblestone streets and charming houses attracted wealthy young couples, and restaurants and shops sprang up on Wisconsin Avenue and M Street. Today Georgetown retains its quiet distinction from the rest of the city, and is a pleasant area in which to stroll for a few hours.

SIGHTS AT A GLANCE

Historic Buildings
Dumbarton Oaks **13**
Georgetown University **9**
Old Stone House **5**
Tudor Place **10**
Washington Post Office **7**

Churches and Cemeteries
Grace Church **3**
Mt. Zion Church **11**
Oak Hill Cemetery **12**

Streets, Canals, and Harbors
Chesapeake and Ohio Canal **4**
M Street **6**
N Street **8**
Washington Harbor **1**
Wisconsin Avenue **2**

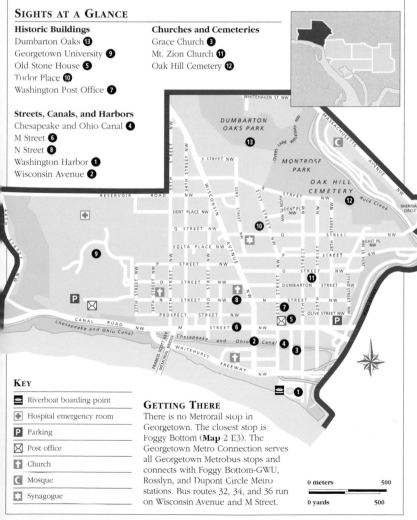

KEY

🚢	Riverboat boarding point
✚	Hospital emergency room
🅿	Parking
⊠	Post office
✝	Church
C	Mosque
✡	Synagogue

GETTING THERE
There is no Metrorail stop in Georgetown. The closest stop is Foggy Bottom (**Map** 2 E3). The Georgetown Metro Connection serves all Georgetown Metrobus stops and connects with Foggy Bottom-GWU, Rosslyn, and Dupont Circle Metro stations. Bus routes 32, 34, and 36 run on Wisconsin Avenue and M Street.

0 meters   500
0 yards   500

◁ **Typical colorful house in Georgetown**

Fountain at Washington Harbor

Washington Harbor ❶

3000-3020 K Street, NW. **Map** 2 D3.

WASHINGTON IS a city where few architectural risks have been taken. However, the approach used by architect Arthur Cotton Moore for Washington Harbor, which is a combination residential and commercial building on the Potomac River, is unusually audacious.

Built on a site that was once filled with factories and warehouses, Moore's creation is a structure that hugs the waterfront and surrounds a semi-circular pedestrian plaza. The architect borrowed motifs from almost every type of design, such as turrets, columns, and even flying buttresses. The harbor has a pleasant boardwalk, a huge fountain, and tall, columned lamp-posts. Under the ground are steel gates that can be raised to protect the building from floods. The top floors of the harbor are apartments. On the bottom floors are office complexes, restaurants, and shops. Sightseeing boats dock at the river's edge for trips to the Mall and back.

Wisconsin Avenue ❷

Wisconsin Ave. **Map** 1 C2.
Ⓜ *Tenleytown, Friendship Heights.*

WISCONSIN AVENUE is one of two main business streets in Georgetown and is home to a wide variety of shops and restaurants. It is also one of the few streets in Washington that pre-dates L'Enfant's grid plan *(see p65).* Once called High Street and then 32nd Street, it starts at the bank of the Potomac River and runs north through Georgetown right up to the

The Chesapeake and Ohio Canal ❹

WHEN IT WAS constructed in 1828, the C&O Canal featured an ingenious and revolutionary transportation system of locks, aqueducts, and tunnels that ran along its 184 miles (296 km) from Georgetown to Cumberland, Maryland. With the arrival of the railroad in the late 19th century, the canal fell out of use. It was only as a result of the efforts of Supreme Court Justice William Douglas that the Chesapeake and Ohio Canal was finally declared a protected national park in 1971. Today visitors come to enjoy its recreational facilities and also to study its fascinating transportation system.

Georgetown
The attractive federal houses of Georgetown line the banks of the canal for about 1.5 miles (2 km).

The Francis Scott Key Memorial Bridge was named after the composer of the American national anthem, *The Star-Spangled Banner.*

Canal Trips
Rides in mule-drawn canal clippers guided by park rangers dressed in period costumes are popular with visitors to the canal.

city line, where it continues as Rockville Pike. On the junction of Wisconsin Avenue and M Street is the landmark gold dome of Riggs National Bank.

During the French and Indian Wars, George Washington marched his troops up the avenue on his way to Pittsburgh to engage the British.

The gold dome of Riggs National Bank

Grace Church **❸**

1041 Wisconsin Avenue, NW. **Map** 1 C3. **☎** *333-7100.* **◯** *call office in advance (office open 10am–4pm Mon, Thu, Fri).* **♿** **W** *www.gracedc.org*

BUILT IN 1866, Grace Church was designed to serve the religious needs of the boatmen who worked on the Chesapeake and Ohio Canal and the sailors of the port of Georgetown. Set on a tree-filled plot south of the canal and M Street, the Gothic Revival church, with its quaint exterior, is an oasis in Georgetown.

The building has undergone few extensive alterations over the years and has a certain timeless quality. The church body, however, has successfuly kept pace with the changing times. Its multi-ethnic congregation makes

Sign for Grace Church

great efforts to reach out to the larger DC community and works with soup kitchens and shelters for the homeless. The church also sponsors the "Thank God It's Friday" lunchtime discussion group which is held on Fridays. Classical concerts, including chamber pieces, organ and piano works, are held here regularly. There is also a popular annual festival devoted to the music of the German composer J.S. Bach.

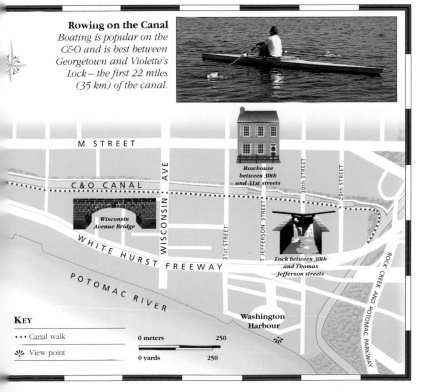

Rowing on the Canal
Boating is popular on the C&O and is best between Georgetown and Violette's Lock – the first 22 miles (35 km) of the canal.

M STREET

C&O CANAL

WISCONSIN AVE

Rowhouse between 30th and 31st streets

30th STREET

29th STREET

Wisconsin Avenue Bridge

31st STREET

T JEFFERSON STREET

WHITE HURST FREEWAY

Lock between 30th and Thomas Jefferson streets

ROCK CREEK AND POTOMAC PARKWAY

POTOMAC RIVER

Washington Harbour

KEY

• • • Canal walk

☀ View point

0 meters 250

0 yards 250

Old Stone House ❺

3051 M St, NW. **Map** 2 D2. 426-6851. phone ahead. 30, 32, 34, 36, 38. limited.
www.nps.gov/rocr/oldstonehouse

THE OLD STONE HOUSE may be the only building in Washington that pre-dates the American Revolution. It was built in 1765 by Christopher Layman, and the tiny two-story cottage has a large garden, which is a welcome respite from the shops of busy M Street.

There is a legend that still persists about the Old Stone House – that it was the Suter's Tavern where Washington and Pierre L'Enfant made their plans for the city. However, most historians today now believe that they met in a tavern located elsewhere in Georgetown.

Over the years, the building has housed a series of artisans, and in the 1950s it even served as offices for a used-car dealership. In 1960 the National Park Service restored it to its pre-Revolutionary War appearance. Today park rangers give talks about what Georgetown would have been like during the Colonial days. The Old Stone House is technically the oldest house in DC, although The Lindens, which is now in Kalorama, was built in Massachusetts in the mid-1750s and later moved to Washington.

The picturesque Old Stone House

M Street ❻

M Street, NW. **Map** 1 C2. 30, 32, 34, 36, 38.

ONE OF TWO MAIN shopping streets in Georgetown, M Street is also home to some of the most historic spots in the city. On the northeast corner of 30th and M Streets, on the current site of a bank, stood Union Tavern. Built in 1796, the tavern played host to, among others, Presidents George Washington and John Adams, Napoleon's younger brother Jerome Bonaparte, author Washington Irving, and Francis Scott Key, the composer of the "Star Spangled Banner." During the Civil War, the inn was turned into a temporary hospital where Louisa May Alcott, the author of *Little Women,* nursed wounded soldiers. In the 1930s the tavern was torn down and replaced by a gas station. Dr. William Thornton, architect of the US Capitol and Tudor Place *(see p120)* lived at 3219 M Street.

On the south side of M Street is Market House, which has been the location of Georgetown's market since 1751. In 1796 a wood frame market house was constructed and later replaced by the

Only the two end houses in this group of fine Federal homes (numbers 3327–3339) are still in their original state.

N Street ❽

1215 31st St, NW. **Map** 1 C2. 30, 32, 34, 36.

N STREET IS A sampler of 18th-century American Federal architecture – a style favored by leaders of the new nation as being of a lighter and more refined design than the earlier Georgian houses.

At the corner of 30th and N Streets is the Laird-Dunlop House. Today it is owned by Benjamin Bradlee, the former editor of the *Washington Post.*

An excellent example of a Federal house is the Riggs-Riley House at 3038 N Street, most recently owned by Averill and Pamela Harriman. At 3041–3045 N Street is Wheatley Row. These houses were designed to provide not only maximum light from large windows but also maximum privacy as they were placed above street level.

Known as Wheatley Row, these three well-designed Victorian town homes were built in 1859.

current brick market in 1865. In the 1930s the market became an auto supply store, and in the 1990s the New York gourmet food store Dean and Deluca opened a branch here.

Today M Street is home to a collection of fashionable stores and restaurants. Young buyers shop for alternative music at Smash and alternative clothing at Urban Outfitters. National chainstores such as Barnes and Noble, Pottery Barn, and Starbucks have branches along M Street.

Clyde's restaurant at number 3236 is a Georgetown institution, famous for its "happy hour." Bill Danoff, of the Starland Vocal Band, wrote his song "Afternoon Delight" about Clyde's; his gold disc hangs in the bar.

The elegant façade of the Post Office in Georgetown

Washington Post Office, Georgetown Branch ❼

1215 31st St, NW. **Map** 2 D2.
🚌 30, 32, 34, 36.

Built in 1857 as a custom-house, the still-functioning Georgetown Branch of the Washington Post Office is interesting both historically and architecturally. A custom-house was a money-producing venture for the Federal government, and the US government's investment in such an expensive building provides evidence of Georgetown's importance

as a viable port for many years. Architect Ammi B. Young, who was also responsible for the design of the Vermont State Capitol building in 1832 and the Boston Custom House in 1837, was called to Washington in 1852. He designed several other Italianate buildings in the capital, but this post office is his finest work. The granite custom-house was converted to a post office when George-town's fortunes declined.

The building underwent a renovation in 1997 that increased its efficiency and accessibility but retained the integrity of Young's simple, functional design.

Attractive houses lining the bustling M Street

The Thomas Beall House (number 3017) was built in 1794 by one of Georgetown's most prominent families. It has since been occupied by the Secretary of War during World War I, and by Jackie Kennedy, who lived here for a year after the death of JFK.

The Laird Dunlop House (number 3014) was built by John Laird who owned many of Georgetown's tobacco warehouses. Laird modeled his home on those in his native Edinburgh. It was subsequently owned by President Lincoln's son, Robert.

Number 3025–3027, with its raised mansard roof, shows the influence of the French during this period.

Unusual flat roof

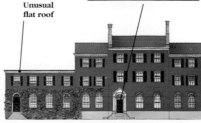

Georgetown University ❾

37th St & O St, NW. **Map** 1 B2.
📞 687-5055. ⏰ *varies, depending on university schedule.* 🎟 *call 687-3600 for details.* ♿
🌐 www.georgetown.edu

GEORGETOWN UNIVERSITY was the first Catholic college to be established in America. Founded in 1789 by John Carroll, and affiliated with the Jesuit Order, the university now attracts students of all faiths from over 100 countries around the world.

The oldest building on the campus is the Old North Building, completed in 1872, but the most recognizable structure is the Healy Building, a Germanic design topped by a fanciful spiral. The university's most famous graduate is President Bill Clinton.

The Gothic-inspired Healy Building, Georgetown University

Tudor Place ❿

1644 31st St, NW. **Map** 1 C2.
📞 965-0400. ⏰ 10am–4pm, Tue–Sat. ● Jan 1, Jul 4, Thanksgiving, Dec 25. 📷 🎟 *by appt only.* 🚻
🌐 www.tudorplace.org

THE MANOR HOUSE and large gardens of this Georgetown estate, designed by William Thornton, offer a unique glimpse into a bygone era.

Martha Washington, the First Lady, gave $8,000 to her granddaughter, Martha Custis Peter, and her granddaughter's husband. With the money, the Peters purchased eight acres and commissioned Thornton, the architect of the Capitol

Stone dog in the garden of Tudor Place

(*see pp48–9*) and the Octagon (*see p108*), to design a house. Generations of the Peters family lived here from 1805 to 1984. It is a mystery as to why this stuccoed, two-story Georgian structure with a "temple" porch is called Tudor Place, but it was perhaps illustrative of the family's English sympathies at the time.

The furniture, silver, china, and portraits provide a glimpse into American social and cultural history; some of the pieces on display come from Mount Vernon (*see pp148–9*).

Mt. Zion Church ⓫

1334 29th St, NW. **Map** 2 D2.
📞 234-0148. ✝ 11am Sun. 🎟 ♿

THIS CHURCH is thought to have had the first black congregation in DC. The first church, at 27th and P Streets, was a "station" on the city's original Underground Railroad.

Altar in Mt. Zion church

It provided shelter for runaway slaves on their journey north to freedom. The present redbrick building was completed in 1884 after the first church burned down.

Mt. Zion Cemetery, the oldest black burial ground in Washington, is located a short distance away, in the middle of the 2500 block of Q Street.

Oak Hill Cemetery ⓬

3001 R St, NW. **Map** 2 D1.
📞 337-2835. ⏰ 10am–4pm Mon–Fri. ● Sat & Sun, Federal hols.

WILLIAM WILSON Corcoran (*see p107*) bought the land for the cemetery and Congress then established Oak Hill Cemetery in 1849. Today there are around 18,000 graves covering the 25-acres site, which is planted with groves of huge oak trees.

Members of some of the city's most prominent families are buried here, their names featuring throughout Washington's history, including Magruder, Thomas, Beall, and Marbury.

At the entrance to the cemetery is an Italianate gatehouse that is still used as the superintendent's lodge and office. Northeast of the gatehouse is the Spencer family monument, designed by Louis Comfort Tiffany. The granite low-relief of an angel is signed by Tiffany.

The conference members in the
music room of Dumbarton Oaks

THE FOUNDING OF THE UNITED NATIONS

In 1944, a conference held at the Dumbarton Oaks
estate laid the groundwork for establishing the United
Nations. President Franklin Roosevelt and the British
Prime Minister, Winston Churchill, wanted to create
a "world government" that would supervise the peace
at the end of World War II. Roosevelt proposed that a
conference be held in Washington, but at the time the
State Department did not have a room big enough to
accommodate all the delegates. As a solution, Robert
Woods Bliss offered the use of the music room in his
former home, Dumbarton Oaks, for the event.

The structure of the United Nations was settled at
the Dumbarton Oaks Conference and then refined at the
San Francisco Conference a year later when the United
Nations' charter was ratified. The UN Headquarters
building, the permanent home of the organization, was
built in New York on the East River site after John D.
Rockefeller donated $8.5 million toward its construction.

Also notable is the Gothic
chapel designed by James
Renwick. Nearby is the grave
of John Howard Payne, composer of "Home, Sweet Home,"
who died in 1852. The bust
that tops Payne's monument
was originally sculpted with a
full beard, but Corcoran
requested a stonemason to
"shave the statue" and so now
it is clean shaven.

Dumbarton Oaks ⑬

1703 32nd St, NW **Map** 2 D2 【 339-
6401. ◯ **House** *2–5pm Tue – Sun.*
Gardens *2–5pm daily.* ● *Federal hols.*
▨ ◪ *for groups call 339-6409* ◻
♿ *house only.* Ⓦ *www.doaks.org*

I N 1703, a Scottish colonist
named Ninian Beall was
granted around 800 acres of
land in this area. In later years
the land was sold off and in
1801, 22 acres were bought by
Senator William Dorsey of
Maryland, who proceeded to
build a Federal-style brick
home here. A year later, financial difficulties caused him to
sell it, and over the next century the property changed
hands many times.

By the time pharmaceutical
heirs Robert and Mildred
Woods Bliss bought the run-
down estate in 1920, it was
overgrown and neglected.
The Blisses altered and
expanded the house, with
the architectural advice of the
prestigious firm McKim, Mead

and White *(see p103)*, to meet
20th-century family needs, and
set to work on the garden.
They engaged their friend,
Beatrix Jones Farrand, one
of the few female land-
scape architects at the
time, to lay out the
grounds. Farrand
designed a series of
terraces that progress
from the formal gar-
dens near the house
to the more informal
landscapes farther
away from it.

In 1940 the Blisses
moved to California
and donated the whole estate
to Harvard University. It was
then converted into a library,
research institution, and
museum. Many of the 1,400
pieces of Byzantine Art on
display were collected by the
Blisses themselves. Examples

**Fountain in
Dumbarton Oaks**

of Greco-Roman coins, late
Roman and early Byzantine
bas-reliefs, Egyptian fabrics,
and Roman glass and bronze-
ware are just some
of the highlights.
In 1962 Robert
Woods Bliss do-
nated his collection
of pre-Columbian
art to the estate as
well. In order to
house it, architect
Philip Johnson
designed a new
wing, consisting
of eight domes sur-
rounding a circular
garden. Although markedly
different from the original
house, the new wing is well
suited to the dramatic art
collection it houses, which
includes masks, stunning gold
jewelry from Central America,
frescoes, and Aztec carvings.

Swimming pool in the grounds of Dumbarton Oaks

FARTHER AFIELD

Zoo sign

ORTH OF THE White House is Dupont Circle, a neighborhood of museums, galleries, and restaurants. The Embassy Row, Kalorama, Adams-Morgan, and Cleveland Park neighborhoods are a walker's paradise, especially for visitors interested in architecture.

Arlington, Virginia, across the Potomac River, was one of DC's first suburbs. Arlington National Cemetery was founded in 1864 to honor those who died for the Union. The Pentagon was built 80 years later by Franklin D. Roosevelt and is the area's most famous landmark.

SIGHTS AT A GLANCE

Museums and Galleries
African American Civil War
  Museum and Memorial **7**
Anacostia Museum **26**
Hillwood Museum **17**
Mary McLeod Bethune
  Council House **16**
National Geographic Society **8**
Phillips Collection **10**
Textile Museum **11**

**Historic Districts,
Streets, and Buildings**
Adams-Morgan **15**
Dupont Circle **9**
Embassy Row **13**
Frederick Douglass House **25**
Heurich Mansion **6**
Kalorama **14**

Lincoln Theatre **18**
National Cathedral pp136–7 **20**
The Pentagon **2**
Southwest Waterfront **3**
Woodrow Wilson House **12**

Monuments
Basilica of the National Shrine
  of the Immaculate
  Conception **23**
Iwo Jima Statue **4**

Parks and Gardens
Cleveland Park **21**
US National Arboretum **24**
*National Zoological Park
  pp132–3* **19**
Rock Creek Park **22**
Roosevelt Island **5**

Cemetery
*Arlington National
  Cemetery pp124–5* **1**

KEY

▨	Central Washington
▢	District of Columbia
▢	Greater Washington
✈	Domestic airport
—	Metro line
═	Freeway (motorway)
═	Major road
═	Minor road

0 kilometers   2.5

0 miles   2.5

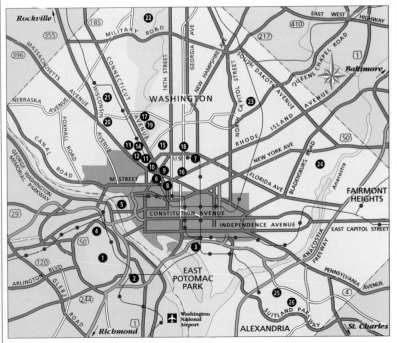

◁ **Chinese-style pagoda in the Asian collection at the National Arboretum**

Arlington National Cemetery ❶

F OR 30 YEARS, CONFEDERATE General Robert E. Lee (1807–70) lived at Arlington House. In 1861 he left his home to lead Virginia's armed forces, and the Union confiscated the estate for a military cemetery. By the end of the Civil War in 1865, 16,000 soldiers were interred in the newly consecrated Arlington National Cemetery. Since then, around another 250,000 veterans have joined them. Simple headstones mark the graves of soldiers who died in every major conflict from the Revolution to the Persian Gulf War. The focus of the cemetery is the Tomb of the Unknowns, which honors the thousands who have died in battle but have no known resting place.

Soldier on guard

Confederate Memorial
This bronze and granite monu ment honors the Confederate soldiers who died in the Civil War. It was dedicated in 1914

Sea of Graves
Over 245,000 servicemen and their families are buried on the 612 acres of Arlington Cemetery.

★ **Tomb of the Unknowns**
This tomb contains four vaults – for World War I and II, Vietnam, and Korea. Each vault held one unidentified soldier until recently when the Vietnam soldier was identified by DNA analysis and reburied in his home town.

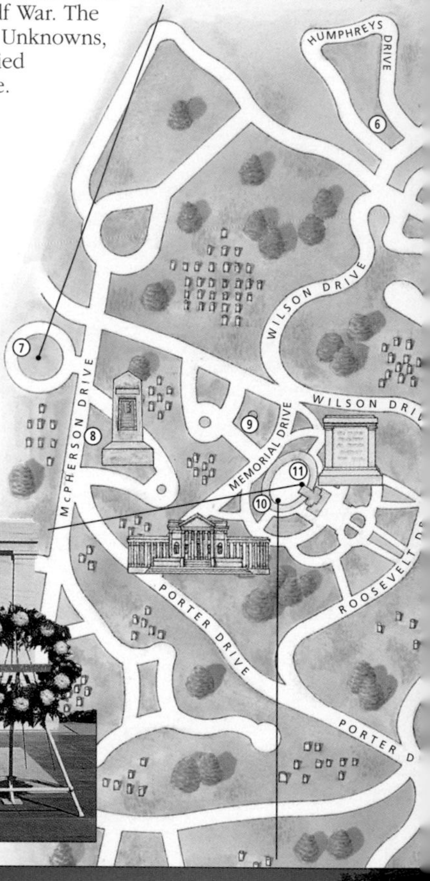

0 meters   200

0 yards   200

★ **Arlington House**

★ **Grave of John F. Kennedy**

★ **Tomb of the Unknowns**

STAR FEATURES

Memorial Amphitheater
This marble amphitheater is the setting of the annual services on Memorial Day (see p34) when the nation's leaders pay tribute to the dead who served their country. It has also hosted many state funerals.

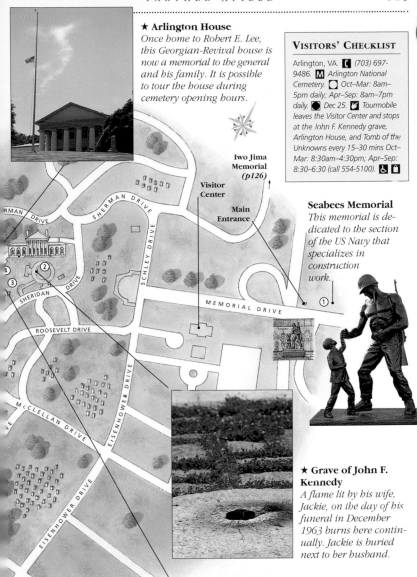

★ Arlington House
Once home to Robert E. Lee, this Georgian-Revival house is now a memorial to the general and his family. It is possible to tour the house during cemetery opening hours.

VISITORS' CHECKLIST

Arlington, VA. **(** (703) 697-9486. **M** *Arlington National Cemetery.* ◯ *Oct–Mar: 8am–5pm daily; Apr–Sep: 8am–7pm daily.* ● *Dec 25.* **T** *Tourmobile leaves the Visitor Center and stops at the John F. Kennedy grave, Arlington House, and Tomb of the Unknowns every 15–30 mins Oct–Mar: 8:30am–4:30pm; Apr–Sep: 8:30–6:30 (call 554-5100).* **&**

Iwo Jima Memorial (p126)

Visitor Center

Main Entrance

Seabees Memorial
This memorial is dedicated to the section of the US Navy that specializes in construction work.

★ Grave of John F. Kennedy
A flame lit by his wife, Jackie, on the day of his funeral in December 1963 burns here continually. Jackie is buried next to her husband.

KEY TO TOMBS AND SITES

Arlington House ⑤
Challenger Shuttle Memorial ⑨
Confederate Memorial ⑦
Grave of John F. Kennedy ②
Grave of Robert F. Kennedy ③
Lockerbie Memorial ⑥
Memorial Amphitheater ⑩
Rough Riders Memorial ⑧
Seabees Memorial ①
Tomb of Pierre L'Enfant ④
Tomb of the Unknowns ⑪

Tomb of Pierre L'Enfant
The architect responsible for planning the city of Washington has a suitably grand burial site in the cemetery (see p65).

View of the Pentagon building's formidable concrete façade from the Potomac River

The Pentagon ❷

1000 Defense Pentagon, Hwy 1-395, Arlington, VA. **C** (703) 695-1776. **M** *Pentagon. Tours were suspended in September 2001. For the latest information call the above number.* **W** www.defenselink.mil

P RESIDENT FRANKLIN Roosevelt decided in the early 1940s to consolidate the 17 buildings that comprised the Department of War (the original name for the Department of Defense) into one building. Designed by army engineers, and built of gravel dredged from the Potomac River and molded into concrete, the Pentagon was completed on January 15, 1943, at a cost of $83 million. As the world's largest office building, it is almost a city in itself. Yet despite its size, the unique five-sided design is very efficient, and it takes only seven minutes to walk between any two points in the building.

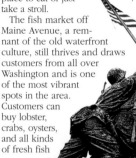

Fish stall at the waterfront's market

The Pentagon is the headquarters of the Department of Defense, a Cabinet-level organization consisting of three military departments, the Army, Navy, and Air Force, as well as 14 defense agencies. Leading personnel are the Secretary of Defense and the Chairman of the Joint Chiefs of Staff.

On September 11, 2001, the building was damaged in a terrorist attack. As a result, public access is restricted and tours have been suspended.

Southwest Waterfront ❸

M *Waterfront.* **Fish Market** ☐ *7:30am–8pm daily.*

I N THE 1960s, urban planners tested their new architectural theories on Washington's southwest waterfront along the Potomac River. Old neighborhoods were torn down, and apartment high-rises put up in their place. Eventually new restaurants developed along the waterfront, and Arena Stage, a popular regional theater company, built an experimental theater here. The area enjoyed a regeneration, and today it is a relaxed place to eat or just take a stroll.

The fish market off Maine Avenue, a remnant of the old waterfront culture, still thrives and draws customers from all over Washington and is one of the most vibrant spots in the area. Customers can buy lobster, crabs, oysters, and all kinds of fresh fish from the vendors selling from their barges on the river. There are also several good restaurants along the waterfront that specialize in freshly caught local fish and seafood.

Iwo Jima Memorial ❹

Meade St, between Arlington National Cemetery & Arlington Boulevard. **Map** 1 B5. **M** *Rosslyn.* &

T HE HORRIFIC battle of Iwo Jima that took place during World War II was captured by photographer Joe Rosenthal. His Pulitzer Prize-winning picture of five Marines and a Navy Corpsman raising the American flag on the tiny Pacific island came to symbolize in the American psyche the heroic struggle of the American forces in the war against Japan. This image was magnificently translated into bronze by sculptor Felix DeWeldon and paid for by private donations. The three

A poignant memorial to the men who died in the battle of Iwo Jima

September 11

On September 11, 2001, one of four airplanes hijacked by terrorists was flown into the Pentagon, resulting in huge loss of life and causing the side of the building to collapse.

Although dedicated crews at the Pentagon are working tirelessly to rebuild the damaged 10 percent of the building (400,000 to 500,000 square feet), it is estimated that repairs will take three years to complete. Today, the area looks much like any other construction site, but the charred walls are a grim reminder of the tragedy.

The damaged Pentagon after the September 11 attack

surviving soldiers from Rosenthal's photograph actually posed for DeWeldon; the other three men, however, were killed in further fighting on the islands. The Iwo Jima Memorial was dedicated on November 10, 1954, to coincide with the 179th birthday of the Marine Corps.

Roosevelt Island ❺

GW Memorial Pkwy, McLean, VA. **Map** 1 C4. 📞 (703) 289-2530. Ⓜ Rosslyn. ⏰ 7am–dusk daily. 🎫 by appt only. 🆆 www.nps.gov/gwmp

A HAVEN FOR naturalists, Roosevelt Island's 88 acres of marshlands and two and a half miles (4 km) of nature trails are home to red-tailed hawks, great owls, groundhogs, wood ducks, and many species of trees and plants. President Theodore Roosevelt (1858–1919), a great naturalist himself, is honored

with a 17-ft (5-m) tall memorial in bronze, and four granite tablets, each inscribed with quotes by the president.

Roosevelt Island is accessible by car via the George Washington Memorial Parkway or by canoe, which can be rented from Thompson's Boathouse *(see p189)* near the Watergate Complex.

Heurich Mansion ❻

1307 New Hampshire Ave, NW. 📞 785-2068. Ⓜ Dupont Circle. 🆆 www.hswdc.org

B REWER CHRISTIAN Heurich built this wonderful Bavarian fantasy for his family just south of Dupont Circle in 1892. The turreted mansion built in the Romanesque Revival architectural style was once home to the Historical Society of Washington, DC. Magnificently preserved, the Heurich Mansion is a

fine example of an upper-middle-class family house in Washington in the late 1800s. Unfortunately, it is no longer open to the public, but is still well worth visiting if only to admire its exterior.

The ornate carving in Heurich's Beer Hall

African American Civil War Museum and Memorial ❼

1200 U Street, NW. **Map** 3 C1 📞 667-2667. Ⓜ U Street. ⏰ 10am–5pm Mon–Fri, 10am–2pm Sat (call to arrange tours). 🆆 www.afroamcivilwar.org

O PENED IN in January 1999, the African American Museum uses photographs, documents and audiovisual equipment to explain the still largely unknown story of African Americans' long struggle for freedom. The Museum's permanent exhibition is entitled "Slavery to Freedom; Civil War to Civil Rights." Interactive kiosks bring together historic documents, photographs, and music in a powerful and evocative way. There is also a service for anyone interested in tracing relatives who may have served with United States Colored Troops during the Civil War. There are computers that can be used to access the National Park Service Civil War Soldiers and Sailors web site. The Museum also hopes to purchase the Gladstone Collection, which is one of the largest collections ever assembled of artifacts relating to the participation of African Americans in the Civil War.

The statue of President Roosevelt and granite tablets on Roosevelt Island

Giant globe in the Explorers Hall at the National Geographic Society

National Geographic Society ❽

1145 17th St at M St, NW.
Map 2 F2 & 3 B2. 📞 857-7588.
Ⓜ Farragut North. 🕐 9am–5pm
Mon–Sat & federal hols, 10am–5pm
Sun. ● Dec 25. ♿ 📷
ⓦ www.nationalgeographic.com

THE NATIONAL Geographic Society has been funding explorers and producing a monthly newsletter, the precursor to its famous yellow-bordered magazine, since 1888.

In 1964 the Society moved into its present headquarters, designed by Edward Durrell Stone, the architect who also designed the Kennedy Center. The upper floors house staff working on magazines and other educational projects.

On the first floor is Explorers Hall, a compact museum that illustrates the Society's mission to explore the earth's land, water, and air masses. Highlights include a simulated tornado that can be touched, holograms that look so life-like visitors try to reach out and grab them, and Earth Station One, an amphitheater that simulates orbital flight. There are also supermicroscopes (or cyberscopes), which visitors can use to look at minerals and plants.

The Explorers Hall has an 10-ft (3-m) high globe, which has become a symbol for the Society. Geographica is an interactive exhibit that allows visitors to experience vicariously undersea exploration,

the force of a tornado, and the land of dinosaurs. The National Geographic's bookstore is a treasure trove of all things related to geography; atlases, videos, books, and maps

Dupont Circle ❾

Map 2 F2 & 3 A1. Ⓜ Dupont Circle.

THIS AREA TO the north of the White House gets its name from the intersection of Massachusetts, Connecticut, and New Hampshire Avenues, and 19th Street, NW. At the heart of this traffic island is the Francis Dupont Memorial Fountain, named for a dishonored Civil War admiral. Built by his family in an effort to restore his good name, the original memorial was a bronze statue that was moved eventually to

Playing chess in Dupont Circle

Wilmington, Delaware. The present marble fountain, which was constructed in 1921, has four figures (which represent the sea, the wind, the stars, and the navigational arts) supporting a marble basin.

The park area around the fountain draws a cross section of the community – chess players engrossed in their games, cyclists pausing at the fountain, picnickers eating alfresco, and tourists taking a break from sightseeing.

In the early 20th century the Dupont Circle area was a place of grand mansions. Its fortunes then declined until the 1970s, when Washingtonians began to buy the decaying mansions. The district is now filled with art galleries, bars, restaurants, and bookstores. The old Victorian buildings have been divided into apartments, restored as single family homes, or converted into small office buildings.

Dupont Circle is also the center of Washington's gay community. The bars and clubs on the section of P Street between Dupont Circle and Rock Creek Park are the most popular area for gay men and women to meet. East along P Street, and past 14th Street, the area changes quite dramatically for the worse. Do not stray into this part of town, especially after dark. However, south of the Circle it changes again, as here the stores and restaurants cater to a wealthier clientele.

The elaborate fountain at the heart of the Dupont Circle intersection

Auguste Renoir's masterpiece, *The Luncheon of the Boating Party* (1881)

Phillips Collection ❿

1600 21st St at Q St, NW. **Map** 2 E2
& 3 A1. 🇨 387-2151. 🇲 *Dupont Circle.* ⭕ *10am–5pm Tue–Sat (10am–8:30pm Thu), 12–7pm Sun.* ⬤ *Mon, Jan 1, Jul 4, Thanksgiving.* 🏷 🎫 *2pm Wed & Sat.* ♿ 🇼 www.phillipscollection.org

T HIS IS ONE of the finest collections of Impressionist works in the world and the first museum devoted to modern art of the 19th and 20th centuries in the United States. Duncan and Marjorie Phillips, who founded the collection, lived in the older of the museum's two adjacent buildings. Following the death of his father in 1917, Duncan Phillips decided to open two of the mansion's rooms as The Phillips Memorial Gallery.

The couple spent their time traveling and adding to their already extensive collection. During the 1920s they acquired some of the most important modern European paintings, including *The Luncheon of the Boating Party* (1881) by Renoir, for which they paid $125,000 (one of the highest prices ever paid at the time). The collection continued to grow to more than 2,000 pieces of art over the next 50 years.

In 1930 the Phillips family moved to a new home on Foxhall Road in northwest Washington and converted the rest of their former 1897 Georgian Revival residence

into a private gallery. The Phillips Gallery was then reopened to the public in 1960 as the newly named Phillips Collection.

The elegant Georgian Revival building that was the Phillips' home makes for a more intimate and personal gallery than the big Smithsonian art museums.

The Collection is best known for its wonderful selection of Impressionist and Post-Impressionist paintings; *Dancers at the Barre* by Degas, *Self-Portrait* by Cézanne and *Entrance to the Public Gardens in Arles* by Van Gogh are just three examples. The museum also has one of the largest collections in the world of pieces by French artist Pierre Bonnard, including *The Open Window* (1921).

Other great paintings to be seen in the collection include El Greco's *The Repentant Saint Peter* (1600), *The Blue Room* (1901) by Pablo Picasso, Piet Mondrian's *Composition No. III* (1921–25), and *Ochre on Red* (1954) by Mark Rothko.

In addition to the permanent exhibits, the museum supports traveling exhibitions, which start at the Phillips Collection before appearing

Collector Duncan Phillips (1886–1966)

in galleries around the country. The exhibitions often feature one artist (such as Georgia O'Keeffe) or one particular topic or period (such as the *Twentieth-Century Still-Life Paintings* exhibition).

The Phillips Collection encourages enthusiasts of modern art to visit the museum for a number of special events. On Thursday evenings the museum hosts "Artful Evenings." These include gallery talks, live jazz music, and light refreshments, and give people the opportunity to discuss the issues of the art world in a relaxed, social atmosphere. On Sunday afternoons from September through May, a series of concerts are staged in the gallery's Music Room. Running since 1941, these popular concerts are free to anyone who has purchased a ticket for the gallery on that day. They range from piano recitals and string quartets to performances by established singers of world renown, such as the famous operatic soprano Jessye Norman.

The gallery shop sells merchandise linked to permanent and temporary exhibitions. Books, posters, and prints can be found as well as ceramics, glassware, and other creations by contemporary artists. There are also hand-painted silks and artworks based on the major paintings in the collection.

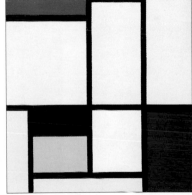

Composition No. III (1921–25) by Piet Mondrian

18th-century Turkish embroidery on silk in the Textile Museum

Textile Museum ⑪

2320 S St, NW. **Map** 2 E1.
📞 667-0441. Ⓜ *Dupont Circle.*
🕐 *10am–5pm Mon–Sat, 1–5pm Sun.* ⬤ *Dec 24, fedcral hols.*
💲 *donation.* 📷 *call 2 weeks in advance; introductory tours Sep–May: 1:30pm Wed, Sat & Sun.*
Library 🕐 *10am–2pm Wed–Fri, 10am–4pm Sat.* 📱 ♿ *call in advance.*
Ⓦ *www.textilemuseum.org*

GEORGE HEWITT Myers, the founder of the Textile Museum, began collecting oriental rugs while he was at college. In 1925 he opened a museum in his home to display his collection of 275 rugs and 60 textiles. It was a private museum, open only by appointment, until Myers' death in 1957.

Today the museum is still housed in Myers' home, which was designed by John Russell Pope, architect of the Jefferson Memorial *(see p75)*. The collection is also now in an adjacent building by Waddy B. Wood, architect of Woodrow Wilson's house.

There are around 17,000 objects in the collection from all over the world, including textiles from Peru, India, Indonesia, and Central America. The museum has a collections database, as well as a library of over 17,000 books on the subject of textiles. Visitors must make an appointment to use the database.

Woodrow Wilson House ⑫

2340 S St, NW. **Map** 2 E1.
📞 387- 4062. Ⓜ *Dupont Circle.*
🕐 *10am–4pm Tue–Sun.*
⬤ *Mon, federal hols.* 💲 📷 ♿

LOCATED IN THE beautiful Kalorama neighborhood, the former home of Woodrow Wilson (1856–1924), who served as president from 1913 to 1921, is the only presidential museum within the District of Columbia.

Wilson led the US through World War I and advocated the formation of the League of Nations, the precursor to the United Nations. Although exhausted by the war effort, Wilson campaigned tirelessly for the League across America.

In 1919 he collapsed from a stroke and became an invalid for the rest of his life. Many believe that Wilson's second wife, Edith Galt, assumed many of the presidential duties herself (she guided his hand when he signed documents). Unable to leave his sickbed, Wilson saw his dream, the League of Nations, defeated in the Senate. In 1920 he was awarded the Nobel Peace Prize – small consolation for the failure of the League.

Wilson and his wife moved to this townhouse, designed by Waddy B. Wood, at the end of his second term in 1921.

Edith Galt Wilson arranged for the home to be bequeathed to the nation. Since then the building has been maintained as it was during the President's lifetime, containing artifacts from his life and reflecting the style of an upper-middle-class home of the 1920s. The house today is the property of the National Trust for Historic Preservation.

Embassy Row ⑬

Massachusetts Avenue. **Map** 2 E1.
Ⓜ *Dupont Circle.*

EMBASSY ROW stretches along Massachusetts Avenue from Scott Circle toward Observatory Circle. It developed during the Depression when many of Washington's wealthy families were forced to sell their mansions to diplomats, who bought them for foreign missions. Since then, many new embassies have been built, often in the vernacular style of their native country, making Embassy Row architecturally fascinating.

At No. 2315 Massachusetts Avenue, the Embassy of Pakistan is an opulent mansion built in 1908, with a mansard roof (four steep sloping sides) and a rounded wall that hugs the corner.

Farther down the road, at No. 2349, is the Embassy of the Republic of Cameroon, one of the Avenue's great

Statue of Churchill, British Embassy

An elaborately decorated room in the Georgian Revival Woodrow Wilson House

early 20th-century Beaux Arts masterpieces. This romantic, Norwegian chateau-style building was commissioned in 1905 to be the home of Christian Hauge, first Norwegian ambassador to the United States, before passing to Cameroon.

Situated opposite the Irish Embassy stands a bronze statue of the hanged Irish revolutionary Robert Emmet (1778–1803). The statue was commissioned by Irish Americans to commemorate Irish independence.

At No. 2536 is the India Supply Mission. Two carved elephants stand outside as symbols of Indian culture and mythology. In the park in front of the Indian Embassy is an impressive bronze sculpture of Mahatma Gandhi.

The British Embassy, at No. 3100, was designed by Sir Edwin Lutyens in 1928. The English-style gardens were planted by the American wife of the then British ambassador, Sir Ronald Lindsay. Outside the embassy is an arresting statue of Sir Winston Churchill by William M. McVey.

Façade of the Croatian Embassy on Massachusetts Avenue

Kalorama ⓮

Map 2 D1 & 2 E1. **M** *Woodley Park or Dupont Circle.*

THE NEIGHBORHOOD of Kalorama, situated north of Dupont Circle, is an area of stately private homes and elegant apartment buildings. From its development at the turn of the 20th century as a suburb close to the city center, Kalorama (Greek for "beautiful view") has been home to the wealthy and upwardly mobile.

The apartments at 2311 Connecticut Avenue, Kalorama

Five presidents had homes here: Herbert Hoover, Franklin D. Roosevelt, Warren Harding, William Taft, and Woodrow Wilson. Only Wilson's home served as his permanent post-presidential residence.

Some of the most striking and ornate apartment buildings in Washington are found on Connecticut Avenue, south of the Taft Bridge that crosses Rock Creek Park. Most notable are the Georgian Revival-style Dresden apartments at No. 2126, the Beaux Arts-inspired Highlands building at number 1914, and the Spanish Colonial-style Woodward apartments at No. 2311 Connecticut Avenue. Also worth viewing is the Tudor-style building at No. 2221 Kalorama Road.

The best views of nearby Rock Creek Park *(see p135)* are from Kalorama Circle at the northern end of 24th Street.

Adams-Morgan ⓯

North of Dupont Circle, east of Rock Creek Park, and south of Mt. Pleasant. **Map** 2 E1 & 2 F1. **M** *Dupont Circle or Woodley Park.*

ADAMS-MORGAN is the only racially and ethnically diverse neighborhood in the city. It was given its name in the 1950s when the Supreme Court ruled that Washington must desegregate its educational system, and forced the combination of two schools in the area – Adams (for white children) and Morgan (an all-black school).

Packed with cafés, bookstores, clubs, and galleries, the district is a vibrant and eclectic mix of African, Hispanic, and Caribbean immigrants, as well as white urban pioneers, both gay and straight. People are attracted by the neighborhood's lively streets and its beautiful, and relatively affordable, early 20th-century houses and apartments.

The area has a thriving music scene and, on any night, rap, reggae, salsa, and Washington's indigenous go-go can be heard in the clubs and bars. The cosmopolitan feel of Adams-Morgan is reflected in its wide variety of restaurants *(see p178)*. Cajun, New Orleans, Ethiopian, French, Italian, Caribbean, Mexican, and Lebanese food can all be found along 18th Street and Columbia Road, the two main streets.

Although the area is becoming increasingly modern and trendy, its 1950s Hispanic roots are still evident. They are loudly celebrated in the Hispanic-Latino Festival that takes place every July and spreads from the Mall up to Adams-Morgan *(see p35).*

It should be noted that this area can be dangerous after dark, so be wary if you are walking around at night. The area is not served by Metrorail and parking, especially on weekends, can be difficult.

Colorful mural on the wall of a parking lot in Adams-Morgan

National Zoological Park ⑲

ESTABLISHED IN 1887 as the Smithsonian's Department of Living Animals and sited on the Mall, the National Zoo moved to its present location in 1891. The park, which covers 163 acres, was designed by Frederick Law Olmstead, the landscape architect responsible for New York's Central Park. Today, the zoo has more than 4,500 animals and is a dynamic "biopark" where animals are studied in environments that replicate their natural habitat. It has a number of breeding programs, one of the most successful of which is the Sumatran tiger program.

Micronesian Kingfisher

Giant Panda Exhibit
Tian Tian and Mei Xiang were given by the Chinese government and arrived in the zoo on December 6, 2001. The giant pandas are one of the zoo's most popular attractions.

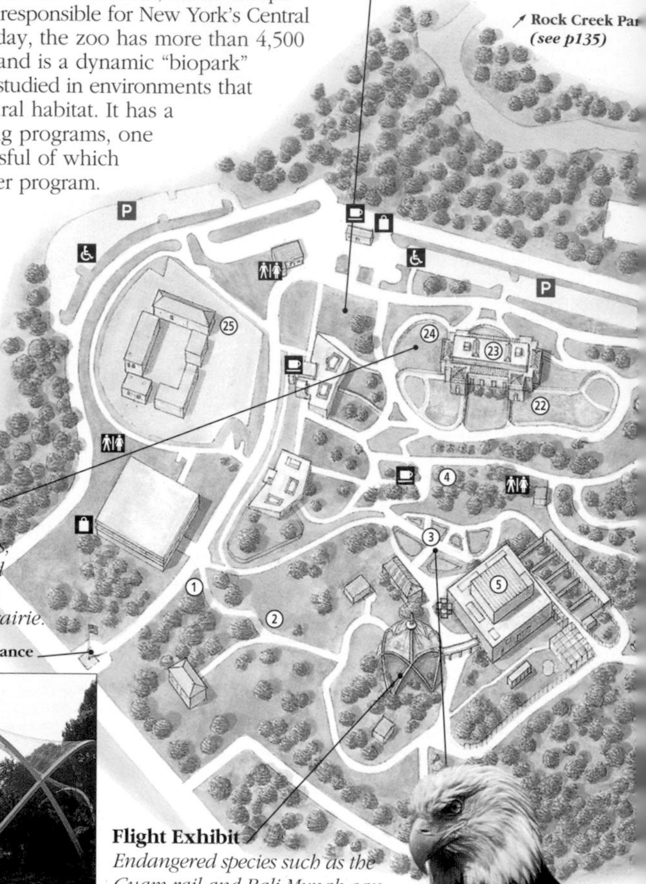

↗ **Rock Creek Park** *(see p135)*

★ **Prairie Exhibit**
This exhibit features plants and creatures, including bison and prairie dogs, from a typical American Prairie.

Main Entrance

Flight Exhibit
Endangered species such as the Guam rail and Bali Mynah can be seen in the Bird House.

Bald Eagle
The only eagle unique to North America, the bald eagle is named for its white head, which appears to be "bald" against its dark body.

KEY TO ANIMAL ENCLOSURES

Amazonia ⑩
Prairie Exhibit ㉔
Bat Cave ⑪
Bears ⑬
Beavers and Otters ⑥
Bird House and Flight Exhibit ⑤
Birds ④
Bongos (rare antelope) ②
Camels ㉑
Cheetahs and Zebras ㉕
Elephants, Giraffes, and Pandas ㉓
Gibbon Ridge ⑲
Great Ape House ⑱

Hippos and Rhinos ㉒
Invertebrate Exhibit ⑰
Lions and Tigers ⑫
Monkey Island ⑭
Red Wolves ⑦
Reptile Discovery Center ⑯
Seals and Sea Lions ⑧
Servals ⑮
Small Mammal House ⑳
Spectacled Bears ⑨
Tapirs ①
Wetlands Exhibit and Eagles ③

0 meters   100
0 yards   100

Golden Lion Tamarins
These endangered mammals are protected by an international conservation program which includes breeding and conservation education.

VISITORS' CHECKLIST

3001 Connecticut Ave, NW.
673-4800. M Cleveland
Park, Woodley Park-Zoo.
May 1–Sep 15: 10am–6pm
daily (buildings), 6am–8pm daily
(grounds); Sep 16–Apr 30:
10am–4:30pm daily (buildings),
8am–6pm daily (grounds).
Dec 25. call 673-4671.
W www.natzoo.si.edu

★ **Great Ape House**
Lowland gorillas – males can weigh up to 400 pounds (180 kg) – can be seen in the Great Ape House. Other occupants include arboreal (tree-dwelling) orangutans.

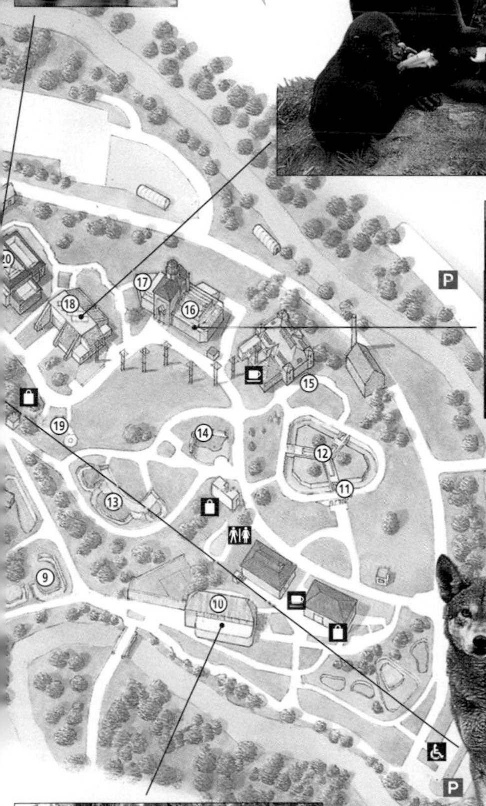

★ **Komodo Dragons**
These rare lizards can grow up to 10 ft (3 m) in length, and weigh up to 200 lbs (90 kg). They are the first to be born in captivity outside Indonesia.

Red Wolves
Related to the gray wolf, the endangered red wolf is native to America. There are only around 300 in existence and of these, 220 live in captivity.

Amazonia
This exhibit re-creates the Amazonian habitat. Visitors can see many creatures from poison arrow frogs to giant catfish.

STAR EXHIBITS

★ **Great Ape House**

★ **Komodo Dragons**

★ **Prairie Exhibit**

Mary McLeod Bethune Council House National Historic Site ⓰

1318 Vermont Ave, NW. **Map** 3 B1. 673-2402. **M** McPherson Square. 10am–4pm Mon–Sat. Sun, federal hols. plus interactive tour for children. **w** www.nps.gov/mamc

BORN IN 1875 to two former slaves, Mary McLeod Bethune was an educator and civil and women's rights activist. In 1904 she founded a college for impoverished black women in Florida, the Daytona Educational and Industrial School for Negro Girls. Renamed the Bethune-Cookman College, it is still going strong.

In the 1930s, President Franklin D. Roosevelt asked her to be his special advisor on racial affairs, and she later became director of the Division of Negro Affairs in the National Youth Administration. As part of Roosevelt's cabinet, Bethune enjoyed the highest position ever held by a black woman in the US government.

Mary McLeod Bethune

Bethune went on to found the National Council of Negro Women, which gives voice to the concerns of black women. The Council grew to have a membership of 10,000, and this house on Vermont Avenue was bought by Bethune and the Council as its headquarters.

It was not until November 1979, 24 years after Bethune's death, that the original Council House was opened to the public, with photographs, manuscripts, and other artifacts from her life on display. In 1982 the house was declared a National Historic Site and was bought by the National Park Service.

Entrance to the Mary McLeod Bethune Council House

The stunning interior of the restored Lincoln Theatre

Hillwood Museum and Gardens ⓱

4155 Linnean Avenue, NW. 1/877 HILLWOOD, 686-5807. **M** Van Ness/ UDC. 9am–5pm Tue–Sat. February, Federal hols. Visits must be booked in advance. **w** www.hillwoodmuseum.org

Hillwood was owned by Marjorie Merriweather Post, and it was opened to the public in 1977. The Museum contains the most comprehensive collection of 18th- and 19th-century Russian imperial costume to be found outside of Russia. It also has a renowned collection of French decorative arts from the 18th century. The Gardens are set within a 25-acre estate, surrounded by woodlands in the heart of Washington, and have important collections of azaleas and orchids.

Lincoln Theatre ⓲

1215 U St, NW. **Map** 2 F1. 328-6000. **M** U Street-Cardozo. 10am–6pm Mon–Fri. Federal hols. groups by appt.

BUILT IN 1922, the Lincoln Theatre was once the centerpiece of cultural life for Washington's downtown African American community. Like the Apollo Theater in New York, the Lincoln presented big-name entertainment, such as jazz singer and native Washingtonian Duke Ellington and his orchestra, Ella Fitzgerald, and Billie Holiday.

By the 1960s the area around the theater began to deteriorate, and the 1968 riots turned U Street into a corridor of abandoned and burned-out buildings and attendance at the theater dropped dramatically. By the 1970s the theater had closed down. Then, in the early 1980s fundraising began for the $10 million renovation. Even the original, highly elaborate plasterwork was carefully cleaned and repaired, and the theater reopened in 1994.

Today the Lincoln Theatre is a center for the performing arts, and one of the linchpins of U Street's renaissance. The magnificent auditorium hosts a program of concerts, stage shows, and events including the DC Film Festival (see p186).

National Zoological Park ⓳

See pp132–3.

National Cathedral ⑳

See pp136–7.

Cleveland Park ㉑

Ⓜ *Cleveland Park.*

CLEVELAND PARK is a beautiful residential neighborhood that resembles the picture on a postcard of small-town America. It was originally a summer community for those wanting to escape the less bucolic parts of the city. In 1885, President Grover Cleveland (1885–9) bought a stone farmhouse here as a summer home for his bride.

The town's Victorian summer houses are now much sought after by people wanting to be close to the city but live in a small-town environment. There are interesting shops and good restaurants, as well as a grand old Art Deco movie theater, called the Uptown, which first opened in 1936.

Rock Creek Park ㉗

Ⓜ *Cleveland Park.* **Rock Creek Park Nature Center** 5200 Glover Rd, NW. **Map** 2 D1–D3. Ⓒ *426-6829.* Ⓜ *Friendship Heights.* ⓞ *9am–5pm Wed–Sun.* ⓦ *federal hols.* ⓖ *4pm Wed–Fri, varied times Sat & Sun* Ⓦ *www.nps.gov/rocr*

NAMED AFTER the creek that flows through it, Rock Creek Park bisects the city of Washington. This 1800-acre

Pierce Mill, the 19th-century gristmill in Rock Creek Park

THE SHAW NEIGHBORHOOD

This neighborhood is named after Union Colonel Robert Gould Shaw, the white commander of an all-black regiment from Massachusetts. He supported his men in their struggle to attain the same rights as white soldiers. Until the 1960s, U Street was the focus of black-dominated businesses and organizations. Thriving theaters, such as the Howard and the Lincoln, attracted top-name performers, and Howard University was the center of intellectual life for black students. The 1968 riots, sparked by the assassination of Dr. Martin Luther King Jr., wiped out much of Shaw's business district, and many thought the area could never be revived. However, the restoration of the Lincoln Theatre, the renewal of the U Street business district, and an influx of homebuyers renovating historic houses, have all contributed to the rejuvenation. In the part of U Street closest to the U Street-Cardoza metro stop, many fashionable bars and clubs have recently opened.

Mural in the Shaw neighborhood depicting Duke Ellington

stretch of land runs from the Maryland border south to the Potomac River and constitutes nearly five percent of the city. Unlike the crowded lawns of Central Park, Rock Creek Park has a feeling of the wilderness. Although the elk, bison, and bears that used to roam the park have vanished, raccoons, foxes, and deer can still be found here in abundance.

The park was endowed in 1880 and is now run by the National Park Service. In addition to hiking and picnicking, the park has a riding stable and horse trails, tennis courts, and an 18-hole golf course. On Sundays, a portion of Beach Drive – one of the main roads running through the park – is closed to cars to allow cyclists and in-line skaters freedom of the road. The creek itself is inviting, with little eddies

and waterfalls, but visitors are advised not to go into the water because it is polluted.

The **Rock Creek Park Nature Center** is a good place to begin an exploration of the park. It includes a small planetarium, and a 1-mile (1.6-km) nature trail, which is very manageable for children.

Pierce Mill near Tilden Street was an active gristmill which was restored by the National Park Service in 1936. It was kept working as a visitor exhibit until 1993 when it was deemed unsafe to work any more. Plans are underway to carry out a second restoration but only once sufficient funding is acquired. The Carter Barron Amphitheater, near 16th Street and Colorado Avenue, stages free performances of Shakespeare's plays and summer jazz concerts.

National Cathedral ⑳

THE BUILDING OF THE Church of Saint Peter and Saint Paul (its official name) was financed entirely by gifts and contributions. The cornerstone was laid by Theodore Roosevelt in 1907 and the final stone was set by George Bush in 1990. It is the world's sixth largest cathedral. Pinnacles measuring 250 ft (76 m), constructed from Indiana limestone, dominate the city's northwest skyline. The succession of architects, including Henry Vaughan, George Bodley, Philip Frohman, and Henry Little, were inspired by 14th-century Gothic style, evident in the pointed arches, rib vaulting, and stained-glass windows. Inside, carvings, sculpture, and needlework depict the nation's history and biblical scenes. It is part of the Protestant Episcopal Archdiocese, and affiliated to the Church of England.

Exterior
A masterpiece of Gothic-style architecture, the towers of the cathedral dominate the skyline.

★ The Creation
Above the west entrance is "The Creation," sculpted by Frederick Hart and carved by Vincent Palumbo, depicting mankind being formed from chaos.

Pilgrim Observation Gallery

George Washington Bay

Main Entrance
The huge Gothic arch, which contains one the Cathedral's beautiful rose windows, is echoed in the smaller arches around the tympanum and central doors. These doors are fronted by bronze gates.

Space Window
This window commemorates the flight of Apollo 11. It contains a piece of moon rock brought back from the first moon landing in 1969.

National Cathedral ⑳

See pp136–7.

Cleveland Park ㉑

Ⓜ *Cleveland Park.*

CLEVELAND PARK is a beautiful residential neighborhood that resembles the picture on a postcard of small-town America. It was originally a summer community for those wanting to escape the less bucolic parts of the city. In 1885, President Grover Cleveland (1885–9) bought a stone farmhouse here as a summer home for his bride.

The town's Victorian summer houses are now much sought after by people wanting to be close to the city but live in a small-town environment. There are interesting shops and good restaurants, as well as a grand old Art Deco movie theater, called the Uptown, which first opened in 1936.

Rock Creek Park ㉒

Ⓜ *Cleveland Park.* **Rock Creek Park Nature Center** 5200 Glover Rd, NW. **Map** 2 D1–D3. 📞 *426-6829.* Ⓜ *Friendship Heights.* 🕐 *9am–5pm Wed–Sun.* ⬛ *federal hols.* 🎟 *4pm Wed–Fri, varied times Sat & Sun.* 🌐 *www.nps.gov/rocr*

NAMED AFTER the creek that flows through it, Rock Creek Park bisects the city of Washington. This 1800-acre

Pierce Mill, the 19th-century gristmill in Rock Creek Park

THE SHAW NEIGHBORHOOD

This neighborhood is named after Union Colonel Robert Gould Shaw, the white commander of an all-black regiment from Massachusetts. He supported his men in their struggle to attain the same rights as white soldiers. Until the 1960s, U Street was the focus of black-dominated businesses and organizations. Thriving theaters, such as the Howard and the Lincoln, attracted top-name performers, and Howard University was the center of intellectual life for black students. The 1968 riots, sparked by the assassination of Dr. Martin Luther King Jr., wiped out much of Shaw's business district, and many thought the area could never be revived. However, the restoration of the Lincoln Theatre, the renewal of the U Street business district, and an influx of homebuyers renovating historic houses, have all contributed to the rejuvenation. In the part of U Street closest to the U Street-Cardoza metro stop, many fashionable bars and clubs have recently opened.

Mural in the Shaw neighborhood depicting Duke Ellington

stretch of land runs from the Maryland border south to the Potomac River and constitutes nearly five percent of the city. Unlike the crowded lawns of Central Park, Rock Creek Park has a feeling of the wilderness. Although the elk, bison, and bears that used to roam the park have vanished, raccoons, foxes, and deer can still be found here in abundance.

The park was endowed in 1880 and is now run by the National Park Service. In addition to hiking and picnicking, the park has a riding stable and horse trails, tennis courts, and an 18-hole golf course. On Sundays, a portion of Beach Drive – one of the main roads running through the park – is closed to cars to allow cyclists and in-line skaters freedom of the road. The creek itself is inviting, with little eddies

and waterfalls, but visitors are advised not to go into the water because it is polluted.

The **Rock Creek Park Nature Center** is a good place to begin an exploration of the park. It includes a small planetarium, and a 1-mile (1.6-km) nature trail, which is very manageable for children.

Pierce Mill near Tilden Street was an active gristmill which was restored by the National Park Service in 1936. It was kept working as a visitor exhibit until 1993 when it was deemed unsafe to work any more. Plans are underway to carry out a second restoration but only once sufficient funding is acquired. The Carter Barron Amphitheater, near 16th Street and Colorado Avenue, stages free performances of Shakespeare's plays and summer jazz concerts.

National Cathedral ⑳

Exterior
A masterpiece of Gothic-style architecture, the towers of the cathedral dominate the skyline.

THE BUILDING OF THE Church of Saint Peter and Saint Paul (its official name) was financed entirely by gifts and contributions. The cornerstone was laid by Theodore Roosevelt in 1907 and the final stone was set by George Bush in 1990. It is the world's sixth largest cathedral. Pinnacles measuring 250 ft (76 m), constructed from Indiana limestone, dominate the city's northwest skyline. The succession of architects, including Henry Vaughan, George Bodley, Philip Frohman, and Henry Little, were inspired by 14th-century Gothic style, evident in the pointed arches, rib vaulting, and stained-glass windows. Inside, carvings, sculpture, and needlework depict the nation's history and biblical scenes. It is part of the Protestant Episcopal Archdiocese, and affiliated to the Church of England.

★ The Creation
Above the west entrance is "The Creation," sculpted by Frederick Hart and carved by Vincent Palumbo, depicting mankind being formed from chaos.

Pilgrim Observation Gallery

George Washington Bay

Main Entrance
The huge Gothic arch, which contains one the Cathedral's beautiful rose windows, is echoed in the smaller arches around the tympanum and central doors. These doors are fronted by bronze gates.

Space Window
This window commemorates the flight of Apollo 11. It contains a piece of moon rock brought back from the first moon landing in 1969.

The pinnacles on the cathedral towers are decorated with leaf-shaped ornaments and topped by elaborately carved finials.

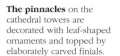

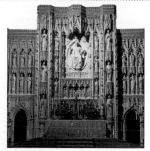

High Altar
Carved on the high altar are 110 figures, surrounding the central statue of Christ. Encased in the floor in front of the altar is stone from Mt. Sinai.

VISITORS' CHECKLIST

Massachusetts Ave & Wisconsin Ave, NW. 537-6200. 537-6616. 32, 34, 36. 10am–4:30pm Mon–Sat, 12:30pm–4:30pm Sun. Group reservations call 537-6207. lower level only. 4:30pm daily (choral evensong), noon Mon–Sat, hourly 8am–11am &, 4pm Sun. ***Children's Medieval Workshop*** 10am–2pm Sat (Jul only: 1–4pm). 537-2934. www.cathedral.org/cathedral

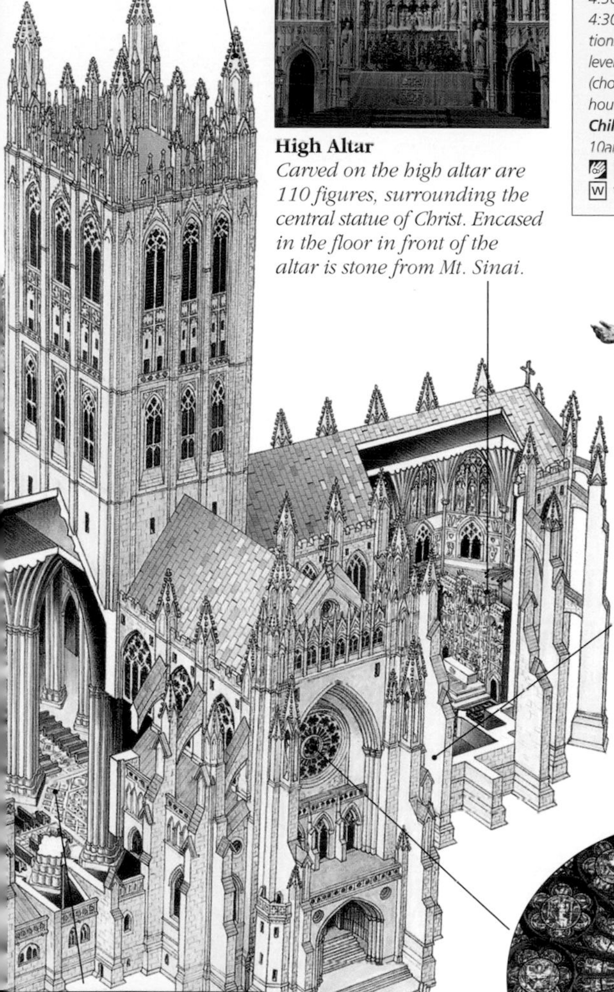

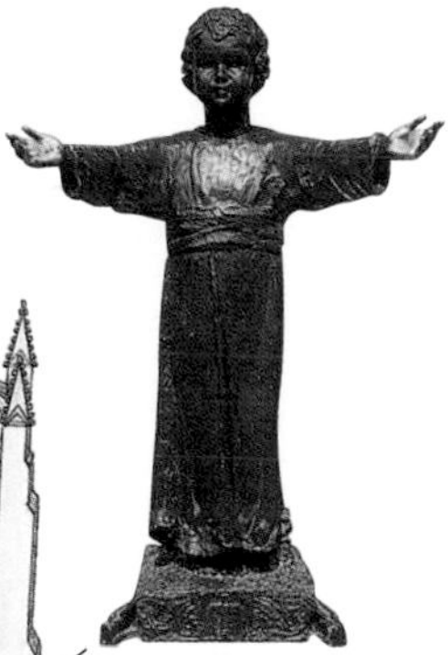

Children's Chapel
A statue of Jesus as a boy stands by this chapel built to the scale of a six-year-old. There are also motifs of baby and mythical animals.

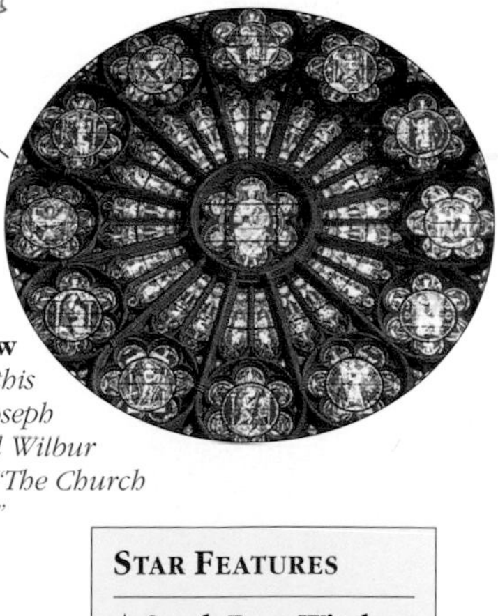

★ South Rose Window
The theme of this window by Joseph Reynolds and Wilbur Burnham is "The Church Triumphant."

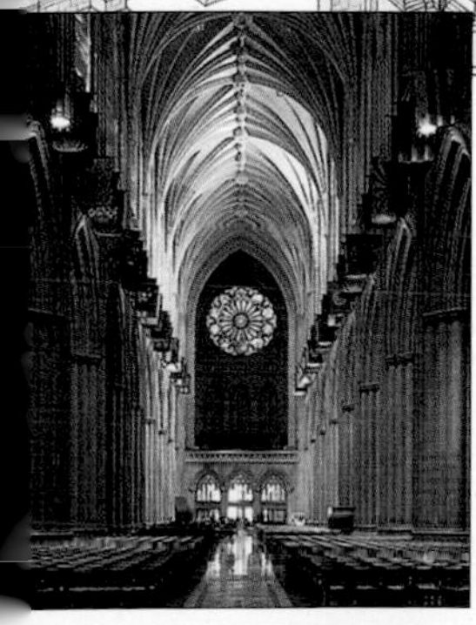

Nave
From the West Portal to the High Altar, the nave stretches a breathtaking one-tenth of a mile (160 m).

STAR FEATURES

- ★ South Rose Window
- ★ *The Creation*

Basilica of the National Shrine of the Immaculate Conception ㉓

Michigan and 4th St. NE.
C 526-8300. **M** Brookland-CUA.
O Apr 1–Oct 31: 7am–7pm daily;
Nov 1–Mar 31: 7am–6pm daily.
↑ C ▣ 🛈 ♿
W www.nationalshrine.com

COMPLETED IN 1959, this enormous Catholic Church is dedicated to the Virgin Mary. The church was designed in the shape of a crucifix and has many stained-glass windows. The building can seat a congregation of 2,500 people or more.

In the early 1900s, Bishop Thomas Shahan, rector of the Catholic University of America, proposed building a national shrine in Washington. Shahan gained the Pope's support in 1913, and in 1920 the cornerstone was laid. The Great Upper Church was dedicated on November 20, 1959. An unusual and striking combination of Romanesque and Byzantine styles, the shrine boasts classical towers as well as minarets in its design. The basilica's large interior includes a number of chapels, each with a distinctive design of its own.

Visitors can also enjoy the peaceful and extensive Prayer Garden which covers almost an acre (4,050sq m).

Entrance to the Chinese Pavilion at the US National Arboretum

US National Arboretum ㉔

Bladensburg Road and R St. **C** 245-2726. **M** Stadium Armory.
O 8am–5pm daily. **●** Dec 25.
📷 by appointment only. **🅿 ♿**
limited. **W** www.usna.usda.gov

TUCKED AWAY in a corner of northeast Washington is the 446-acre US National Arboretum – a center for research, education, and the preservation of trees, shrubs, flowers, and other plants. The magnificent columns, in a setting by English landscape architect Russell Page, were once part of the east entrance to the US Capitol building but now stand on a bluff in the Arboretum. The many different collections here mean that the Arboretum is an ever-changing, year round spectacle, magnificent even during the winter. In January and February, conifers, holly, wintersweet, and winter jasmine flourish. Early bulbs, such as daffodils, start appearing in March and, by the end of the month, pussywillows and wild flowers are burgeoning. April and May are the prime times to see the Arboretum's many varieties of crocus, magnolias, forsythia, flowering cherries, and rhododendrons. The

Bonsai tree in the Arboretum

azaleas in May are especially spectacular. In the summer, the heat-resistant plants such as daylilies, waterlilies, and roses bloom. The fall brings fruit on the firethorn, the dogwood, and the viburnum.

The Japanese Garden, which encompasses the National Bonsai and Penjing Museum, has a huge collection of Japanese, Chinese, and American bonsai that range from 20 to 380 years in age. The 2-acre herb garden comprises ten specialty gardens, where herbs are grouped according to use and historical significance. At the entrance to the garden is a 16th-century European-style "knot garden," which is elaborately designed with around 200 varieties of old roses.

The Perennial Collection includes peonies, daylilies, and irises, all of which bloom in late spring and summer. The National Grove of State Trees has trees representing every US state, along with DC itself, and there is a picnic area adjacent to the Grove.

The Washington Youth Garden was set up for inner-city children. They are given their own vegetable plots to look after and learn how to plant, tend, and harvest crops.

An ideal way to see as much of the Arboretum as possible without exhausting yourself is to take a tram tour, though this operates only seasonally and on the weekend.

View down the nave to the Basilica's altar

FREDERICK DOUGLASS (1817–95)

Born a slave around 1818, Frederick Douglass became the leading voice in the abolitionist movement that fought to end slavery in the United States. Douglass was taught to read and write by his white owners. At the age of 20 he fled to Europe. British friends in the anti-slavery movement purchased him from his former masters, and he was at last a free man. For most of his career he lived in New York, where he worked as a spokesman for the abolitionist movement. A brilliant speaker, he was sent by the American Anti-Slavery Society on a lecture tour and won added fame with the publication of his autobiography in 1845. In 1847 he became editor of the anti-slavery newspaper *The North Star*, named after the constellation point followed by escaping slaves on their way to freedom. During the Civil War *(see p19)*, Douglass was an advisor to President Lincoln and fought for the constitutional amendments that guaranteed equal rights to freed blacks.

Frederick Douglass

Frederick Douglass House 25

1411 W St, SE. 426-5961. Anacostia. Apr–Oct: 9am–5pm; Nov–Mar 9am–4pm. Jan 1, Thanksgiving, Dec 25. call ahead. www.nps.gov/frdo/freddoug.htm

THE ABOLITIONIST leader Frederick Douglass lived in Washington only toward the end of his illustrious career. After the Civil War he moved first to a townhouse on Capitol Hill, and then to Anacostia. In 1877 he bought this white-framed house, named it Cedar Hill, and lived here, with his family, until his death in 1895.

Douglass's widow opened Cedar Hill for public tours in 1903, and in 1962 the house was donated to the National Park Service, which is now responsible for maintaining it. Most of the furnishings are original to the Douglass family and include gifts to Douglass

"The Growlery" in the garden of the Frederick Douglass House

from President Lincoln and the writer Harriet Beecher Stowe, author of *Uncle Tom's Cabin* (1852). In the garden is a small stone building that Douglass used as an alternative study, and which he nicknamed "The Growlery." From the front steps of the house there is a magnificent view across the Anacostia River to the center of Washington.

Anacostia Museum 26

1901 Fort Place, SE. 357-2700. Anacostia. 10am–5pm Mon–Fri. Dec 25. by appointment only. www.si.edu/anacostia

THE FULL NAME of this museum is the Anacostia Museum and Center for African-American History and Culture. It is part of the Smithsonian Institution *(see p68)*, and is dedicated to increasing public understanding and awareness of the history and culture of people of African descent and heritage living in the Americas.

Basic needs such as housing, transportation, healthcare, and employment were long denied to members of the African-American community, and the Anacostia Museum sponsors exhibits addressing these concerns. Two of its major initiatives have been *Black Mosaic*, a research project on Washington's diverse Afro-Caribbean culture, and *Speak to My Heart: African American Communities of Faith and Contemporary Life*.

After a two-year renovation, in particular of its library and computers, the museum is now as much a resource center as it is a space for art and history exhibitions. Its collections include historical objects, documents, videos, and works of art. A nationally traveling exhibit, *Reflections in Black*, traces the history of African-American photography from 1840 to the present.

Façade of Cedar Hill, the Frederick Douglass House

EXCURSIONS BEYOND WASHINGTON, DC

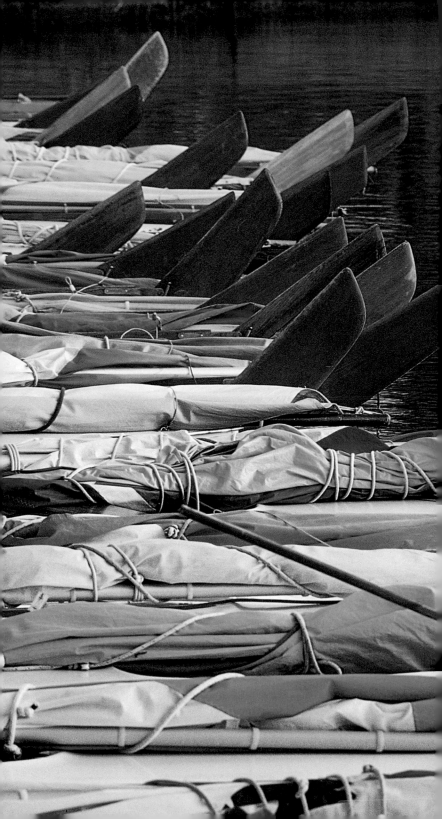

BEYOND WASHINGTON, DC

WITHIN A HALF-DAY'S DRIVE *of Washington lies enough history and natural beauty to satisfy the most insatiable sightseer. Alexandria and Williamsburg are a must for history buffs, while Chesapeake Bay and the islands of Chincoteague and Assateague offer a wealth of natural beauty. This area of Virginia and Maryland, along with parts of West Virginia and Pennsylvania, has been at the center of 400 years of turbulent American history.*

Founded in 1623, Jamestown was the first permanent English settlement in America. In the 18th century, Williamsburg became the capital of Virginia and the first colony to declare independence from England. Today, Williamsburg is a living museum of the Colonial era.

A Civil War Howitzer cannon

The cultural influence of Europe is clearly seen in the architecture of this region. The two presidents largely responsible for crafting the character of the early republic lived in Virginia – George Washington at Mount Vernon, and Thomas Jefferson at Monticello. These homes reveal the lives their occupants led, at once imaginative, agrarian, inventive, comfortable – and, like many wealthy landowners, relying on slavery.

Cities and towns throughout the area have attractive historic districts that are a welcome contrast to the modern commercial strips on their outskirts.

Annapolis, for example, is a pleasant Colonial and naval port city. Baltimore also has a diverse charm, combining working-class neighborhoods and Old World character, and the town of Richmond blends the Old South's Victorian gentility with the luxuries of modern life.

Civil War battlefields are spread over the map as far as Gettysburg and tell the war's painful story with monuments, museums, cemeteries, and the very contours of the land itself.

The 105-mile (170-km) Skyline Drive through Shenandoah National Park, situated west of DC, makes the beautiful Blue Ridge Mountains accessible to hikers, cyclists, and drivers alike. To the east of the city, the Chesapeake Bay region attracts sailors and fishermen, as well as seafood lovers who can indulge in the delicious local specialty – blue crabs.

Farm fields in front of the treading barn at Mount Vernon

◁ **Colorful furled sails at the Dangerfield Island marina**

Exploring Beyond Washington, DC

JUST MINUTES OUTSIDE the bustling center of Washington is a striking and varied area of mountains, plains, and historic towns. To the west are Virginia's Blue Ridge Mountains, the setting for Shenandoah National Park. To the south is the Piedmont, an area of gently rolling hills that supports the vineyards of Virginia's burgeoning wine industry. To the east, the Chesapeake Bay divides Maryland almost in two, and to the south it travels the length of the Virginia coastline. To the north is the big port city of Baltimore, with its pleasant waterfront promenade, shops, museums, and stunning National Aquarium.

The Philadelphia Brigade Monument at Gettysburg

A re-created fort in Jamestown

The dramatic Bearfence Mountain, part of Shenandoah National Park

Harrisburg York

6 GETTYSBURG PENNSYLVANIA

MANCHESTER (83)

(15) (140)

Philadelphia

EDERICK (795) ●ABERDEEN (95)

5 BALTIMORE

●COLUMBIA

(270)

●GAITHERSBURG (301) *Delaware Bay*

EAT FALLS ANNAPOLIS
PARK **4**

10 ●WASHINGTON, DC (50)(301)

1 ALEXANDRIA OLD TOWN

2 MOUNT VERNON (13)

3
GUNSTON
HALL (50)

(301) ATLANTIC
OCEAN

(235) CAMBRIDGE

●GOLDEN BEACH ●SALISBURY

REDERICKSBURG

Potomac River

17 CHINCOTEAGUE
AND ASSATEAGUE

(17)

Rappahannock River

301 **16**
CHESAPEAKE
BAY (13)

KEY

	Freeway/Interstate highway
	Major highway
	Secondary route
	Scenic route
	River
---	State boundary
※	Viewpoint

RICHMOND (64)

York River

(295) (5)

James River **18** WILLIAMSBURG

ERSBURG **19** YORKTOWN
AND JAMESTOWN

HAMPTON
(664)

CHESAPEAKE

Franklin (58)

TTING THERE

good interstate highways lace the area: I-95
south and north on the eastern side of Virginia;
runs south and north in western Virginia; I-66
ls west from Washington; and I-270 goes toward
erick. Trains depart from Union Station to most
e main towns, such as Baltimore, Alexandria,
mond, Williamsburg, and Harpers Ferry, which
so served by the MARC *(see pp202–3)*. Virginia
vay Express goes from Union Station to Alex-
ia and Fredericksburg. Greyhound buses also
el to most towns.

Boats moored in the Chesapeake Bay area

Old Town Alexandria ❶

Detail from the Apothecary Shop

OLD TOWN Alexandria has kept a special historical flavor, dating back to its incorporation in 1749. It is still a busy seaport and offers many historic sights, as well as shops selling everything from antique hat racks to banana splits. Restaurants are abundant, art thrives here, and the socializing goes on day and night, in and around Market Square.

Exploring Alexandria

Alexandria's tree-lined streets are filled with elegant, historic buildings and make for a pleasant stroll. Alternatively, a boat tour on the Potomac River offers an attractive prospect as does a leisurely lunch on the patio overlooking the waterfront. Nearby Founder's Park is the perfect place to bask on the grass by the river.

Façade of the elegant Carlyle House

🏛 Carlyle House

121 N Fairfax St. ☎ (703) 549-2997. ☐ 10am–4:30pm Tue–Sat, noon–5pm Sun; Nov–Mar 10am–4pm Tue–Sat, noon–4pm Sun. ● Mon, Thanksgiving, Dec 25, Jan 1. 🎫 ♿ 🛇 🛈

This elegant Georgian Palladian mansion was built by wealthy Scottish merchant John Carlyle in 1753.

The house fell into disrepair in the 19th century but was purchased in 1970 by the Northern Virginia Regional Park Authority; it has since been beautifully restored. A guided tour provides fascinating details about 18th-century daily life. One room, known as the "architecture room," has been deliberately left unfinished to illustrate the original construction of the house. The back garden is being replanted with 18th-century plant species.

🏛 Stabler-Leadbeater Apothecary Shop

105–107 S Fairfax St. ☎ (703) 836-3713. ☐ 10am–4pm Mon–Sat, 1–5pm Sun. ● Thanksgiving, Dec 25, Jan 1. 🎫 🛇 🛈

Established in 1792, this family apothecary was in business for 141 years. When it closed in 1933, the doors were locked with all of the contents intact. Now reopened as a museum, the shop's mahogany drawers still contain the potions noted on their labels. Jars containing herbal remedies line the shelves. Huge mortars and pestles and a collection of glass baby bottles are among the shop's 8,000 original objects. George Washington was a patron, as was Robert E. Lee, who bought the paint for his Arlington house here.

🏛 Gadsby's Tavern Museum

134 N Royal St. ☎ (703) 838-4242. ☐ Apr–Sep: 10am–5pm Tue–Sat, 1–5pm Sun; Oct–Mar: 11am–4pm Tue–Sat, 1–4pm Sun. ● Mon, federal hols. 🎫 🛇 🛈

Dating from 1770, this tavern and the adjoining hotel, owned by John Gadsby, were the Waldorf-Astoria of their day. Now completely restored, they evoke the atmosphere of a hostelry in this busy port.

Interesting rooms include the dining room with its buffet and gaming tables, the bedrooms where travelers reserved not the room but a space in a bed, and the private dining room for the wealthy, or the rare woman traveler. The hotel's ballroom, where George and Martha Washington were fêted on his last birthday in 1799, can be rented out.

Interior of the Old Presbyterian Meeting House

🏛 Old Presbyterian Meeting House

321 S Fairfax St. ☎ (703) 549-6670. ☐ 9am–5pm Mon–Fri. 🛇 by appt. ♿

Memorial services for George Washington were held in this meeting house, founded in 1772. In the churchyard are buried Dr. John Craig, a close friend of Washington who was at the president's deathbed, merchant John Carlyle, and the Reverend Muir, who officiated at Washington's funeral.

🏛 Boyhood Home of Robert E. Lee

Unfortunately, the boyhood home of Robert E. Lee is currently a private residence and not open to the public. General Lee lived in this 1795 Federal townhouse from the age of 11 until he went to West Point Military Academy. The drawing room was the setting for the marriage of Mary Lee Fitzhugh to Martha Washington's grandson, George Washington Parke Custis. The house is elegantly furnished with antiques and was sometimes used for weddings.

Bedroom of Robert E. Lee

🏛 Lee-Fendall House Museum

614 Oronoco St. ☎ *(703) 548-1789.* ⏰ *10am–4pm Tue–Sat, 1–4pm Sun.* ⏺ *Dec 25–Jan 31 (except 3rd Sun, Lee's birthday celebration).* 🎫 🖼

Philip Fendall built this stylish house in 1785, then married the sister of Revolutionary War hero "Light Horse" Harry Lee. Lee descendants lived here until 1904. Restored to its early Victorian motif, the house is rich with artifacts from the Revolution to the 1930s Labor Movement.

Lee-Fendall House Museum

🏛 Torpedo Factory Art Center

105 N. Union St. ☎ *(703) 838-4565.* ⏰ *10am–5pm daily.* ⏺ *Easter, July 4, Thanksgiving, Dec 25, Jan 1.* ♿ 🖥 www.torpedofactory.org

Originally a real torpedo factory during World War II, it was converted into an arts center by a partnership between the town and a group of local artists in 1974. Today there is gallery and studio space for over 150 artists to create and exhibit their work. Visitors can watch a potter at his wheel, sculptors, print-makers, and jewelry-makers.

⛪ Christ Church

Cameron & N Washington Sts. ☎ *(703) 549-1450.* ⏰ *9am–4pm Mon–Sat, 2–4:30pm Sun.* ⏺ *Thanksgiving, Dec 25, Jan1.* ♿

The oldest church in continu-ous use in the town, this Georgian edifice was com-pleted in 1773. George Wash-ington's square pew is still preserved with his nameplate, as is that of Robert E. Lee.

On the other side of this Episcopalian church, a label

reads "William E. Cazenove." Free pew for strangers." In the churchyard 18th-century gravestones wear away under the weather of the centuries.

🛒 Farmers Market

Market Square, King & Fairfax Sts. ☎ *(703) 838-4770. 5am–10am Sat.*

This market dates back to the city's incorporation in 1749. George Washington, a trustee of the market, regularly sent produce to be sold at the market from his farm at Mount Vernon *(see pp148–9)*. One of the most pleasant aspects of the market square today is its central fountain. Shoppers can find fresh fruits and vegetables, preserves, cut flowers, herbs, baked goods, meats, and crafts.

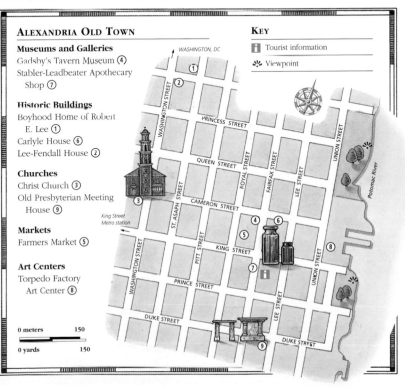

ALEXANDRIA OLD TOWN

Museums and Galleries
Gadsby's Tavern Museum ④
Stabler-Leadbeater Apothecary Shop ⑦

Historic Buildings
Boyhood Home of Robert E. Lee ①
Carlyle House ⑥
Lee-Fendall House ②

Churches
Christ Church ③
Old Presbyterian Meeting House ⑨

Markets
Farmers Market ⑤

Art Centers
Torpedo Factory Art Center ⑧

KEY
🛈 Tourist information
🌿 Viewpoint

0 meters   150
0 yards   150

Mount Vernon ❷

Cameo of Washington

THIS COUNTRY ESTATE on the Potomac River was George Washington's home for 45 years. Originally built as a farmhouse by his father, Augustine, Washington made many changes, including adding architectural elements such as the cupola and curving colonnades. The house is furnished as it would have been during Washington's presidency (1789–97) and the 500-acre grounds (8,000 acres in his time) still retain aspects of Washington's farm, such as the flower and vegetable gardens, the sheep paddock, and quarters for the many slaves who worked the plantation.

Kitchen
Set slightly apart from the main house, the kitchen has been completely restored.

★ **Mansion Tour**
Visitors can see the study and the large dining room, as well as Washington's bedroom and the bed in which he died.

The Museum displays belongings of George and Martha Washington, as well as Houdon's famous bust of Washington.

Overseer's House

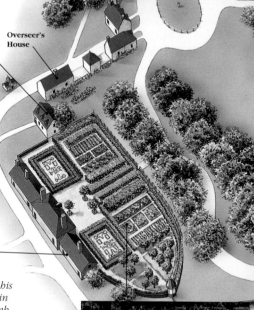

Slave Quarters
Washington freed all his slaves in his will. A memorial to them, erected in 1983, stands near Washington's tomb.

★ **Upper Garden**
The plants in this colorful flower garden are known to have grown here in Washington's time. The audio-visual presentation "Washington Is No More" can be seen in the small auditorium here.

Wharf

Daytrip boats from central DC bring visitors to this wharf, which is on the same site as it was in Washington's time. Potomac cruise boats also stop off here.

Pioneer Farm

Stable

Coach House

The Lower Garden was used for growing vegetables and berries. The boxwood bushes surrounding it were planted in Washington's time.

★ **Pioneer Farm**
This exhibit demonstrates farming techniques that were pioneered by George Washington. There is also a replica of his unique 16-sided treading barn, which was created using authentic tools.

Washington's Tomb
In his will, Washington requested that a new brick tomb be built for his family at Mount Vernon. Washington died in 1799 but the tomb was not completed until 1831.

The Bowling Green was added to the estate by George Washington.

STAR SIGHTS

★ **Mansion Tour**

★ **Pioneer Farm**

★ **Upper Garden**

Gunston Hall ❸

10709 Gunston Road, Mason Neck, Fairfax County, VA. ☎ *(800) 811-6966;* *(703) 550-9220.* ◐ *9:30am–5pm daily.* ▨ *Jan 1, Thanksgiving, Dec 25.* ▨ ▨ ▨ ▨ W www.GunstonHall.org

THIS GEORGIAN HOUSE, built in 1755, was the home of George Mason, author of the 1776 Virginia Declaration of Rights. Situated 20 miles (32 km) south of Washington, DC, it is an exquisite example of careful historic restoration.

Of particular interest is the finely carved woodwork in the entrance hall, the chinoiserie mantel and fireplace in the formal dining room, and the servants' staircase which was used by the slaves so that they wouldn't be seen by guests. Outside are the beautiful boxwood gardens.

Annapolis ❹

Anne Arundel County, MD. ▨ *33,300.* ▮ *Annapolis and Anne Arundel County Visitors Bureau, 26 West St. (410) 280-0445.* ◐ *9am–5pm.* W *www.visit-annapolis.org*

THE CAPITAL OF Maryland, Annapolis is the jewel of Chesapeake Bay. It is defined by the nautical character that comes with 17 miles (27 km) of shoreline and the longtime presence of the US Naval Academy.

A walk down Main Street takes you past the 200-year-old Maryland Inn, and the shops and restaurants, to the City Dock lined with boats. It is then a short walk to the 150-year-old **US Naval Academy**. Inside the visitor center is the Freedom 7 space capsule that carried the first American, Alan Shepard, into space. The US Naval Academy Museum in Preble Hall is also worth visiting, especially to see the gallery of detailed ship models.

Tiffany window in the Naval Academy, Annapolis

The beautiful formal gardens of the William Paca House, in Annapolis

The **Maryland State House** is the oldest state capitol in continuous use. Its Old Senate Chamber is where the Continental Congress (delegates from each of the American colonies) met when Annapolis was briefly the capital of the United States in 1783–4.

Annapolis teems with Colonial-era buildings, most still in everyday use. The **William Paca House**, home of Governor Paca, who signed the Declaration of Independence, is a fine Georgian house with an enchanting garden, both of which have been lovingly restored recently. The **Hammond Harwood House** has also been restored. This masterpiece of Georgian design was named after the Hammond and Harwood families, both prominent in the area. Cornhill and Duke of Gloucester streets are beautiful examples of the city's historic residential streets.

Many tours are offered in Annapolis, including walking, bus, and boat tours. It is particularly enjoyable to view the city from the water, be it by sightseeing boat, chartered schooner, or even by kayak.

🏛 **US Naval Academy**
Corner of King George, east of Randall St. ☎ *(410) 293-2108.* ◐ *9am–5pm Mon–Sat, 11am–5pm Sun.* ● *Thanksgiving, Dec 25, Jan 1.* ▨ ▨
🏛 **Maryland State House**
State Circle. ☎ *(410) 974-3400.* ◐ *9am–5pm (call ahead).* ● *Dec 25.* ▨ *11am & 3pm.* ▨
🏛 **William Paca House**
186 Prince George St. ☎ *(410) 263-5553.* ◐ *Mar–Dec: 10am–4pm Mon–Sat, noon–4pm Sun; Jan–Feb: Sat & Sun.* ▨ ▨
🏛 **Hammond Harwood House**
19 Maryland Ave. ☎ *(410) 269-1714.* ◐ *10am–4pm Mon–Sat, noon–4pm Sun (Jan–Feb: Fri–Sun only).* ● *Thanksgiving, Dec 25, Jan 1.* ▨

Baltimore ❺

Chesapeake Bay, MD. ▨ *675,500.* ▮ *Inner Harbor West Wall (410) 837-4636 or (800) 282-6632.* ▨ ▨ W *www.baltimore.org*

THERE IS MUCH to do and see in this pleasant city. A good place to start is the Inner Harbor, the city's redeveloped waterfront, with the harborside complex of shops and restaurants. The centerpiece is the **National Aquarium**, which has many fish and mammal exhibits, including a seal pool and dolphin show. The Harbor is home to the **Maryland Science Center**, where "do touch" is the rule. The

People walking along Baltimore's pleasant Inner Harbor promenade

planetarium and an IMAX® theater thrill visitors with images of earth and space.

The **American Visionary Art Museum** houses a collection of extraordinary works by self-taught artists whose materials range from matchsticks to faux pearls.

Uptown is the **Baltimore Museum of Art**, with its world-renowned collection of modern art, including works by Matisse, Picasso, Degas, and Van Gogh. There is also a large collection of Warhol pieces and two sculpture gardens featuring work by Rodin and Calder.

The collection in the **Walters Art Gallery**, on Mount Vernon Square, spans around 5,000 years. It is home to pieces by Fabergé, Rubens, and Monet and houses the beautiful painting *Sappho and Alcaeus* (1881) by Alma-Tadema.

The neighborhood of Little Italy is also worth a visit, not only for its knock-out Italian restaurants but also for the games of bocce ball (Italian lawn bowling) played around Pratt or Stiles Street on warm evenings.

🐟 National Aquarium
N side of Inner Harbor. 📞 (410) 576-3800. ⏰ 10am–5pm Mon–Thu, Sat & Sun;10am–8pm Fri. ● Thanksgiving, Dec 25. 🅿️ ♿ 🅿️ W www.aqua.org

🏛 Maryland Science Center
601 Light St. 📞 (410) 685-5225. ⏰ 10am–5pm Mon–Fri, 10am–6pm Sat, 12am–6pm Sun. ● Thanksgiving, Dec 25. 🅿️ ♿ 🅿️ W www.mdsci.org

🏛 American Visionary Art Museum
800 Key Highway at Inner Harbor. 📞 (410) 244-1900. ⏰ 10am–6pm Tue–Sun. ● Mon, Thanksgiving, Dec 25. 🅿️ ♿ 🅿️ 🅿️

🏛 Baltimore Museum of Art
N Charles St & 31st St. 📞 (410) 396-7100. ⏰ 11am–5pm Wed–Fri, 11–6 Sat–Sun. ● Jul 4, Thanksgiving, Dec 25, Jan 1. 🅿️ 🅿️ ♿ 🅿️ 🅿️

🏛 Walters Art Museum
600 N Charles St. 📞 (410) 547-9000. ⏰ 10am–5pm Tue–Sun, 11–5 Sat & Sun; 1st Thu each month 10am–8pm. ● Mon, Thanksgiving, Dec 25, Jan 1, July 4. 🅿️ except 10–1pm Sat. ♿ 🅿️

Gettysburg National Military Park ❻

97 Taneytown Rd, Gettysburg, Adams County, PA. 📞 (717) 334-1124. **Park** ⏰ 6am–10pm daily. **Visitor Center** ⏰ 8am–5pm daily (6pm in summer). ● Jan 1, Thanksgiving, Dec 25. 🅿️ ♿ 🅿️ 🅿️ W www.nps.gov/gett

THIS 6,000-acre park, south of the town of Gettysburg, Pennsylvania, marks the site of the three day Civil War battle on July 1–3, 1863. It was the bloodiest event ever to take place on American soil, with 51,000 casualties.

A two- or three-hour driving tour begins at the visitor

THE GETTYSBURG ADDRESS

The main speaker at the dedication of the National Cemetery in Gettysburg on November 19, 1863 was the orator Edward Everett. President Lincoln had been asked to follow with "a few appropriate remarks." His two-minute, 272-word speech paid tribute to the fallen soldiers, restated his goals for the Civil War, and re-phrased the meaning of democracy: "government of the people, by the people, for the people." The speech was inaudible to many, and Lincoln declared it a failure. However, once published, his speech revitalized the North's resolve to preserve the Union. Today it is known to every schoolchild in America.

Abraham Lincoln

center. The National Cemetery, where Abraham Lincoln gave his Gettysburg Address, is opposite. Other sights on the 18-mile tour include the Eternal Light Peace Memorial, the Pennsylvania Memorial, and Confederate Avenue.

Frederick ❼

Frederick County, MD. 👥 50,000. 🚏 19 E Church St (301) 228-2888. ⏰ 9am–5pm daily W www.visitfrederick.org

DATING BACK to the mid-18th century, Frederick's historic center was renovated in the 1970s and is now a popular tourist attraction.

This charming town is a major antique center and home to hundreds of antique dealers. Its shops, galleries, and eateries are all in 18th-and 19th-century settings. Francis Scott Key, author of "The Star Spangled Banner," is buried in Mt. Olivet Cemetery.

The eye-catching architecture of the National Aquarium, Baltimore

Antietam National Battlefield ❽

Route 65, 10 miles (16 km) S of Hagerstown, Washington County, MD. 📞 *(301) 432-5124.* ⏰ *Jun–Aug: 8:30am–6pm daily; Sept–May: 8:30am–5pm.* ⬤ *Thanksgiving, Dec 25, Jan 1.* 🎫 🏠 ♿
🌐 www.nps.gov/anti

ONE OF THE worst battles of the Civil War was waged here on September 17, 1862. There were 23,000 casualties but no decisive victory.

An observation tower offers a panoramic view of the battlefield. Antietam Creek runs peacefully under the costly Burnside Bridge. General Lee's defeat at Antietam inspired President Lincoln to issue the Emancipation Proclamation. The Visitors' Center movie recreating the battle is excellent.

John Brown's Fort in Harpers Ferry National Historic Park

Harpers Ferry ❾

Route 340, Harpers Ferry, Jefferson County, WV. 📞 *(304) 535-6298.* ⏰ *8am–5pm daily.* ⬤ *Thanksgiving, Dec 25, Jan 1.* 🎫 🗂 *Spring–Fall.*
🌐 www.nps.gov/hafe

NESTLED AT the confluence of the Shenandoah and Potomac rivers in the Blue Ridge Mountains is Harpers Ferry National Historical Park. The town was named after Robert Harper, a builder from Philadelphia who established a ferry across the Potomac here in 1761. There are stunning views from Maryland Heights to the foot of Shenandoah Street, near abolitionist John Brown's fort. Brown's ill-fated raid in 1859 on the Federal arsenal, established by George Washington, became tinder in igniting the Civil War.

The great importance of the town led to the area being designated a national park in 1944. It has been restored by the National Park Service.

Great Falls Park ❿

Georgetown Pike, Great Falls, Fairfax County, VA. 📞 *(703) 285-2966.* ⏰ *daily.* ⬤ *Dec 25.* 🎫 🗂 ♿
🌐 www.nps.gov/gwmp/grfa

THE FIRST VIEW of the falls, near the visitor center, is absolutely breathtaking. The waters of the Potomac roar through a gorge of jagged rock over a 76-ft (23-m) drop at the point that divides Virginia's undulating Piedmont from the coastal plain. Only experienced kayakers are permitted to take to the tubulent whitewater below, which varies with rainfall upstream.

The park is crisscrossed by 15 miles of hiking trails, some showing evidence of the commerce from the early 19th-century Patowmack, America's first canal. Guided history and nature walks are offered.

Situated just across the river, in Maryland, is the C&O Canal National Historical Park, entry to which is free for visitors to Great Falls Park.

The Red Fox Inn in Middleburg

Middleburg ⓫

Route 50, Loudoun County, VA. 🚶 *600.* ℹ️ *Visitors' Center, 12 N Madison St. (540) 687-8888.* ⏰ *11am–3pm Mon–Fri, 11am–4pm Sat–Sun.*
🌐 www.middleburgonline.com

HORSE AND FOX are king in this little piece of England in the Virginia countryside. Middleburg's history began in 1728, with Joseph Chinn's fieldstone tavern on the Ashby's Gap Road, still operating today as the Red Fox Inn. Colonel John S. Mosby and General Jeb Stuart met here to plan Confederate strategy during the Civil War.

The exquisite countryside is known for its thoroughbred horse farms and estates, some of which open during the Hunt Country Stable Tour in May.

Foxcroft Road, north of the town, winds past perfectly groomed horse farms. The same road to the south leads to **Meredyth Vineyards**. On the lovely Plains Road at the west end of town is **Piedmont Vineyards**, and a mile east of Middleburg is **Swedenburg Winery**. All three vineyards provide tours and tastings.

🍷 **Meredyth Vineyards**
Route 628. 📞 *(540) 347-3475.* ⏰ *daily.* ⬤ *Thanksgiving, Dec 25, Jan 1.* 🎫 ♿
🍷 **Piedmont Vineyards**
Off Route 626. 📞 *(540) 687-5528.* ⏰ *daily.* ⬤ *Thanksgiving, Dec 24, 25, 31, Jan 1.*
🍷 **Swedenburg Winery**
Off Route 50
📞 *(540) 687-5219.* ⏰ *daily.* ⬤ *Thanksgiving, Dec 25, Jan 1.*

The roaring waterfalls in Great Falls Park

Skyline Drive ⑫

SKYLINE DRIVE RUNS along the backbone of the Shenandoah National Park's Blue Ridge Mountains. Originally farmland, the government designated the area a national park in 1926. Deer, wild turkey, bears, and bobcats inhabit the park, and wildflowers, azaleas, and mountain laurel are abundant. The park's many hiking trails and its 75 viewpoints offer stunning natural scenery.

North entrance station

Whiteoak Canyon ②
The Whiteoak Canyon Trail passes six waterfalls on its route.

Pinnacles Overlook ①
The view of Old Rag Mountain with its outcroppings of granite is spectacular.

Bearfence Mountain ⑤
Although it is a bit of a climb up this mountain, partly on rock scramble, it is not too difficult, and the reward is a breathtaking 360-degree view of the surrounding landscape.

Big Meadows ③
Close to the Visitor Center, this meadow is kept in its centuries-old state. It was probably kept clear by fire from lightning or Indians. Deer can easily be seen here.

Camp Hoover ④
At the end of Mill Prong Trail, this 160-acre resort was President Hoover's weekend retreat until 1933, when he donated it to the Park.

KEY

- - - Walk route

‒‒‒‒ Lookout point

▬▬▬ Road

0 kilometers   10

0 miles   10

TIPS FOR DRIVERS

Starting points: north at Front Royal, central at Thornton Gap, south at Rockfish Gap.
Length: 105 miles (168 km), duration of 3–8 hrs depending on how many stops are taken.
When to go: Fall leaf colors draw crowds in mid-October. Wildflowers bloom through spring and summer. .
What it costs: toll charge of $10 per car (valid for 7 days).

Lewis Mountain ⑥
This awe-inspiring view from Lewis Mountain shows Shenandoah Valley in spring, when the lush scenery is interspersed with beautiful wildflowers.

Charlottesville ⑬

Virginia. 🏛 40,700. 🚌 🚍 🛈
Charlottesville-Albemarle Convention and Visitors Bureau, Monticello Visitors Center, Route 20 South (434) 977-1783, (877) 386-1102 (toll free).
Ⓦ www.charlottesvilletourism.org

CHARLOTTESVILLE was Thomas Jefferson's hometown. It is dominated by the University of Virginia, which he founded and designed, and also by his home, **Monticello**.

Jefferson was a Renaissance man – author of the Declaration of Independence, US president, farmer, architect, inventor, and vintner. It took him 40 years to complete Monticello, beginning in 1769 when he was 25. It is now one of the most celebrated houses in the country. The entrance hall doubled as a private museum, and the library held a collection of around 6,700 books.

The grounds include a 1,000-sq ft (93-sq m) terraced vegetable garden where Jefferson grew and experimented with hundreds of varieties.

The obelisk over Jefferson's grave in the family cemetery

lauds him as "Father of the University of Virginia." Tours of the university are available year round.

Vineyards and wineries surround Charlottesville. Michie Tavern, joined to the Virginia Wine Museum, has been restored to its 18th-century appearance, and serves a buffet of typical Southern food.

Montpelier, on a 2,500 acre site 25 miles (40 km) to the north, was the home of former US president James Madison.

🍽 Monticello

Route 53, 3 miles (5 km) SE of Charlottesville. 📞 (434) 984-9822.
◘ Mar–Oct: 8am–5pm; Nov–Feb: 9am–4:30pm. ● Dec 25. 🎫 🛍 🔗 🛈

Fredericksburg ⑭

Virginia. 🏛 22,600. 🚌 🚍 🛈 *Fredericksburg Visitor Center, 706 Caroline St. (800) 678-4748.* ◘ 9am–5pm daily, Memorial Day, Labor Day until 7pm.
● Thanksgiving, Dec 25, 31, Jan 1.
Ⓦ www.fredericksburgvirginia.com

FREDERICKSBURG'S attractions are its historic downtown district, and four Civil War

The elegant dining room at Kenmore House

battlefields, including The Wilderness and Chancellorsville. The Rising Sun Tavern and Hugh Mercer Apothecary Shop offer living history accounts of life in a town that began as a 50-acre port on the Rappahannock River. **Kenmore Plantation and Gardens** is famous for its beautiful rooms.

The visitor center offers useful maps as well as horse-and-carriage or trolley tours.

🍽 Kenmore Plantation and Gardens

1201 Washington Ave, Fredericksburg.
📞 (540) 373-3381. ◘ 10am–5pm Mon–Sat, noon–5pm Sun; Jan & Feb: 10am–5pm Sat, noon–5pm Sun.
Ⓦ www.kenmore.org

MONTICELLO, CHARLOTTESVILLE

Situated in the leafy foothills of the Blue Ridge Mountains, this Palladian masterpiece was built between 1769 and 1809 by Thomas Jefferson.

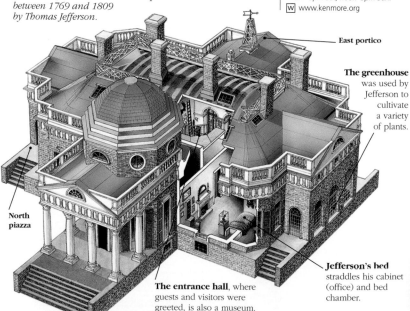

East portico

The greenhouse was used by Jefferson to cultivate a variety of plants.

North piazza

The entrance hall, where guests and visitors were greeted, is also a museum.

Jefferson's bed straddles his cabinet (office) and bed chamber.

Richmond ⓯

Virginia. 🏛 *198,300.* 🚊 ➤
ℹ️ *Metropolitan Richmond Convention and Visitors Bureau, 550 E Marshall St. (804) 782-2777.* ◑ *8:30am–5pm Mon–Fri.* 🖳 *www.richmondva.org*

RICHMOND, THE OLD capital of the Confederacy *(see p19)*, still retains an Old South aura. Bronze images of Civil War generals punctuate Monument Avenue. Brownstones and Victorian houses testify to this area's postwar prosperity.
   The Museum of the Confederacy contains Civil War artifacts, including Robert E. Lee's coat and sword. The restored White House of the Confederacy is next door. Another popular museum is the fascinating **Science Museum of Virginia**.
   The Neoclassical State Capitol, inside which is the life-sized Houdon sculpture of George Washington, was designed by Thomas Jefferson. Hollywood Cemetery is the resting place of presidents John Tyler and James Monroe, and also 18,000 Confederate soldiers under a communal pyramid. The view from Palmer Chapel Isle is superb.

Statue of Robert E. Lee in Richmond

🏛 **Museum of the Confederacy**
1201 E Clay St. 📞 *(804) 649-1861.* ◑ *10am–5pm Mon–Sat, noon–5pm Sun.* ● *Thanksgiving, Dec 25, Jan 1.* 🈴 🎦
🏛 **Science Museum of Virginia**
2500 W Broad St. 📞 *(804) 864-1400.* ◑ *9:30am–5pm Mon–Sat, 11:30am–5pm Sun; Jun–Aug until 7pm Fri & Sat.* ● *Thanksgiving, Dec 25.* 🈴 ♿ 🖵 🎦 🖳 *www.smv.org*

Chesapeake Bay ⓰

🖳 *www.wwlandmarks.com*

KNOWN AS "the land of pleasant living," Chesapeake Bay offers historic towns, fishing villages, bed-and-breakfasts, seafood restaurants, beaches, wildlife, and farmland. Much of its Colonial history is preserved in towns such as Cambridge and Easton. The Chesapeake Bay Maritime Museum, in the town of St. Michael's, depicts life on the bay, both past and present. Watermen unload the catch in Crisfield, where cruises depart for Smith Island. The place really feels like a step back in time, particularly with the local Elizabethan dialect.

Chincoteague and Assateague ⓱

Chincoteague, Accomack County, VA. 🏛 *4,000.* Assateague, Accomack County, VA and MD *(unpopulated).* ℹ️ *Chincoteague Visitors Center, 6733 Maddox Blvd. (757) 336-6161.* 🖳 *www.chincoteaguechamber.com*

THESE SISTER ISLANDS offer a wealth of natural beauty. Chincoteague is a town situated on the Delmarva (Delaware, Maryland and Virginia) Peninsula. Assateague is an unspoiled strip of nature with an ocean beach and hiking trails that wind through woods and marshes. It is famously populated by wild ponies, thought to be descended from animals grazed on the island by 17th-century farmers. The woodlands and salt marshes of Assateague attract over 300 species of birds, and in fall peregrine falcons and snow geese fly in. Monarch butterflies migrate here in October, on a backdrop of burr marigolds and goldenrod. There are several campgrounds in the area, and the ocean beach is ideal for swimming and surf fishing. **Toms Cove Visitor Center** and **Chincoteague Refuge Visitor Center** can provide extra information.

ℹ️ **Toms Cove Visitor Center**
📞 *(757) 336-6577.*
ℹ️ **Chincoteague Refuge Visitor Center**
📞 *(757) 336-6122.*

Yorktown and Jamestown ⓳

York County, VA, and James City County, VA. ℹ️ *York County Public Information Office (757) 890-3300.*

ESTABLISHED in 1607, Jamestown was the first permanent English settlement in America. It has 1,500 acres of marshland and forest, threaded with tour routes. There are ruins of the original English settlement and a museum. There is a re-creation of James Fort, and full-scale reproductions of the ships that brought the first colonists to America. An Indian village invites visitors to experience traditional Indian culture.
   Yorktown was the site of the decisive battle of the American Revolution in 1781. **Colonial National Historical Park**'s battlefield tours and exhibits explain the siege at Yorktown.

🏛 **Jamestown Settlement**
📞 *(757) 253-4838.* ◑ *9am–5pm; June 15–Aug 15 9am–6pm.* ● *Dec 25 and Jan 1.* 🈴 ♿ 🎦
♣ **Colonial National Historical Park**
📞 *(757) 898-3400 or (757) 229-1733.* ◑ *9am–5pm daily.* ● *Dec 25.* 🈴 ♿ 🖳 *www.nps.gov/colo*

Jamestown Settlement, a re-creation of Colonial James Fort

Colonial Williamsburg ⑱

Colonial couple

As Virginia's capital from 1699 to 1780, Williamsburg was the hub of the loyal British colony. After 1780 the town went into decline. Then in 1926, John D. Rockefeller embarked on a massive restoration project. Today, in the midst of the modern-day city, the 18th-century city has been re-created. People in colonial dress re-enact the lifestyle of the original townspeople; blacksmiths, silversmiths, cabinet makers, and bakers show off their skills while horse-drawn carriages pass through the streets, providing visitors with a fascinating insight into America's past.

Courthouse
Built in 1770–71 this was the home of the county court for more than 150 years.

NASSAU STREET

PALACE STREET

PALACE STREET

NORTH ENGLAND

QUEEN ST

★ Governor's Palace
Originally built in 1720 by Governor Alexander Spotswood, the palace has been reconstructed in its full pre-Revolution glory.

0 meters	200
0 yards	200

Nursery
Costumed living-history interpreters work the land in Colonial Williamsburg using replica tools and the same techniques as the original settlers.

STAR SIGHTS

★ Governor's Palace

★ Robertson's Windmill

★ Capitol

★ Robertson's Windmill
The windmill has daily demonstrations of the settlers' crafts, such as basket-making and barrel-making. The cart was a traditional means of transporting materials.

Print Office
This store stocks authentic 18th-century foods, including wine, Virginia ham, and peanuts.

Milliner
Owned by Margaret Hunter, the milliner shop stocked a wide range of items. Imported clothes for women and children, jewelry, and toys could all be bought here.

Raleigh Tavern
The Raleigh was once an important center for social, political and commercial gatherings. The original burned in 1859, but this reproduction has its genuine flavor.

★ **Capitol**
The capitol is a 1945 reconstruction of the original 1705 building. The government resided in the West Wing, while the General Court was in the East Wing.

KEY

– – – – Suggested route

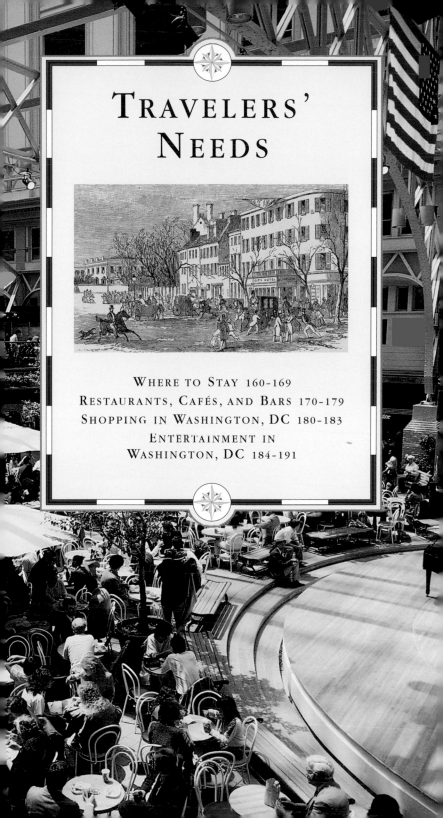

TRAVELERS' NEEDS

WHERE TO STAY

IF YOU PLAN to be doing the sights in Washington from dawn until midnight, you may simply need a roof over your head and a bed for your weary body. If you intend to take your time and relax, you may want to have a hotel with all the amenities: pool, health club, deluxe restaurant, room service. Washington can offer a wide range of accommodations. Generally, hotels that are closer to downtown and the

Hotel doorman

Mall are more expensive, and those in the city suburbs are more affordable. Being a tourist destination as well as a business center, Washington's room rates are the second highest in the United States next to New York City. However, there are bargains to be had, especially during the off season and on weekends. Package deals are advertised regularly in the Sunday travel sections of *The New York Times* and the *Washington Post*.

Lobby of the plush Hilton Hotel

HOW TO RESERVE

MANY HOTELS have toll-free numbers for making reservations. It is also often possible to preview the accommodations on the hotel's website. If you want to stay at a bed-and-breakfast, either reserve one through an agent or pick one from the phone book. Many hotels sell unreserved rooms at a discount, just as airlines sell unsold tickets. Some companies specialize in offering hotel discounts, including **Capitol Reservations**, **Washington**, **DC Accommodations**, and **Hotel Discounts**.

HOTEL GRADING AND FACILITIES

A FIVE-STAR HOTEL will offer everything the visitor could wish for. Room service, health facilities, bathrooms with a jacuzzi, valet parking, and 24-hour maid and butler service are just some of the luxury services provided, but at a price. At the opposite

end of the spectrum, a one-star hotel will have a television and a telephone in the bedroom but may have shared bathrooms. Hotels of all price ranges are available in the city.

DISCOUNTS

WASHINGTON HAS different "seasons" from other cities. When the cherry blossoms around the Tidal Basin bloom in April, it is impossible to find a reasonably priced room in the city. Then in June the city is full of school groups taking end-of-the-year trips. Despite often broiling temperatures, families are lured to the capital in the summer. Labor Day in September is very big for tourists as is, of course, the Fourth of July.

However, you can find bargains during the winter months from November through March. Washington is a Monday-through-Friday convention town, so the best prices are on the weekend, often at a fraction of the vacation season, midweek rate.

HIDDEN EXTRAS

BEWARE THE hefty 14.5% tax levied on hotels in Washington. Also note that most hotels will invariably charge you extra for parking in the hotel's parking lot. There is no way to escape the tax, but you can shop around for a hotel with free parking. If you have to park your car in a garage, you can expect to have another $7 to $15 added to each night's tab.

CHAINS AND BOUTIQUE HOTELS

STAYING AT either a **Hilton**, **Best Western**, **Marriott**, or **Howard Johnson** hotel will guarantee a level of service and cleanliness mandated by the chain. An alternative to the large chain hotels are the increasingly popular boutique hotels. These small, unique places all have their own personalities. The Hotel George in Old Downtown has undergone a sleek modern renovation. It also houses Bis, one of the city's most talked-about new restaurants. The Henley Park has the décor of a British aristocratic home and serves afternoon tea. The Morrison

The George, a boutique hotel

Clark Inn on Massachusetts Avenue is a restored mansion filled with Victorian antiques. The Phoenix Park Hotel on Capitol Hill has an Irish theme and staff – and a pub popular with Irish nationals and Irish-American politicians.

BUSINESS TRAVELERS

WASHINGTON HOTELS increasingly accommodate the sophisticated communications needs of the business traveler. Modems and fax machines are often installed in rooms, and secretarial services are available through the (often multilingual) concierge. **Meeting Solutions** (a division of Washington DC Accommodations) can help arrange block bookings for a business convention.

Entrance to the Hay-Adams hotel

BED-AND-BREAKFASTS

ALTHOUGH bed-and-breakfast accommodations are not as popular or as plentiful in the United States as they are in Europe, both American and foreign travelers are starting to seek them out as an alternative to the more sterile and expensive hotels. There are two services that will try to match visitors with the perfect room in either a bed-and-breakfast, an apartment or small hotel, or even a private home. **Bed-and-Breakfast Accommodations Ltd.** has 85 properties in the city and suburbs. The **Bed-and-Breakfast League/**

Sweet Dreams & Toast has properties in central Washington and in Arlington, Virginia. Both charge a one-time booking fee of $10.

BUDGET OPTIONS

THE BEST VALUE accommodation option for young travelers in Washington is the Youth Hostel. It is located in the center of the city in an area that is currently being rehabilitated. Young travelers are advised to be cautious when returning after dark. The rate is around $25 per night for a bunk bed in a single-sex dormitory room.

Camping is another inexpensive alternative. There are no campgrounds in the city itself, but camping facilities are available in the outer suburbs. The closest facility approved by Kampgrounds of America is in Millersville, Maryland, 17 miles (27 km) from central DC.

DISABLED TRAVELERS

NEARLY ALL the large, modern hotels are wheelchair accessible, but the independent hotels and bed and breakfasts may not be. Call in advance to ask about stairs, elevators, and door widths if you have special needs.

CHILDREN

TRAVELING WITH children may dictate your hotel reservations. There are many hotels such as Embassy Suites that have kitchens or kitchenettes and living rooms with sofabeds that provide space and privacy for parents. After walking around the Mall, children may crave a hotel with a pool or a game room. Consider a more expensive room in town rather than a less expensive room in the suburbs. The suburban rates may look appealing until you face a long drive back to your hotel during Washington's unpleasant rush hour.

Some hotels may ban children completely, but these are few and far between. More often than not hotels will be very accommodating toward young guests.

Doormen at the Willard Hotel

Choosing a Hotel

THESE HOTELS have been selected across a wide price range for their good value, facilities, and location; they are listed area by area, starting with central Washington, DC and moving on to hotels farther outside the city. All hotel rooms have air conditioning and private bathrooms unless stated otherwise. The number of rooms is followed by the number of suites in parentheses.

	CREDIT CARDS	GARDEN OR TERRACE	CHILDREN'S FACILITIES	RECOMMENDED RESTAURANT

CAPITOL HILL

BULL MOOSE BED-AND-BREAKFAST ON CAPITOL HILL $$
101 5th St, NE (at A St). **Map 4 F4.** 547-1050 or (800) 261-2768. FAX 548-9741.
W www.BullMoose-B-and-B.com
This turn-of-the-century bed-and-breakfast, five blocks from the Capitol, has original oak woodwork and turreted bedrooms. The theme throughout is Teddy Roosevelt. Some of the rooms have a shared bath. 9 (1)
Credit Cards: AE DC MC V

CAPITOL HILL SUITES $$$
200 C St, SE (at 2nd St). **Map 4 F5.** 543-6000 or (800) 424-9165. FAX 547-2608.
@ capitolhillsuites.reservations@starwoodhotels.com
This modern, boutique-style hotel has a large but cozy lobby area with an open fire. The continental breakfast is free. (152)
Credit Cards: AE D DC MC V

HOLIDAY INN ON THE HILL $$$$
415 New Jersey Ave, NW (between D St & E St). **Map 4 E3.** 638-1616 or (800) 638-1116
FAX 638-0707. W www.holiday-inn.com/was-onthehill
A good choice for both business travelers and families – children under 19 stay free. During the summer season there is a play area for children called the Discovery Zone. Children 12 and under dine free. 343 (9)
Credit Cards: AE D DC MC V • ▪

HOTEL GEORGE $$$$$
15 E St, NW (between N Capitol St & New Jersey Ave). **Map 4 E3.**
347-4200 or (800) 576-8331. FAX 347-4213. W www.hotelgeorge.com
A modern boutique hotel with large, airy rooms and a trendy French restaurant on the premises called Bis. 139 (3)
Credit Cards: AE D DC MC V ▪

HYATT REGENCY CAPITOL HILL $$$$
400 New Jersey Ave, NW (at D St). **Map 4 E3.** 737-1234 or (800) 233-1234.
FAX 393-7927. W www.hyatt.com
Entrance to the Hyatt is through a superbly elegant plant-filled atrium. Children under 15 stay for free. 834 (32)
Credit Cards: AE D DC MC V •

PHOENIX PARK HOTEL $$$$
520 N Capitol St, NW (at F St and N Capitol). **Map 4 E3.** 638-6900 or (800) 824-5419.
FAX 393-3236. W www.phoenixparkhotel.com
An intimate hotel, the rooms are furnished in an 18th-century Irish Manor style. Three of the suites have spiral staircases, three have balconies. Irish entertainers perform nightly in the pub. 149 (9)
Credit Cards: AE D DC MC V •

THE MALL

LOEWS L'ENFANT PLAZA HOTEL $$$$
480 L'Enfant Plaza, SW. **Map 3 C4.** 484-1000 or (800) 235-6397. FAX 646-5060.
W www.loewshotels.com   Named after Pierre L'Enfant, architect of the original city plans, this luxury 3-star hotel is one of the top properties in DC. Many of the rooms have spectacular views of the city. 370 (21)
Credit Cards: AE D DC MC V ▪ • ▪

OLD DOWNTOWN

GRAND HYATT $$$$
1000 H St, NW (at 11th St). **Map 3 C3.** 582-1234 or (800) 223-1234. FAX 637-4797.
W www.washington.hyatt.com
The Grand Hyatt has a fanciful interior featuring a waterfall-fed lagoon surrounding an island where a pianist plays. 888 (58)
Credit Cards: AE D DC MC V • ▪

HOTEL HARRINGTON $
436 11th St, NW (at E St NW). **Map 3 C3.** 628-8140. FAX 347-3924.
W www.hotel-harrington.com
The Harrington is clean and comfortable but not fussy. Popular with tourists and students, the central location and low prices offset the rather threadbare décor. 250
Credit Cards: AE D DC MC V •

<table>
<tr><td colspan="2">

Price categories for a standard double room per night, inclusive of service charges and any additional taxes; some hotels also include continental breakfast:
Ⓢ under $100
ⓈⓈ $100–$150
ⓈⓈⓈ $150–$200
ⓈⓈⓈⓈ $200–$300
ⓈⓈⓈⓈⓈ $300 plus.

</td></tr>
</table>

CREDIT CARDS
Indicates credit cards accepted: *AE* American Express; *D* Discover; *DC* Diners Club; *MC* MasterCard/Access; *V* VISA.

GARDEN OR TERRACE
Hotels with a garden, courtyard, or terrace.

CHILDREN'S FACILITIES
Cribs and a baby-sitting service available. Some hotel restaurants have children's portions and high chairs.

RECOMMENDED RESTAURANT
Hotel restaurant or dining room highly recommended and open to non-residents unless otherwise stated.

	CREDIT CARDS	GARDEN OR TERRACE	CHILDREN'S FACILITIES	RECOMMENDED RESTAURANT
HOTEL WASHINGTON ⓈⓈⓈ 515 15th St, NW (at Pennsylvania Ave). **Map** 3 B3. 📞 638-5900 or (800) 424-9540. FAX 638-4275. W www.hotelwashington.com One of the oldest hotels in Washington, this is a registered historic landmark. The rooms have been renovated. 🔧 📺 🔽 ♿ 🍽 340 (16)	AE D DC MC V	■	●	■
J.W.MARRIOTT ⓈⓈⓈⓈ 1331 Pennsylvania Ave, NW (at 14th St). **Map** 3 B3. 📞 393-2000 or (800) 228-9290. FAX 626-6991. W www.marriotthotels.com Rooms at the Marriott are plush, with luxurious furnishings and décor. The columned lobby is luxurious. 🔧 🍸 ≋ 📺 🔽 P ♿ 🍽 772 (25)	AE D DC MC V	■	●	■
RED ROOF INN ⓈⓈ 500 H St, NW (at 5th St). **Map** 4 D3. 📞 289-5959. FAX 682-9152. W www.redroof.com Although it is not in the best neighborhood, this hotel has a good coffee shop. The rooms are inexpensive and simple. 🔧 📺 ♿ 🍽 195	AE D DC MC V			
WASHINGTON INTERNATIONAL YOUTH HOSTEL Ⓢ 1009 11th St, NW (at K St, NW). **Map** 3 C2. 📞 737-2333. FAX 737-1508. W www.hiwashingtondc.org Very inexpensive accommodation for the thrifty young traveler, the dormitory rooms sleep up to 12 people. 🔧 ♿ 🍽 270	MC V			
WILLARD INTER-CONTINENTAL HOTEL ⓈⓈⓈⓈⓈ 1401 Pennsylvania Ave, NW (at 14th St). **Map** 3 B2. 📞 628-9100 or (800) 327-0200. FAX 637-7326. W www.washingtoninterconti.com This lavish hotel *(see p89)* offers rooms with marble bathrooms. The public areas feature chandeliers and mosaic floors. 24 🔧 🍸 📺 🔽 P ♿ 🍽 340 (40)	AE D DC MC V			■

THE WHITE HOUSE AND FOGGY BOTTOM

	CREDIT CARDS	GARDEN OR TERRACE	CHILDREN'S FACILITIES	RECOMMENDED RESTAURANT
CAPITAL HILTON ⓈⓈⓈⓈ 16th St and K St, NW. **Map** 3 B2. 📞 393-1000 or (800).445-8667. FAX 639-5784. W www.hilton.com This large, bustling hotel has been completely refurbished. The helpful staff is multi-lingual. 24 🔧 🍸 📺 🔽 P ♿ 🍽 544 (15)	AE D DC MC V		●	■
DOUBLETREE GUEST SUITES ⓈⓈⓈ 801 New Hampshire Ave (at H St). **Map** 2 D3. 📞 785-2000 or (800) 222-8733. FAX 785-9485. W www.doubletree.com A full kitchen, pull-out sofa beds and two televisions per suite make this a good choice for families. The staff are friendly and efficient. 🔧 ≋ P ♿ 🍽 (105)	AE D DC MC V		●	
GEORGE WASHINGTON UNIVERSITY INN ⓈⓈⓈⓈⓈ 824 New Hamphire Ave, NW (between H St & I St). **Map** 2 E3. 📞 337 6620 or (800) 426-4455. FAX 298-7499. W www.gwuinn.com An upscale boutique-style hotel with a marble lobby. Its rooms have been recently renovated in Williamsburg-inspired décor. 🔧 ≋ 📺 🔽 P ♿ 🍽 48 (47)	AE DC MC V			■
HAY-ADAMS HOTEL ⓈⓈⓈⓈⓈ 800 16th St, NW (at H St). **Map** 3 B2. 📞 638-6600 or (800) 424-5054. FAX 638-2716. W www.hayadams.com Italian Renaissance-style property located directly across from the White House. Rooms with antiques and ornamental ceilings. 24 🔧 🍸 🔽 P 🍽 (143)	AE D DC MC V			■
HOTEL LOMBARDY ⓈⓈⓈ 2019 Penn. Ave, NW (at I St, NW). **Map** 2 E3. 📞 828-2600 or (800) 424-5486. FAX 872 0503. W www.hotellombardy.com A European-style, boutique hotel with a restaurant in the building and an accommodating multilingual staff. 🔧 🍸 🍽 130 (38)	AE D DC MC V			■
ONE WASHINGTON CIRCLE ⓈⓈⓈ One Washington Circle, NW. **Map** 2 E3. 📞 828-1680 or (800) 424-9671. FAX 887-4989. W www.onewashcirclehotel.com This is an all-suite hotel, all with balconies, and has been recently renovated. 🔧 ≋ 📺 P ♿ 🍽 151	AE D DC MC V		●	■

Price categories for a standard double room per night, inclusive of service charges and any additional taxes; some hotels also include continental breakfast:
$ under $100
$$ $100–$150
$$$ $150–$200
$$$$ $200–$300
$$$$$ $300 plus.

CREDIT CARDS
Indicates credit cards accepted: *AE* American Express; *D* Discover; *DC* Diners Club; *MC* MasterCard/Access; *V* VISA.

GARDEN OR TERRACE
Hotels with a garden, courtyard, or terrace.

CHILDREN'S FACILITIES
Cribs and a baby-sitting service available. Some hotel restaurants have children's portions and high chairs.

RECOMMENDED RESTAURANT
Hotel restaurant or dining room highly recommended and open to non-residents unless otherwise stated.

	CREDIT CARDS	GARDEN OR TERRACE	CHILDREN'S FACILITIES	RECOMMENDED RESTAURANT

LINCOLN SUITES $$$
1823 L St, NW (between 18th St & 19th St). Map 3 A2. 223-4320 or (800) 424-2970. FAX 223-8546. W www.lincolnhotels.com
All the rooms in this modern, boutique hotel are large studio apartments with full-size kitchens. Friendly staff offer a free daily *Washington Post* newspaper, and freshly baked cookies and milk every evening. (99)
AE D DC MC V — Recommended Restaurant ▪

ST. REGIS WASHINGTON $$$$$
923 16th St, NW (at K St). Map 3 B2. 638-2626 or (800) 325-3535.
W www.stregis.com A luxury hotel with more character than some of the chain hotels. Eating in the upscale restaurant on the premises makes for a romantic evening. 180 (14)
AE D DC MC V — Recommended Restaurant ▪

WASHINGTON MARRIOTT $$$
1221 22nd St, NW (between M St and Ward Place). Map 2 E2. 872-1500 or (800) 228-9290. FAX 872-1424. W www.marriotthotels.com/
The Washington Marriott has a prime, central downtown location and the comfortable facilities expected of a hotel from a large chain. 418 (4)
AE D DC MC V — Children's Facilities ● Recommended Restaurant ▪

THE MONARCH HOTEL $$$$$
2401 M Street, NW (at 24th St). Map 2 E2. 429-2400 or (877) 222-2266. FAX 457-5010. W www.monarchdc.com
This contemporary hotel, located halfway between the White House and Georgetown, has luxurious, airy rooms, some overlooking the central courtyard and gardens. The service is impeccable. 415 (28)
AE D DC MC V — Garden or Terrace ▪ Recommended Restaurant ▪

THE WATERGATE SWISSÔTEL $$$$$
2650 Virginia Avenue, NW. Map 2 D3. 965-2300 or (800) 424-2736. FAX 337-7915. W www.swissotel.com Despite the notoriety of the Watergate name *(see p111)*, the views of the Potomac River along with the genteel décor and subdued lighting lend the hotel a peaceful air. The beautifully renovated rooms have walk-in closets and luxurious baths. 250 (144)
AE D DC MC V — Children's Facilities ● Recommended Restaurant ▪

THE WESTIN GRAND $$$$$
2350 M St, NW (between 23rd St & 24th St). Map 2 E2. 429-0100 or (800) 848-0016. FAX 429-9759. W www.westin.com
Luxurious marble bathrooms with extra-deep bath tubs, minibars, coffeemakers, and CD players are just a few of the amenities in the rooms of this well-appointed hotel. 263 (8)
AE D DC MC V — Garden or Terrace ▪ Children's Facilities ● Recommended Restaurant ▪

WYNDHAM CITY CENTRE $$$$
1143 New Hampshire Ave (between 22nd St & M St). Map 2 E3. 775-0800. FAX 331-9491. W www.windom.com
The Wyndham City Centre is in a very good location for the busy tourist, close to all amenities and main sights. 337 (15)
AE D DC MC V — Recommended Restaurant ▪

THE MELROSE HOTEL $$$$
2430 Pennsylvania Ave, NW (between 24th St & 25th St). Map 2 E3. 955-6400 or (800) 635-7673. FAX 775-8489. W www.melrosehotel.com
A comfortable hotel, this is often the choice of artists performing at the Kennedy Center. The décor is European contemporary in style, with fine furnishings and textiles in all the rooms. 239 (42)
AE D DC MC V — Recommended Restaurant ▪

GEORGETOWN

FOUR SEASONS HOTEL $$$$$
2800 Pennsylvania Ave, NW (between M St NW and Rock Creek & Potomac Parkway NW). Map 2 D3. 342-0444 or (800) 332-2443. FAX 944-2076.
W www.fourseasons.com A modern exterior belies the old-world elegance of this luxurious hotel, which prides itself on its excellent service. The rooms are spacious, with mahogany paneling, antiques, and flower displays. 260 (55)
AE D DC MC V — Garden or Terrace ▪ Children's Facilities ● Recommended Restaurant ▪

THE GEORGETOWN INN ⑤⑤⑤⑤
1310 Wisconsin Ave, NW (between N St & O St). **Map** 1 C2. 333-8900
or (800) 368-5922. FAX 338-8308. W www.georgetowninn.com
A small, boutique hotel built in the style of historic Georgetown. The large
rooms have Colonial-style décor and luxurious bathrooms. The restaurant has
scenes of old Washington on the walls. 🔳🔳🔳🔳🔳🔳🔳 86 (10)

| | AE D DC MC V | | | ■ |

HOTEL MONTICELLO ⑤⑤⑤
1075 Thomas Jefferson St, NW. **Map** 2 D3. 337-0900 or (800) 388-2410. FAX 333-6526.
W www.hotelmonticello.com Located below M Street, near the C&O Canal, this
Georgian-style inn has a lobby furnished with 18th-century antiques. It has
one-bedroom suites and two-story penthouses. 🔳🔳🔳🔳🔳 (47)

THE LATHAM HOTEL ⑤⑤⑤⑤
3000 M St, NW (at 30th St). **Map** 2 D2. 726-5000 or (800) 368-5922. FAX 337-4250.
An upscale European-style, boutique hotel with a luxurious lobby, and an
excellent French restaurant called Citronelle. There are four poolside bungalows
and nine suites, in addition to beautifully decorated rooms, some overlooking
the C&O Canal. 🔳🔳🔳🔳 143 (9)

FARTHER AFIELD

BRICKSKELLER INN ⑤⑤
1523 22nd St, NW (between P St & Q St NW). **Map** 2 E2. 293-1885. FAX 293-0996.
An old, quaint hotel with an old-fashioned elevator dating from 1950. The
restaurant offers over 1,000 kinds of beer from all around the world. 🔳 40

THE DUPONT AT THE CIRCLE ⑤⑤⑤
1604 19th St, NW (at Dupont Circle). **Map** 2 F2. 332-5251. FAX 332-3244.
W www.dupontatthecircle.com This luxurious bed-and-breakfast is set in a
restored 1883 townhouse, close to Dupont Circle. 🔳🔳 7 [1]

EMBASSY SQUARE SUMMERFIELD SUITES BY WYNDHAM ⑤⑤
2000 N St, NW (at 20th St). **Map** 2 E2. 659-9000 or (800) 424-2999.
W www.staydc.com This is an all-suite hotel with modern furnishings. Each unit
has a kitchenette. 🔳🔳🔳🔳 (278)

EMBASSY SUITES HOTEL ⑤⑤⑤⑤
1250 22nd St, NW (between M St & N St). **Map** 2 E2. 857-3388 or (800) 362-2779.
FAX 293-3173. W www.embassysuitesdcmetro.com
With suites that accommodate up to five people, this hotel is very suitable for
families. The modern atrium has a waterfall, columns, and palm trees. A free
full breakfast, cooked to order, is included. 🔳🔳🔳🔳🔳 (318)

EMBASSY SUITES HOTEL AT THE CHEVY CHASE PAVILION ⑤⑤⑤⑤
4300 Military Rd, NW (at Wisconsin & Western Ave). 362-9300 or (800) 362-2779.
FAX 686-3405. W www.embassysuitesdcmetro.com/chevychase Situated in the popular
Chevy Chase Shopping District, the hotel accesses a wide range of shops, as
well as a Metrorail stop within the Pavilion. 🔳🔳🔳🔳🔳 (198)

CLARION HAMPSHIRE HOTEL ⑤⑤⑤
1310 New Hampshire Ave, NW (at 13th St). **Map** 2 E2. 296-7600 or (800) 368-5691.
FAX 293-2476. W www.clarioninn.com
A small, simple hotel in a great location near both Dupont Circle and the White
House. This is an all-suite hotel, most with kitchenettes. 🔳🔳🔳🔳 (82)

THE HENLEY PARK HOTEL ⑤⑤⑤
926 Massachusetts Ave, NW (between 9th St & 10th St). **Map** 3 C2. 638-5200
or (800) 222-8474. FAX 414-0513. @ reservations@henleypark.com W www.henleypark.com
An English manor-style building that is part of the National Historic Trust, this
hotel has the air of an English country house. 🔳🔳🔳🔳🔳🔳 96 (15)

HOTEL CHURCHILL ⑤⑤⑤⑤
1914 Connecticut Ave, NW (between Leroy Place & California St). **Map** 2 E1.
797-2000 or (800) 424-2464. FAX 462-0944. W www.churchillhotel.com
A French-owned luxury hotel with a predominantly European clientele. Each
suite has a separate study. 🔳🔳🔳🔳🔳🔳 144 (36)

THE HYATT REGENCY BETHESDA ⑤⑤⑤⑤⑤
1 Bethesda Metro Center (Wisconsin Ave & Old Georgetown Rd).
(301) 657 1234 or (800) 233-1234. FAX 657-6478. W www.hyatt.com
This luxurious hotel is in the suburbs but conveniently located directly above
a Metrorail stop for easy access into central Washington.
🔳🔳🔳🔳🔳🔳🔳 384 (6)

Price categories for a standard double room per night, inclusive of service charges and any additional taxes; some hotels also include continental breakfast: ⑤ under $100 ⑤⑤ $100–$150 ⑤⑤⑤ $150–$200 ⑤⑤⑤⑤ $200–$300 ⑤⑤⑤⑤⑤ $300 plus.	**CREDIT CARDS** Indicates credit cards accepted: *AE* American Express; *D* Discover; *DC* Diners Club; *MC* MasterCard/Access; *V* VISA. **GARDEN OR TERRACE** Hotels with a garden, courtyard, or terrace. **CHILDREN'S FACILITIES** Cribs and a baby-sitting service available. Some hotel restaurants have children's portions and high chairs. **RECOMMENDED RESTAURANT** Hotel restaurant or dining room highly recommended and open to non-residents unless otherwise stated.		

	CREDIT CARDS	GARDEN OR TERRACE	CHILDREN'S FACILITIES	RECOMMENDED RESTAURANT
JEFFERSON HOTEL ⑤⑤⑤⑤ 1200 16th St, NW (at M St). **Map** 2 F2. 🎔 347-2200 or (800) 368-5966. **FAX** 331-7982. **W** www.loewshotels.com Built in 1923, this hotel is part of the America Hotel Historic Association. The rooms are decorated in Federal-style elegance, with antiques and original art, and some have fireplaces. The service is unquestionably outstanding. 🛗 🚼 🍸 🍴 🍽 P ♿ ✿ 100 (35)	AE D DC MC V			▪
JURYS WASHINGTON HOTEL ⑤⑤⑤ 1500 New Hampshire Ave, NW (near Dupont Circle). **Map** 2 F2. 🎔 483-6000 or (800) 423-6953. **FAX** 328-3265. **W** www.jurysdoyle.com An Irish hotel, with fine dining and an Irish pub, the Biddy Mulligan's, on the premises. Situated just a block away from Dupont Circle. 🍸 🍽 🔋 P ♿ ✿ 314 (6)	AE D DC MC V			▪
JURYS NORMANDY INN ⑤⑤⑤ 2118 Wyoming Ave, NW (between Connecticut Ave & 23rd St). **Map** 2 E1. 🎔 483-1350 or (800) 424-3729. **FAX** 387-8241. **W** www.jurysdoyle.com Converted from a dormitory in a private school, this is a small, cozy hotel. Books can be borrowed from the hotel library and read by the fireside. The building is surrounded by stately apartment buildings and elegant homes. P ♿ ✿ 75	AF D DC MC V			
KALORAMA GUEST HOUSE ⑤⑤ 1854 Mintwood Pl, NW (between Columbia Rd & 19th St). **Map** 2 E1. 🎔 667-6369. **FAX** 319-1262. **W** www.washingtonpost.com/yp/kgh A Victorian townhouse in a residential neighborhood, the rooms are tastefully decorated in period décor. No children under six allowed. 🚼 P ✿ 30 (5)	AE D DC MC V			
MADISON HOTEL ⑤⑤⑤⑤ 1177 15th St, NW (at M St). **Map** 3 B2. 🎔 862-1600 or (800) 424-8577. **FAX** 785-1255. **W** www.themadisonhotel.net The lobby of this hotel is filled with beautiful antiques, including a Louis XVI commode. Though modern on the outside, the hotel specializes in old-world luxury and meticulous service, and often accommodates high-ranking guests, such as heads of state, in its special top-security rooms. 🛗 🚼 🍸 🍽 🔋 P ♿ ✿ 311 (32)	AE D DC MC V			
MANSION ON O STREET ⑤⑤⑤⑤ 2020 O St, NW (at 20th St NW). **Map** 2 E2. 🎔 496-2000. **FAX** 659-0547. **W** www.mansion.com Originally separate Victorian townhouses, the all-suite Mansion on O Street is run by a lady who has decorated it with great character. It is particularly delightful to stay in at Christmas time. 🍴 🔋 P ♿ ✿ 12	AE D DC MC V	▪	●	
MARRIOTT WARDMAN PARK HOTEL ⑤⑤⑤⑤⑤ 2660 Woodley Rd, NW (between Connecticut Ave & Woodley Rd). 🎔 328-2000 or (800) 325-3535. **FAX** 234-0015. **W** www.marriott.com Set in 16 acres of parkland, the original apartment building has been extended with a modern glass complex. 🚼 🍸 🍴 🍽 🔋 P ♿ ✿ 1213 (125)	AE D DC MC V	▪		▪
MORRISON-CLARK INN ⑤⑤⑤⑤ Massachusetts Ave & 11th St , NW. **Map** 3 C2. 🎔 898-1200 or (800) 332-7898. **FAX** 289-8576. **W** www.morrisonclark.com This historic 1864 inn was originally two separate townhouses. The rooms are furnished with antiques and either Neoclassic, French rustic, or Victorian décor. 🚼 🍸 🍽 🔋 P ✿ 41 (13)	AE D DC MC V	▪		▪
OMNI SHOREHAM HOTEL ⑤⑤⑤⑤⑤ 2500 Calvert St, NW (between Conneticut & 22th St NW). 🎔 234-0700 or (800) 843-6664. **FAX** 756-5145. **W** www.omnihotels.com Set in 11 acres of grounds, this renovated hotel includes an Art Deco-style lobby and marble-floored bathrooms. 🛗 🚼 🍸 🍴 🍽 🔋 P ♿ ✿ 836 (35)	AE D DC MC V		●	▪

RENAISSANCE MAYFLOWER $$$$ 1127 Connecticut Ave, NW (at Desales St). **Map 2 F3.** 【 347-3000 or (800) 468-3571. FAX 466-9083. W www.renaissancehotels.com The Mayflower was built in 1925 and is on the National Register of Historic Places. 🈷 🏨 🍸 🍴 🛌 P 🚻 ❖ 660 (80)	AE D DC MC V			■
SWANN HOUSE $$$ 1808 New Hampshire Ave, NW (between S St & Swann St). **Map 2 F1.** 【 265-7677. FAX 265-6755. W www.swannhouse.com This bed-and-breakfast, in a Romanesque-style house built in 1883, is within walking distance of Dupont Circle. 🏨 🏊 🛌 ❖ 9 (4)	AE D DC MC V			
SWISS INN $ 1204 Massachusetts Ave, NW (at 12th St NW). **Map 3 C2.** 【 371-1816 or (800) 955-7947. FAX 371-1138. W www.theswissinn.com A brownstone building containing very reasonably priced studio apartments. The location is central and is four blocks north of the White House. 🏨 ❖ (7)	AE D DC MC V			
TABARD INN $$ 1739 N St, NW (between 17th St & 18th St). **Map 2 F2.** 【 785-1277. FAX 785-6173. W www.tabardinn.com This country-style inn, converted from three townhouses, is named after the inn in *The Canterbury Tales.* 🏊 🍴 🛌 ❖ 40 (2)	AE D DC MC V	■		■
THE TAFT BRIDGE INN $$ 2007 Wyoming Ave, NW (at 20th St). **Map 2 E1.** 【 387-2007. W www.taftbridgeinn.com This Georgian-style mansion is within walking distance of Adams-Morgan. Some rooms have a shared bathroom. 🔌 🛌 ❖ 12	MC V	■		
TOPAZ HOTEL $$$ 1733 N St, NW (between 17th St & 18th St). **Map 2 F2.** 【 393-3000 or (800) 424-2950. FAX 785-9581. W www.topazhotel.com An old European-style inn providing stylish, elegant accommodation with modern facilities in an atmosphere of Eastern-inspired calm. 🏨 🍸 🍴 🛌 P 🚻 ❖ (99)	AE D DC MC V			■
WASHINGTON COURTYARD BY MARRIOTT $$$ 1900 Connecticut Ave, NW. **Map 2 E1.** 【 332-9300 or (800) 842-4211. FAX 328 7039. W www.marriotthotels.com This hotel features a dark wood-paneled lobby and large rooms. Free cookies and coffee are available in the afternoon. 🏨 🍸 🏊 🍴 🛌 P 🚻 ❖ 145 (2)	AE D DC MC V			■
HILTON WASHINGTON $$$$ 1919 Connecticut Ave, NW (at Columbia Rd NW). **Map 2 E1.** 【 483-3000 or (800) 445-8667. FAX 265-8221. W www.hilton.com This massive hotel has just been recently renovated. Rooms are compact and bright. 🏨 🍸 🏊 🍴 🛌 🚻 ❖ 1,118 (44)	AE D DC MC V			■
THE WESTIN FAIRFAX HOTEL $$$$$ 2100 Massachusetts Ave (at 21st St). **Map 2 E2.** 【 293-2100 or (800) 937-8461. FAX 293-0641. W www.westin.com The Embassy Row location draws a mixture of foreign ministers and tourists. Cabo's restaurant serves French and California cuisine. 🈷 🏨 🍸 🍴 🛌 P 🚻 ❖ 131 (75)	AE D DC MC V		●	■
THE WYNDHAM, WASHINGTON, DC $$$$$ 1400 M St, NW (at Thomas Circle). **Map 3 B2.** 【 429-1700 or (800) 847-8232. FAX 872-1506. W www.wyndham.com The Wyndham has a large central atrium and all the amenities you would expect for a largely business clientele. 🈷 🏨 🍸 🍴 🛌 P 🚻 ❖ 400 (13)	AE D DC MC V			■

BEYOND WASHINGTON, DC

BALTIMORE, MD: *Ann Street Bed-and-Breakfast* $$ 804 South Ann St. 【 (410) 342-5883. Originally two separate 18th-century town houses, this bed-and-breakfast offers an authentic Colonial atmosphere with open fires and antique furniture. ❖ 2 (1)					
BALTIMORE, MD: *Clarion Hotel* $$$ 612 Cathedral St (between W Centre St & W Monument St). 【 (410) 727-7101 or (800) 292-5500. FAX (410) 789-3312. W www.clarionhotel.com A boutique-style hotel offering excellent service and located close to the Walters Art Gallery. A free continental breakfast is provided. 🏨 🍴 🛌 P 🚻 ❖ 104 (5)	AE D DC MC V			

For key to symbols see back flap

<table>
<tr><td>

Price categories for a standard double room per night, inclusive of service charges and any additional taxes; some hotels also include continental breakfast:

Ⓢ under $100
ⓈⓈ $100–$150
ⓈⓈⓈ $150–$200
ⓈⓈⓈⓈ $200–$300
ⓈⓈⓈⓈⓈ $300 plus.

</td><td>

CREDIT CARDS
Indicates credit cards accepted: *AE* American Express; *D* Discover; *DC* Diners Club; *MC* MasterCard/Access; *V* VISA.

GARDEN OR TERRACE
Hotels with a garden, courtyard, or terrace.

CHILDREN'S FACILITIES
Cribs and a baby-sitting service available. Some hotel restaurants have children's portions and high chairs.

RECOMMENDED RESTAURANT
Hotel restaurant or dining room highly recommended and open to non-residents unless otherwise stated.

</td></tr>
</table>

	CREDIT CARDS	GARDEN OR TERRACE	CHILDREN'S FACILITIES	RECOMMENDED RESTAURANT

BALTIMORE, MD: *Hyatt Regency Baltimore* ⓈⓈⓈⓈ
300 Light St (between E Conway St & E Pratt St). 【 *(410) 528-1234 or (800) 233-1234.*
FAX *(410) 685-3362.* W *www.hyatt.com*
This 14-story hotel overlooks the harbor. The rooms have marble bathrooms, cherry-wood furniture, and glass elevators. 🏢 🍽 🏊 🍴 🍷 **P** 🔥 ♦ *486 (26)*
AE D DC MC V — Children's ●, Recommended ■

BALTIMORE, MD: *Renaissance Harborplace Hotel* ⓈⓈⓈⓈ
202 E Pratt St (between South St & S Calvert St). 【 *(410) 547-1200 or (800) 535-1201.*
FAX *(410) 539-5780.* W *www.renaissancehotels.com*
The rooms in this hotel have a view either of the harbor or of the indoor courtyard. The staff are attentive and cordial and the restaurant specializes in excellent seafood from the Chesapeake Bay. 🕑 🏢 🍽 🏊 🍴 🍷 **P** 🔥 ♦ *622 (30)*
AE D DC MC V

BERLIN, MD: *Merry Sherwood Plantation* ⓈⓈ
8908 Worcester Hwy (nr Assateague). 【 *(410) 641-2112 or (800) 660-0358.*
FAX *(301) 797-4978.* W *www.merrysherwood.com*
This inn is a restored 1850s Italianate Revival-style mansion, set on 17 acres. The rooms have working fireplaces and Victorian-style furniture. 🏢 ♦ *8 (1)*
MC V — Garden ■

EASTON, MD: *Tidewater Inn* ⓈⓈ
101 East Dover St (near Chesapeake Bay). 【 *(410) 822-1300 or (800) 237-8775.*
W *www.tidewaterinn.com*
A charming, historic inn furnished with antiques. The restaurant serves all types of food but the crab cakes are the specialty. 🏢 🏊 **P** 🔥 ♦ *114 (18)*
AE D DC MC V — Recommended ■

TILGHMAN ISLAND, MD: *Chesapeake Wood Duck Inn* ⓈⓈⓈ
Gibsontown Rd, at Dogwood Harbor. 【 *(410) 886-2070 or (800) 956-2070.* FAX *(410) 886-2263.*
An 1890 Victorian bed-and-breakfast with period furnishings, oriental rugs, and original works of art. The house is immaculately kept. 🏢 ♦ *6 (1)*
MC V

GETTYSBURG, PA: *Baladerry Inn* ⓈⓈⓈ
40 Hospital Rd. 【 *(717) 337-1342.* FAX *call first.*
Nestling in the countryside, the cozy Baladerry Inn dates back to 1812, when it served as a hospital in the Civil War *(see p17)*. There are four rooms in the original house and four in the recently renovated carriage houses. 🏢 ♦ *8*
AE D DC MC V

ALEXANDRIA, VA: *Holiday Inn of Old Town* ⓈⓈⓈⓈ
480 King St (at S Pitt St). 【 *(703) 549-6080 or (800) 465-4329.*
W *www.axe-oldtown.hiselect.com* A huge, old-fashioned lobby greets guests at this hotel. The refurbished rooms are Victorian in style. 🏢 🏊 🍴 🍷 **P** 🔥 ♦ *227 (2)*
AE D DC MC V — Garden ■

ALEXANDRIA, VA: *Morrison House* ⓈⓈⓈⓈ
116 S Alfred St (between Prince St & King St), Old Town. 【 *(703) 838-8000 or (800) 367-0800.* FAX *(703) 684-6283.* W *www.morrisonhouse.com*
Modeled after a Federal manor home, the hotel's rooms are very ornate with four-poster beds, armoires, and Italian marble bathrooms. 🕑 🍷 🔥 ♦ *42 (3)*
AE DC MC V — Recommended ■

ARLINGTON, VA: *Arlington Crystal City Marriott Hotel* ⓈⓈⓈⓈ
1999 Jefferson Davis Hwy (at S 20th St). 【 *(703) 413-5500 or (800) 228-9290.*
FAX *(703) 413-0185.* W *www.marriotthotels.com* The lobby has a marble floor and art deco fixtures. Recently renovated rooms are elegant. 🏢 🏊 🍴 🍷 **P** 🔥 ♦ *338 (8)*
AE D DC MC V — Children's ●, Recommended ■

ARLINGTON, VA: *Ritz-Carlton Pentagon City* ⓈⓈⓈⓈⓈ
1250 S Hayes St (between S 15th St & Army Navy Dr). 【 *(703) 415-5000 or (800) 241-3333.* FAX *(703) 415-5061.* W *www.ritzcarlton.com*
The rooms in this hotel are furnished with antiques and fine art inspired by Virginia horse country. Afternoon tea is served. 🕑 🍽 🏊 🍴 🍷 **P** 🔥 ♦ *366 (21)*
AE D DC MC V — Children's ●, Recommended ■

CHARLOTTESVILLE, VA: *The Boar's Head Inn* ⓈⓈⓈ
Route 250 West. 【 *(804) 296-2181 or (800) 476-1988.* FAX *(804) 972-6024.*
W *www.boarsheadinn.com* A luxurious inn, with two lakes in the grounds. Facilities include an 18-hole golf course, tennis, fishing, biking, and a spa. Rooms have been recently renovated. 🏢 🍽 🏊 🍴 🍷 **P** 🔥 ♦ *160 (11)*
AE D DC MC V — Children's ●, Recommended ■

FREDERICKSBURG, VA: *Dunning Mills Inn All-Suite Hotel* $
2305-C Jefferson Davis Highway. (540) 373-1256. www.dunningmills.com
Set in the woods, this inn offers suites at a reasonable price. All accommodations include a queen size bed, a sofa bed, a full kitchen, and a dining
area (suites with Jacuzzi are available). (54)

AE D DC MC V

FREDERICKSBURG, VA: *Kenmore Inn* $$
1200 Princess Anne St. (540) 371-7622.
An historic inn with rooms decorated in either Victorian or Colonial style.
Many of the rooms have working fireplaces. There are two dining facilities –
formal dining upstairs and a pub downstairs. 12 (1)

AE DC MC V

LURAY, VA: *Big Meadows Lodge* $$
PO Box 727, Luray, VA 22835 (Skyline Drive). (540) 999-2221 or (800) 999-4714.
www.visitshenandoah.com
The accommodations here offer an attractive view of either the forest or
the valley.
92 (5) Nov–early April.

AE MC V

LURAY, VA: *Skyland Lodge* $$
PO Box 727, Luray, VA 22835 (Skyline Drive). (540) 999-2221 or (800) 999-4714.
www.visitshenandoah.com
The Skyland Lodge is on the highest point of the mountain, and most rooms
have a view of the valley below. Horseback riding is available.
171 (6) Dec–early March.

AE MC V

PARIS, VA: *The Ashby Inn* $$$
692 Federal St (near Middleburg). (540) 592-3900. www.ashbyinn.com
A renovated house dating back to 1829, the inn is decorated with period
pieces, and the rooms have a breathtaking view of the foothills of the Blue
Ridge mountains. Some rooms have their own private porches.
10

MC V

RICHMOND, VA: *The Berkeley Hotel* $$$
1200 East Cary St. (804) 780-1300. www.berkeleyhotel.com
A warm welcome is given at this gracious hotel, with its lavish, traditional
furnishings. The most popular rooms are, not surprisingly, those with
balconies. Situated in the heart of downtown Richmond.
55 (1)

AE D DC MC V

RICHMOND, VA: *The Jefferson Hotel* $$$$
101 W. Franklin St. (804) 788-8000 or (800) 424-8014.
www.jefferson-hotel.com
One of the oldest hotels in the area, the Jefferson was built in 1895. The lobby
boasts a breathtaking stained-glass ceiling.
260 (37)

AE D DC MC V

TREVILIANS, VA: *Prospect Hill* $$$$$
2887 Poindexter Rd (near Charlottesville). (540) 967-0844 or (800) 277-0844.
FAX (540) 967-0102.
This inn is situated on a 40-acre former plantation, and the house dates back
to 1732. Those rooms located outside the house are old slave quarters; all the
rooms have fireplaces. 10 (3)

AE D MC V

WASHINGTON, VA: *Inn at Little Washington* $$$$$
Main St & Middle St (Skyline Drive). (540) 675-3800.
No two rooms are alike at this imaginatively furnished and luxurious hotel.
The famous restaurant on the premises offers an excellent and generously
proportioned fixed price multi-course meal.
14 (4)

MC V

WILLIAMSBURG, VA: *Colonial Houses* $$$$
136 East Francis St. 1-800-HISTORY. www.colonialwilliamsburg.com
Restored 18th-century houses with traditional furnishings and modern
amenities. You can rent a whole house or a room in a house. The facilities of
the nearby Williamsburg Inn are also available to the guests of the Colonial
Houses. 77 (28 houses)

AE D DC MC V

WILLIAMSBURG, VA: *The Williamsburg Inn* $$$$$
136 East Francis St. 1-800-HISTORY. www.colonialwilliamsburg.com
This famous hotel offers all the luxuries of a modern hotel in a Regency-style
setting. The acclaimed Regency Room provides fine dining and afternoon tea
is served in the Terrace Room. Golf, croquet, and tennis are available in the
grounds. (62)

AE D DC MC V

For key to symbols see back flap

RESTAURANTS, CAFÉS, AND BARS

JOSEPH ALSOP, a renowned Washington host of the early 1960s, routinely gave lavish dinner parties in his Georgetown home. When asked why he gave so many parties, Alsop replied that it was because Washington had no good restaurants. Today the capital rivals New York, offering restaurants of every cuisine and price range. It is largely due to

Façade of Ben's Chili Bowl

Washington's cosmopolitan population that the city offers such a wide array of cuisines, from Ethiopian to Vietnamese, with many new styles of "fusion food" in between. The seafood is also superb, freshly caught from the nearby waters of Chesapeake Bay. Crab and shellfish feature regularly on menus, especially in coastal areas outside the city.

The elegant Matisse restaurant

PLACES TO EAT

WASHINGTON'S restaurants are a reflection of its neighborhoods. Adams-Morgan has a mix of ethnic establishments, especially Salvadoran and Ethiopian, and cutting-edge cuisine. Perry's, Cashion's Eat Place, and Felix Restaurant and Bar offer inventive fusion food with Asian and French influences, and the crowd is young and hip. An easy walk from the Mall, Washington's compact Chinatown has some of the best bargains for families. Meals are inexpensive and often served family style. Next to Chinatown is the restored Old Downtown district on Seventh Street. Chic restaurants like The Mark, Coco Loco, and the District Chophouse are in restored early 19th-century buildings. Georgetown has a mix of expensive and inexpensive places. Good value can be

found at its many Indian and Vietnamese restaurants. North of the White House and south of Dupont Circle, Downtown restaurants cater to business travelers and high-powered lobbyists. More reasonable places, again mostly ethnic restaurants, are found closer to the Circle.

With very few exceptions, all restaurants in Washington are air conditioned. This has changed the city from one where most of the population used to escape in the summer to a lively, year-round capital.

RESERVATIONS

RESERVATIONS MAY be necessary for popular restaurants; the most fashionable can get booked up weeks in advance. Call ahead if there is somewhere you really want to go. However, walk-in diners are expected in most places. You may be placed on a waiting list and expected to return at the appointed time or wait in the adjacent bar, but you will usually be guaranteed a table within a fairly short time.

PRICES AND PAYING

RESTAURANT PRICES range from the very cheap to the very expensive in Washington. Prices vary according to location, cuisine, and décor. Most restaurants take major credit cards, although street vendors and fast food places may only accept cash. A 15 percent tip is expected for good service in

restaurants; some places even recommend 20 percent. The tip is seldom automatically added to the bill except in the case of large parties, which may incur an automatic 15 percent gratuity.

Unlike many European cities, the fixed price meal is uncommon in Washington. Items are usually listed à la carte unless specified in the menu. Diners should expect to spend between $20 and $30 for dinner and a drink, including tip, at a moderate restaurant. However Indian, Ethiopian, Chinese, and Vietnamese restaurants are often considerably less expensive. It is also worth knowing that you will generally be charged about 25 percent less for the same meal if you eat at lunchtime rather than in the evening, so visitors on a budget may choose to eat their main meal at lunchtime. Breakfasts are usually under $10 for bacon and eggs with coffee and juice, but many hotels include a free continental breakfast (rolls, coffee, and juice) in the cost of the room.

B. Smith's grand Beaux Arts style dining room at historic Union Station

Mural on the side of Madam's Organ bar in Adams-Morgan

OPENING HOURS

IT IS UNUSUAL for a restaurant to be open 24 hours, except for those in very large hotels. Restaurants also rarely serve food continuously throughout the day; they usually have a break of several hours between lunch and dinner. Most restaurants are open all year (except Christmas Day) but a few may be closed on Sunday or Monday It is best to call in advance. Restaurants often open for dinner between 5pm and 6pm, with the busiest period usually between 7pm and 8pm. The last seating is often at 9pm, and the last customers usually leave by 11pm. Bars are open until 2am. Remember that Metrorail trains stop running at 2am on Friday and Saturday, and at midnight the rest of the week.

ALCOHOL

RESTAURANTS ARE required by law to have a liquor license in order to sell alcohol so you will notice that some do not offer it. Others may serve wine only but not hard liquor or mixed drinks.

Bars rarely serve food other than perhaps some appetizers Other restaurants may have a a separate bar as well as a dining section. Patrons are not permitted to bring their own drinks to a restaurant.

The drinking age in DC, in Maryland, and in Virginia is 21. Restauranteurs can and will ask for proof of age in the form of a driver's license or passport since the penalty for serving alcohol to underage drinkers is severe.

SMOKING

IN THE DISTRICT of Columbia smoking is still permitted in restaurants but may be restricted to designated areas. Americans are very conscious of smoking, especially in eating establishments, and smoking in a nonsmoking area may mean a fine of several hundred dollars.

DRESS CODE

DRESS VARIES from the very casual (shorts, t-shirt, and sneakers) to the very formal. In some restaurants men will not be admitted without a jacket and tie (the maitre d' may have spares). But as a general guide, the more expensive the restaurant, the more formal the dress code will be. Some bars also have a very strict dress code, and customers may not be admitted in very casual dress. Respectable but casual attire is acceptable in the majority of establishments.

WHAT TO EAT

WASHINGTON OFFERS a vast range of types of food to the visitor, but like most American cities it has a high concentration of fast-food establishments. Chains like McDonalds, Burger King, and Wendy's serve the same food worldwide and can be a reliable and popular source of sustenance for a family on the move. The hotdog vendors along the Mall offer an alternative. Other than fast food, Washington's cuisine is immensely multicultural, and you will find French, Chinese, Ethiopian, and Vietnamese restaurants, among others.

CHILDREN

THE BEST INDICATION as to whether children are welcome in a restaurant is the presence of a children's menu or the availability of high chairs. When dining in more formal places with children, it is best to reserve the earliest seating when the restaurant will not be too busy.

Tony and Joe's bar on the side of Washington harbor

WHEELCHAIR ACCESS

RESTAURANTS ARE not required to be wheelchair accessible. In general, restaurants in older neighborhoods like Dupont Circle and Adams-Morgan are less likely to accommodate wheelchairs than modern establishments on K Street. The Smithsonian Museum restaurants are all accessible for the disabled.

Street vendor selling hot dogs, pretzels, ice cream, and drinks

What to Eat in Washington, DC

Hot dog

WASHINGTON OFFERS an eclectic choice of foods. There are many traditional restaurants and diners that serve classic American dishes such as T-bone steak and Caesar salad, but the city's cosmopolitan population is reflected in the vast number of ethnic restaurants, including Ethiopian, Vietnamese, Italian, and Greek. The local seafood, fresh from nearby Chesapeake Bay, is world famous; try the blue claw crabs, oysters, clams, and mussels, at least once.

Pancakes, *served in a stack with maple syrup and whipped butter, are eaten for breakfast, often with side orders of fruit.*

Southern Breakfast *is a hearty meal with eggs, bacon, and grits (a corn porridge), delicious served with butter and black pepper.*

Senate Bean Soup, *made with white beans and onions cooked with ham hocks, used to sustain senators during all-night sessions.*

Maryland Crab Soup *is a thick and creamy soup containing chunks of white crab meat, served with crackers.*

Caesar Salad *is made with Romaine lettuce and croutons, with a fresh, tangy dressing of anchovy, Parmesan cheese, lemon juice, and olive oil.*

Steamed Blue Claw Maryland Crabs *are delicious served simply with slices of brown bread and lemon wedges.*

Oysters *caught locally are served with a choice of dips – vinaigrette, mayonnaise, chili, and spicy tomato.*

Panfried Squash, *common as a side order, is served with broiled or roasted meats, broiled fish, or cornbread.*

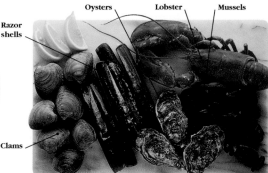

Oysters   Lobster   Mussels

Razor shells

Clams

Chesapeake Bay Grill *is a platter of seafood from the beaches and shallow waters of Chesapeake Bay.*

Southern Fried Chicken *is a highly seasoned dish served with mustard greens.*

Grilled T-Bone Steak *is an American classic. The steak is grilled to your specification and then served with corn on the cob, a baked potato, and steak sauce.*

Poussin and Wild Rice *is a classic East Coast dish often found on menus in the fall.*

Spaghetti Bolognese *is a classic Italian pasta dish with meat in a tomato sauce.*

Ethiopian Injera *is a dish of vegetables in a hot chili sauce, served on a "plate" of bread.*

Bourtheto *is a dish of fish in a spicy tomato sauce, introduced by Greek immigrants.*

Vietnamese Roast Pork *is a DC favorite. The pork is marinated before roasting and served with white rice. A side dish of pickled vegetables complements the meat.*

COCKTAILS

Bars serve an enormous variety of cocktails, such as the traditional vodka martini. "Specials" and nibbles are usually offered during "cocktail hour" (6–7pm).

Apple Pie *is an all-American favorite, best served warm and either à la mode (with a scoop of vanilla ice cream) or with whipped cream.*

Old Fashioned **Whiskey Sour** **Vodka Martini**

Banana Split *is a popular ice cream concoction that will feed a family. No one will mind if you order extra spoons and share.*

Choosing a Restaurant

THE RESTAURANTS in this guide have been selected across a range of price categories for their exceptional food, good value, and interesting location. Entries are arranged alphabetically within each district, both for the central areas of Washington, DC and for towns and cities in the surrounding states. Map references refer to the Street Finder, pages 210–13.

Restaurant	Credit Cards	Outdoor Tables	Vegetarian Dishes	Late-Night Menu	Good Wine List
CAPITOL HILL					
AMERICA $ Union Station, 50 Massachusetts Ave, NE. **Map 4 E3.** ☎ *682-9555.* The 200-item menu, including all the American classics, is sure to please everybody, and makes the choice both easy and inexpensive.	AE D DC MC V	●	■		■
ANATOLIA $ 633 Pennsylvania Ave. **Map 4 F4.** ☎ *544-4753.* Excellent Turkish food, served in intimate surroundings, with coffee that almost lets you stand your spoon in it.	AE D MC V		■		
B. SMITH'S $$ Union Station, 50 Massachusetts Ave, NE. **Map 4 E3.** ☎ *289-6188.* The ornate setting of the former Presidential Waiting Room of Union Station is now one of the best places for Southern Creole cooking.	AE D DC MC V		■		■
CAPITOL HILL BREWING COMPANY $ 2 Massachusetts Ave, NE (near 1st St). **Map 4 E3.** ☎ *842-2337.* Situated above the National Postal Museum, this restaurant/bar offers good pub food and an excellent selection of beers.	AE D DC MC V	●	■	●	
HAWK AND DOVE $ 329 Pennsylvania Ave, SE (between 3rd St & 4th St). **Map 4 F4.** ☎ *543-3300.* This is a British-style pub, but it offers a typically American menu. It has 11 TVs with satellite programming, and usually contains an interesting mixture of locals and politicians. There is a children's menu.	AE D DC MC V	●		●	
MARKET LUNCH $ Eastern Market, 225 7th St, SE (at C St). **Map 4 F4.** ☎ *547-8444.* Authentic regional food, such as crab cakes and crab sandwiches, are offered here. The cafeteria-style breakfast and lunch is as casual as it is delicious. Expect a long wait on Sunday mornings. Mon.		●			
TUNNICLIFF'S $ 222 7th St, SE (opposite Eastern Market). **Map 4 F4.** ☎ *544-5680.* The old wooden interior attracts a casual and diverse crowd. The cuisine is American pub-type food.	AE D DC MC V	●	■	●	
TWO QUAIL $$ 320 Massachusetts Ave, NE (between 3rd St & 4th St). **Map 4 F3.** ☎ *543-8030.* This refreshing American Bistro has a cozy atmosphere (the most romantic in Washington). Specialties include the quail, and homemade desserts.	AE D DC MC V		■		■
THE MALL					
CASCADE CAFÉ $ National Gallery of Art, Concourse Level, Constitution Ave, NW (between 4th St & 7th St). **Map 4 D4.** ☎ *216-5966.* One of the better options for hungry museum-goers, this café offers fast and convenient buffet-style food, including salads and great desserts.	AE D DC MC V		■		
THE PALM COURT ICE CREAM PARLOR AND CAFE $ National Museum of American History, Constitution Ave, NW (between 12th St & 14th St). **Map 3 B4.** ☎ *357-2700.* A typical American selection of cuisine is offered, but this is a bit more pricey than some of the other Mall eateries.	AE MC V		■		
FLIGHT LINE CAFE $ National Air and Space Museum, Independence Ave (between 4th St & 7th St). **Map 4 D4.** ☎ *357-2700.* The only restaurant in the museum, it offers a range of hamburgers, pizzas, and sandwiches.	AE MC V				

Price categories are for a three-course meal for one, with a glass of wine, including cover, service, and tax:
($) less than $20
($)($) $20–$30
($)($)($) $30–$45
($)($)($)($) $45–$60
($)($)($)($)($) $60 plus.

CREDIT CARDS
Indicates credit cards accepted: *AE* American Express; *D* Discover; *DC* Diners Club; *MC* MasterCard/Access; *V* VISA.

OUTDOOR TABLES
The restaurant has a garden, terrace, or boardwalk area for eating outside.

VEGETARIAN DISHES
The menu includes some vegetarian options.

LATE-NIGHT MENU
Snacks and light meals are available until late in the evening.

GOOD WINE LIST
The restaurant offers an exceptional choice of wines.

OLD DOWNTOWN

Restaurant	Price	Credit Cards	Outdoor Tables	Vegetarian Dishes	Late-Night Menu	Good Wine List
BISTRO BIS	($)($)	AE D DC MC V	●	■		■
COCO LOCO	($)	AE MC V		■	.	■
DISTRICT CHOPHOUSE	($)($)	AE DC MC V				■
FADÓ	($)	AE D DC MC V		■	●	
FULL KEE	($)			■		
HARD ROCK CAFÉ	($)	AE D DC MC V		■		
JALEO	($)($)	AE D DC MC V		■	●	■
OLD EBBITT GRILL	($)	AE D DC MC V		■	●	■
RED SAGE	($)($)	AE D DC MC V		■	●	■
SKY TERRACE	($)	AE D MC V	●	■		■

BISTRO BIS
15 E Street, NW (between N. Capitol & New Jersey). **Map** 4 D4. *661-2700.*
French food with an American twist, served in a beautiful, cozy dining area. The duck confit and salmon Provençal come highly recommended. 🄿 🍸 ♿

COCO LOCO
810 7th St, NW (between H St & I St). **Map** 3 C2. *289-2626.*
Tex-Mex, Brazilian BBQ, and a late night party are on the menu at Coco Loco. The atmosphere is fun and colorful. 🄿 🍸 🎵 🧒 ♿

DISTRICT CHOPHOUSE
509 7th St, NW (between E St & F St). **Map** 3 C3. *347-3434.*
This upscale hangout echoes the style and ambience of the 1940s with a cigar bar, pool tables, and swing music. Huge portions of steak, burgers, and pizza can be washed down by the beers, which are brewed on the premises. 🍸 🎵 🧒 ♿

FADÓ
808 7th St, NW (between H St & I St). **Map** 3 C3. *789-0066.*
Fadó has the look of an authentically traditional Irish pub, with furnishings shipped over from Ireland. Typical and fusion Irish dishes are served. 🍸 🎵 ♿

FULL KEE
509 H St, NW (between 5th St & 6th St). **Map** 4 D3. *371-2233.*
The Cantonese noodles and dumplings are excellent in this rather sparsely decorated restaurant. A great place to grab a cheap meal before an MCI Center event. ♿

HARD ROCK CAFÉ
999 E Street, NW (at 10th Street). **Map** 3 C3. *737-7625.*
All the American classics are available, including burgers, sandwiches, and salads. Videos, music, and memorabilia make the two floors of this restaurant an exciting tourist experience, though it can get a little hectic. 🍸 🧒 ♿

JALEO
480 7th St, NW. **Map** 3 C3. *628-7949.*
Not far from the monuments, and a stone's throw from the MCI Center, this Spanish *tapas* restaurant is a refreshing alternative with its colorful menu and décor. 🄿 🍸 🎵 🧒 ♿

OLD EBBITT GRILL
675 15th St, NW (between Pennsylvania Ave & G St). **Map** 3 B3. *347-4801.*
Expect this upbeat American grill to be packed with both locals and tourists – in fact, anyone who enjoys a great meal. It's a chance to sample the DC scene as well as quality seafood, pasta, and steaks. 🄿 🍸 🧒 ♿

RED SAGE
605 14th St, NW (between F St & G St). **Map** 3 B3. *638-4444.*
Upstairs is a Southwestern café, downstairs a formal dining room with Western-influenced modern American dishes, including game. 🄿 🍸 🧒 ♿

SKY TERRACE
Hotel Washington, 515 15th St, NW (between Pennsylvania Ave and G St). **Map** 3 B3. *638-5900. Open Apr–Oct only.*
The Sky Terrace has one of the best views of the city's monuments and the White House, and offers a light Continental menu. 🍸 🧒 ♿

For key to symbols see back flap

Price categories are for a three-course meal for one, with a glass of wine, including cover, service, and tax:
$ less than $20
$$ $20–$30
$$$ $30–$45
$$$$ $45–$60
$$$$$ $60 plus.

CREDIT CARDS
Indicates credit cards accepted: *AE* American Express; *D* Discover; *DC* Diners Club; *MC* MasterCard/Access; *V* VISA.

OUTDOOR TABLES
The restaurant has a garden, terrace, or boardwalk area for eating outside.

VEGETARIAN DISHES
The menu includes some vegetarian options.

LATE-NIGHT MENU
Snacks and light meals are available until late in the evening.

GOOD WINE LIST
The restaurant offers an exceptional choice of wines.

THE WHITE HOUSE AND FOGGY BOTTOM

Restaurant	Price	Credit Cards	Outdoor Tables	Vegetarian Dishes	Late-Night Menu	Good Wine List
AROMA	$	AE D DC MC V		■		
ASIA NORA	$$$$	AE D MC V		■		■
BOMBAY CLUB	$	AE DC MC V	●	■		■
GALILEO	$$	AE D DC MC V	●	■		■
GEORGIA BROWN'S	$$	AE D DC MC V		■		■
HORS D'OEUVRERIE	$	AE DC MC V		■	●	■
JEFFREY'S	$$	AE D DC MC V		■		■
KC CAFÉ	$	AE D DC MC V		■		
KINKEAD'S	$$$	AE D DC MC V	●	■		■
PRIMI PIATTI	$$$	AE DC MC V	●	■		
RENAISSANCE MAYFLOWER, CAFÉ PROMENADE	$$	AE D DC MC V		■		■

AROMA $
1919 I Street, NW (between 19th St & 20th St). **Map** 2 E3. **(** 833-4700.
This North Indian restaurant is one of the best-kept secrets in Washington. It is casual yet elegant, and the food is excellent. ▮ ♿

ASIA NORA $$$$
2213 M St, NW (between 22nd St & 23rd St). **Map** 2 E2. **(** 797-4860.
A creative selection of Asian fusion cuisine using organic ingredients. The setting is intimate and serene, with carvings decorating the walls. P ▮

BOMBAY CLUB $
815 Connecticut Ave, NW (between H St & I St). **Map** 2 F3. **(** 659-3727.
Exotic Indian food in a Colonial setting. The attentive service and exclusive clientele provide a glimpse of upper-crust Washington. P ▮ ♫ ♿

GALILEO $$
1110 21st St, NW (between L St & M St). **Map** 2 E3. **(** 293-7191.
The most talked-about Italian restaurant in DC, Galileo is famous for its innovative and elaborate dishes, such as homemade pastas, risottos, and game dishes, as well as its fine selection of wines. P ▮ ⚘ ♿

GEORGIA BROWN'S $$
950 15th St, NW (between I St & K St). **Map** 3 B3. **(** 393-4499.
Anyone who craves Carolina shrimp, grits (fried, coarse grain), or fried green tomatoes should come here. Southern cooking with style in an inviting but hectic atmosphere. P ▮ ♫ ⚘ ♿

HORS D'OEUVRERIE $
Kennedy Center. **Map** 2 D4. **(** 416-8560.
The Kennedy Center location for light fare, such as salads and pasta. It is open after the last show on Thu, Fri & Sat. P ▮ ⚘ ♿

JEFFREY'S $$
Watergate Hotel, 2650 Virginia Ave, NW. **Map** 2 D3. **(** 298-4455.
The infamous Watergate building houses this contemporary American restaurant. The name, prices, and staff attitude are not always justified by the food, but the view across the Potomac river is spectacular.
P ▮ ♫ ⚘ ♿

KC CAFÉ $
Kennedy Center. **Map** 2 D4. **(** 416-8560.
The most casual venue of the Kennedy Center, this self-service café offers a wide selection of inexpensive food, from pastas to chili. P ⚘ ♿

KINKEAD'S $$$
Red Lion Row, 2000 Pennsylvania Ave, NW (between 20th St & 21st St).
Map 2 E3. **(** 296-7700.
A fantastic seafood restaurant without the price inflation that can come with a big name. Bob Kinkead's creations, such as the pepita-crusted salmon, are wonderfully complemented by the extensive wine list. P ▮ ♫ ♿

PRIMI PIATTI $$$
2013 I St, NW (between 20th St & Pennsylvania Ave). **Map** 2 E3. **(** 223-3600.
This Northern Italian restaurant has a menu offering pasta and meat dishes. The food is reliably good, and the atmosphere sophisticated.
P ▮ ♿

RENAISSANCE MAYFLOWER, CAFÉ PROMENADE $$
1127 Connecticut Ave, NW (at DeSales St). **Map** 2 F3. **(** 347-3000.
A Mediterranean-accented menu that includes crab cakes and red snapper is offered at this hotel restaurant. Reservations recommended. P ▮ ♫ ⚘ ♿

ROOF TERRACE $$
Kennedy Center. **Map** 2 D4. 416-8555
Theater-goers can enjoy a contemporary American meal of such dishes as
salmon, crab cakes, and delicious pecan tart, coupled with a fabulous view
of the Virginia skyline. The Sunday brunch buffet is superb.
Cards: AE DC MC V

GEORGETOWN

1789 $$
1226 36th St, NW, at Prospect St. **Map** 1 B2. 965-1789.
Excellent, modern American food served in four separate dining areas
with a Colonial theme.
Cards: AE D DC MC V

AU PIED DE COCHON $
1335 Wisconsin Ave NW (at Dumbarton St). **Map** 1 C2. 337-6400.
This French café is not noted for its décor or quick service, but it is one of
the only restaurants in Georgetown that is open 24 hours a day. At the end
of a night out on the town, try the eggs Benedict for an early breakfast.
Cards: AE MC V

CAFÉ LA RUCHE $
1039 31st St, NW (between K St & C&O Canal). **Map** 2 D3. 965-2684.
A typical Parisian bistro with a comfortable atmosphere that is great for
chatting with friends. There is a wide range of dishes available, including
rainbow trout, crab cakes, mussels niçoise, and soups and salads.
Cards: AE MC V

CITRONELLE $$$$$
Latham Hotel, 3000 M St, NW (at 30th St). **Map** 2 D2. 625-2150.
This excellent restaurant serves sophisticated French dishes, such as pastry
"cigars" stuffed with wild mushrooms, and potato-crusted halibut.
Cards: AE D DC MC V

CLYDE'S OF GEORGETOWN $$
3236 M Street, NW. **Map** 1 C2. 333-9180.
A Washington institution in the heart of Georgetown that has been
popular since it first opened 40 years ago. It popularized saloon food and
could claim to have invented Sunday brunch.
Cards: AE D DC MC V

JAPAN INN $$
1715 Wisconsin Avenue, NW (corner R St & S St). **Map** 1 C1. 337-3400.
Authentic food and plenty of options give you the choice of either sitting
at a communal table while your dinner is grilled in front of you,
or ordering from a more traditional menu.
Cards: AE MC V

MARTIN'S TAVERN $
1264 Wisconsin Ave, NW (at N St). **Map** 1 C2. 333-7370.
Martin's is the oldest family-owned restaurant in DC, and one of the most
charming locations for American pub food.
Cards: AE D DC MC V

OLD GLORY ALL AMERICAN BARBECUE $
3139 M St, NW (between Wisconsin Ave & 31st St). **Map** 1 C2. 337-3406.
This homey restaurant serves traditional American fare, such as spare ribs,
hickory-smoked chicken, wood-fried shrimp, and apple crisp.
Cards: AE D DC MC V

PAOLO'S $
1303 Wisconsin Ave, NW (at N St). **Map** 1 C2. 333-7353.
This Italian- and Californian-style restaurant is as trendy and international
as its Georgetown surroundings – a place to be seen and to enjoy a light
salad, a pasta dish, or a grilled pizza.
Cards: AE D DC MC V

TAHOGA $$
2815 M St NW (at 28th St). **Map** 2 D2. 338-5380.
This restaurant has a minimalist, contemporary dining room, serving new
American regional cuisine, featuring seafood, and an award-winning wine
list. In season, tables are available in a brick-walled garden.
Cards: AE DC MC V

ZED'S ETHIOPIAN CUISINE $
1201 28th St, NW. **Map** 1 C2. 333-4710.
An Ethiopian restaurant, popular with vegetarians, Zed's offers traditional
wats (red pepper sauces), *alechas* (stews), and *injera* (bread).
Cards: AE D DC MC V

SEQUOIA $$
Washington Harbor, 3000 K St, NW. **Map** 2 D3. 944-4200.
A trendy restaurant combining American cuisine with fabulous
views of the Potomac and Virginia skyline
Cards: AE D DC MC V

For key to symbols see back flap

		Credit Cards	Outdoor Tables	Vegetarian Dishes	Late-Night Menu	Good Wine List

Price categories are for a three-course meal for one, with a glass of wine, including cover, service, and tax:

$ less than $20
$$ $20–$30
$$$ $30–$45
$$$$ $45–$60
$$$$$ $60 plus.

CREDIT CARDS
Indicates credit cards accepted: *AE* American Express; *D* Discover; *DC* Diners Club; *MC* MasterCard/Access; *V* VISA.

OUTDOOR TABLES
The restaurant has a garden, terrace, or boardwalk area for eating outside.

VEGETARIAN DISHES
The menu includes some vegetarian options.

LATE-NIGHT MENU
Snacks and light meals are available until late in the evening.

GOOD WINE LIST
The restaurant offers an exceptional choice of wines.

FARTHER AFIELD

Restaurant	Price	Credit Cards	Outdoor Tables	Vegetarian Dishes	Late-Night Menu	Good Wine List
ARDEO 3311 Connecticut Ave, NW (between Macomb St & Ordway St). 244-6750. This trendy and busy modern American restaurant features an interesting and innovative menu and is located in Cleveland Park. P Y ⚥ ♿	$	AE DC MC V		■		
BEN'S CHILI BOWL 1213 U St, NW (between 12th St & 13th St). 667-0909. A favorite for anyone who loves a good, high-calorie meal. The chili dogs are known nationally. It is Bill Cosby's favorite haunt when he visits DC.	$			■	●	
CASHION'S EAT PLACE 1819 Columbia Rd NW. 797-1819. New American cuisine, with French, Italian, and Spanish influences, and an award-winning wine list. P Y ♫ ♿ ● Mon.	$$	MC V	●	■		■
CITIES 2424 18th St, NW (at Columbia Rd). 328-7194. There is a change of cuisine and décor almost every year here to honor the taste and style of a different international city. Expect a dress code at night (business casual) and a yuppie, Euro crowd. P Y ⚥ ♿	$$	AE D DC MC V	●	■	●	■
CITY LIGHTS OF CHINA 1731 Connecticut Ave, NW (between R St & S St). **Map 2 E1.** 265-6688. Many people attest that the crowds and waiting in line are worth it for the inexpensive and delicious Chinese food. Delivery is available too. ⚥	$	AE D DC MC V		■		
GEORGETOWN SEAFOOD GRILL 1200 19th St, NW (between M St & N St). **Map 2 F2.** 530-4430. High-quality seafood at a moderate price – the crab cakes are said to be the best in town. The service is quick and friendly. P Y ⚥ ♿	$$	AE D DC MC V	●	■		■
KRAMERBOOKS AND AFTERWORDS CAFÉ 1517 Connecticut Ave, NW (between Dupont Circle & Q St). **Map 2 E2.** 387-1462. This café serves salads, pasta, and Asian-influenced vegetarian dishes. Open 24 hours on weekends. Y ♫ ♿	$	AE D MC V	●	■	●	
LA TOMATE 1701 Connecticut Ave, NW, (between R St & S St). **Map 2 E1.** 667-5505. This Italian restaurant's prime location near Dupont Circle makes it a summer favorite with the locals for outdoor eating. P Y ♫	$$	AE DC MC V	●	■		■
LAVANDOU 3321 Connecticut Ave, NW (between Macomb St & Ordway St). 966-3002. The atmosphere and food of Provence, with over 90 wines to complement the fresh grilled seafood and soups. ⚥ ♿	$$	AE DC MC V		■		■
MATISSE 4934 Wisconsin Ave, NW (at Fessenden St). 244-5222. Visually arresting décor inspired by Matisse, and delicious innovative French food, but the service lacks finesse. P Y ♿ ● Mon lunchtime.	$$$$	AE DC MC V		■		■
MORRISON-CLARK RESTAURANT 1015 L St, NW (between 10th St & 11th St). **Map 3 C2.** 898-1200. Modern American food with a Southern influence in a restored 1864 dining room. Impeccable service and a relaxing atmosphere. P Y ⚥ ♿	$$$$$	AE D DC MC V	●	■		■
NORA'S 2132 Florida Ave, NW (between Connecticut Ave & Massachusetts Ave). **Map 2 E1.** 462-5143. W www.noras.com One of the stalwarts of Washington dining, Nora's features organic ingredients and a varied menu of contemporary American cuisine. P ⚥ Y ♿	$$$$$	AE D MC V		■		■

PESCE $$\small\text{(\$)(\$)}$$
2016 P St, NW (between 20th St & 21st St). **Map 2 E2.** (466-3474.
The French and Italian menu changes daily but always includes delicious seafood and a fabulous wine list. Great food at a reasonable price.

Credit cards: AE, D, DC, MC, V

RUPPERTS $$\small\text{(\$)(\$)(\$)}$$
1017 7th St, NW (between L St & New York Ave). **Map 3 C2.** (783-0699.
A constantly changing menu focuses on fresh, seasonal American fare. The décor is hip but simple.

Credit cards: AE, DC, MC, V

EXCURSIONS

ANNAPOLIS, MD: *Middletown Tavern Oyster Bar & Restaurant* (\$)(\$)
2 Market Space. (410) 263-3323.
Located across the street from the harbor, this outdoor restaurant is a perfect spot to soak up the view. The oysters come with beer; also on the menu are crab cakes, seafood, and pasta dishes.

Credit cards: AE, D, MC, V

BALTIMORE, MD: *Obrycki's Crab House* (\$)(\$)
1727 East Pratt St. (410) 732-6399.
A seasonal restaurant offering superb seafood dining. A favorite of the house is the hard-shell steamed crabs. ● Dec–Mar.

Credit cards: AE, DC, MC, V

CHESAPEAKE BAY, MD: *The Crab Claw* (\$)(\$)
Navy Point, St. Michaels. (410) 745-2900.
A seasonal restaurant located on the harbor, with spectacular views. Fresh seafood dishes are the specialty. ● Dec–Feb.

GREAT FALLS PARK, MD: *Old Angler's Inn* (\$)(\$)(\$)(\$)
10801 MacArthur Blvd, Potomac. (301) 365-2425. Closed Mon.
This quaint English pub-style restaurant is a short trip from the city. Next to the C&O Canal, it is a traditional place for a hot cider by the fire. The sophisticated kitchen serves new American cuisine with flair.

Credit cards: AE, DC, MC, V

GETTYSBURG, PA: *Farnsworth House Inn* (\$)
401 Baltimore St. (717) 334-8838.
The theme of this restaurant is Civil War/Victorian. Waiters dress in period clothes and the menu features Civil War dishes. Favorites are the game pie, spoon bread, sweet potato pudding, and pumpkin fritters.

Credit cards: AE, D, MC, V

ALEXANDRIA, VA: *Gadsby's Tavern* (\$)(\$)(\$)
N Royal St, at Cameron St. (703) 548-1288.
Here the waiters are in Colonial costume, and the décor in the style of the late 1700s. The menu includes duck, venison, seafood, and pies.

Credit cards: AE, DC, MC, V

CHARLOTTESVILLE, VA: *Michie Tavern* (\$)
683 Thomas Jetterson Parkway. (804) 977-1234.
Casual dining with a Colonial touch – serving staff dress in Colonial outfits, and the décor is on the rustic side. The traditional Southern fried chicken is outstanding.

Credit cards: AE, MC, V

RICHMOND, VA: *Southern Culture* (\$)(\$)
2229 West Main St. (804) 355-6939.
This restaurant serves a wide variety of regional Southern food, ranging from Virginia fried chicken to seafood dishes from the Gulf of Mexico, and is relatively inexpensive.

Credit cards: AE, MC, V

SKYLINE DRIVE, VA: *Inn at Little Washington* (\$)(\$)(\$)(\$)(\$)
Middle St & Main St, Little Washington. (540) 675-3800.
This five-star and five-diamond restaurant offers regional, eclectic, American cuisine. The 90-minute drive might be discouraging, but the inviting country house makes it worthwhile *(see p169).*

Credit cards: MC, V

WILLIAMSBURG, VA: *Chowning's Tavern* (\$)(\$)
109 Duke of Gloucester St (at Queen St). (1-800-HISTORY.
This Colonial restaurant is a step back into the 18th century. Gambols (18th-century entertainments) take place nightly, and the food is old-fashioned, with such dishes as Welsh rarebit and stew.

Credit cards: AE, D, DC, MC, V

WILLIAMSBURG, VA: *The Trellis* (\$)(\$)(\$)
403 Duke of Gloucester St. (757) 229-8610.
Regional cuisine which concentrates on fresh food – the menu changes every season. Located in the heart of the historic district, it offers an extensive wine list with more than 20 wines from Virginia.

Credit cards: AE, D, DC, MC, V

SHOPPING IN WASHINGTON, DC

WASHINGTON'S VAST selection of stores makes shopping in the capital a pleasurable experience. Souvenirs can be found anywhere from fashion boutiques and specialist food stores to museum and gallery gift shops. The many museums on the Mall and around the city sell a wide variety of unusual gifts, reproduction prints, and replica artifacts selected from all over the world.

US Capitol in straw-work

Although the many smart shopping malls and department stores in the DC area can provide hours of shopping, Georgetown offers visitors a far more lively and authentic environment in which to browse. It is a neighborhood packed with fashionable clothing boutiques and endless interesting shops that sell everything from antiques to hair dye, from one-dollar bargains to priceless works of art.

East Hall of the Union Station shopping mall

OPENING HOURS

MOST DEPARTMENT stores, shopping malls, and other centers are open from 10am until 8 or 9pm, Monday through Saturday, and from noon until 7pm on Sunday. Smaller shops and boutiques are generally open from noon until 6pm on Sundays, and from 10 until 6 or 7pm on all other days. Convenience stores such as supermarkets and local grocery stores may open for longer hours. Drugstores (pharmacies) are also often open for extended hours.

HOW TO PAY

GOODS MAY BE paid for in cash, in traveler's checks (in US dollars), or by credit card. VISA and MasterCard are the most popular credit cards in the United States, while American Express is often, but not always, accepted. A tax of 5.75% is added to all purchases at the cash register.

SALES

DEPARTMENT STORES, such as **Hecht's** in the Old Downtown area and **Nordstrom** farther out in Arlington, often hold sales during holiday weekends, including Memorial Day, the 4th of July, Labor Day, and Columbus Day. Check the newspapers for advertisements to find good prices on electronics, jewelry, kitchenwares, shoes, and clothing. White sales (towels and bedlinen) occur in January.

Stalls selling an eclectic range of goods at Eastern Market

MUSEUM SHOPS

ALL THE MUSEUMS on the Mall have an incredibly wide selection of products on sale in their museum shops. The **National Gallery of Art** shop sells artwork reproductions, books, art-related games and children's toys, and the **Museum of African Art** shop offers a range of African textiles, ceramics, basketry, musical instruments, and books.

The **National Museum of American History** shop is the largest of the Smithsonian museum shops and carries a range of souvenirs, including American crafts, reproductions, and T-shirts, as well as a range of books on American history. The museum's music shop sells recordings from the 1940s to the 1970s, including Doo Wop, Motown, and Disco, from the Smithsonian Recordings and Smithsonian Folkways labels.

Also well worth a visit are two museum shops near the White House. **The Renwick Gallery** museum shop sells contemporary crafts made from glass, wood, fiber, metal, and ceramic, as well as silk scarves and tapestry purses. The shop at the **Decatur House Museum**, home of Stephen Decatur, a naval hero from the War of 1812, has a collection of items for sale related to Washington's history, art, and architecture.

For a selection of interesting books on architecture, contemporary design, and historic preservation, as well as a range of toys, ties, frames, and gifts, pay a visit to the **National Building Museum** shop at Judiciary Square.

Entrance to Hecht's Department Store on G Street, NW

MALLS AND DEPARTMENT STORES

THERE ARE a few small-scale shopping malls in central Washington, such as Georgetown Park and Union Station. **Georgetown Park** combines modern retail shops with a Victorian-style interior. It is situated at the intersection of Wisconsin Avenue and M Street, right in the heart of Georgetown. **Union Station**, the beautifully renovated train station in the Capitol Hill area *(see p53)*, houses 130 shops and restaurants on three levels, in a very pleasant environment. There are name-brand stores as well as an extensive collection of specialty shops that sell clothing, gifts, souvenirs, crafts, jewelry, and more.

Two small shopping malls are located on upper Wisconsin Avenue in the Friendship Heights neighborhood – **Mazza Gallerie** and **Chevy Chase Pavilion**. The metro is very convenient, but there is also plenty of parking for cars. Visitors can shop at Hecht's, one of several department stores, or the specialty boutiques and name-brand stores.

The larger malls are located in the Maryland and Virginia suburbs. The **Fashion Center at Pentagon City** is easily reached by metro. Discount-hunters should head for the 230 outlets at **Potomac Mills**, situated 30 miles (48 km) south of the city on I-95.

GALLERIES, ARTS, AND CRAFTS

VISITORS WILL discover a cornucopia of art galleries and crafts shops in three of Washington's neighborhoods – Georgetown, Dupont Circle, and Adams-Morgan. Here visitors can spend a few hours feasting their eyes on the delightful objects on display.

Work by several local artists is on sale in the **Addison/Ripley Galleries**, located in Dupont Circle and Georgetown. Some of the best pottery can be found in the **Appalachian Spring** shops in Georgetown and at Union Station. **Eastern Market** in Capitol Hill offers a vibrant mix of stalls from antiques to ethnic artifacts, and is best at weekends.

Art lovers should browse along 7th Street, NW, between D Street and the MCI Center. Among the highlights are pieces of sculpture and contemporary art at **Zenith Gallery** for sale from $50 to $50,000. Out of town, in Alexandria, the **Torpedo Factory Art Center** is excellent for lovers of all kinds of arts and crafts.

Torpedo Factory Art Center logo

SOUVENIRS

COLLECTORS' ITEMS and DC memorabilia are abundant at Political Americana and Made in America, two shops in **Union Station**. The **Old Post Office Pavilion** near Metro Center is also worth a visit for DC souvenirs. The gift shops in the **Kennedy Center** sell gifts and books about the performing arts and Washington in general. People looking for religious items or unusual souvenirs should try the **Washington National Cathedral** museum and book shop in the basement of the cathedral or the Herb Cottage, a renovated octagonal baptistry in the Cathedral grounds.

CLOTHES

WISCONSIN AVENUE and M Street in Georgetown are home to a wide range of clothing stores. National high-street chains include **The Gap** and **Eddie Bauer**, while those seeking something a little out of the ordinary should visit **Urban Outfitters**.

Among the many women's boutiques is **Betsey Johnson**, which specializes in sleek city fashions. Unique designs in ladieswear can be purchased at **Gazelle** in Chevy Chase Pavilion as well as at **Relish** on Wisconsin Avenue. Classic, well-tailored menswear can be bought from **Britches of Georgetown**. There is also a great variety of clothes shops at Friendship Heights.

FOOD AND WINE

FOR SOMETHING unusual, tasty, or exotic in the culinary field, there are several delicatessens worth visiting in Washington. In particular, try **Dean & Deluca** in Georgetown, or alternatively visit **Sutton Place Gourmet** at American University Park, near Massachusetts Avenue. Both have an excellent selection of gourmet foods and offer a fine range of American and European wines. While there, it is possible to sample the food and drinks available in their pleasant on-site cafés.

The Old Post Office Pavilion

One of many antique centers in Frederick

ANTIQUES

THERE ARE SOME wonderful hidden treasures to be discovered in the many antique stores scattered throughout Washington. Along Wisconsin Avenue, between P and S streets and also along M and O streets, there are around 20 antique shops. Some specialize in expensive antiques, others in prints, lamps, silverware, perfume bottles, or just interesting knick-knacks.

Adams-Morgan and Dupont Circle are also good neighborhoods for antique hunting. **Brass Knob Architectural Antiques**, on 18th Street, is worth visiting for their range of salvaged curiosities, including clawfoot bathtubs and unusual antique light fixtures. Customers are bound to leave with just the perfect relic for their home, which could be

anything from a chandelier to an iron gate.

There is also a number of centers for antiques outside central Washington. Kensington in Maryland and Old Town Alexandria in Virginia are areas rich in antiques. **Bird-in-the-Cage Antiques** in Alexandria sells all kinds of antiques, such as dolls, china, and silver, but specializes in books. In Frederick, Maryland, is the enormous **Emporium at Creekside Antiques**. This paradise for antiques lovers houses over 100 shops that sell everything from huge pieces of furniture through household wares to jewelry.

BOOKS AND MUSIC

BOOK LOVERS will enjoy spending time browsing in the myriad bookstores that can be found in Washington. As well as the large chainstores, such as **Barnes and Noble**, there are several excellent independent and second-hand bookstores, especially in the Dupont Circle area, such as **Olsson's Books and Records**, and **Kramerbooks & Afterwords Café**, where customers can sit with their new purchase and a coffee. **Second Story Books** is DC's biggest second-hand store.

Farther north, on Connecticut Avenue, is the **Politics & Prose Bookstore**, a favorite among Washingtonians for its

combination of books and coffee. Customers can chat with the knowledgeable staff, browse, or attend a reading. (The Sunday book review section of the *Washington Post* lists readings.)

The chainstore **Borders**, like Olsson's, sells both books and compact discs, which are competitively priced. Located near George Washington University is the music store **Tower Records**, which has the largest choice of compact discs in Washington, while **Melody Record Shop** sells music at discount prices.

MISCELLANEOUS

FOR CHINA AND bric-a-brac, shoppers should go no farther than **Little Caledonia** in Georgetown, which also stocks furniture. The many department stores in and around Washington, such as **Hecht's** and **Neiman-Marcus**, are well-stocked with good quality household wares from linens to cutlery and crockery. They are also prepared to order any out-of-stock items for customers.

Wake Up Little Suzie sells unusual and unique gifts, such as handmade books, jewelry, and hanging mobiles. Similarly, **Chocolate Moose**, on M Street, is a treasure trove of the unusual and unconventional, including ceramics, chocolates, jewelry, ceramics, and children's toys, amongst other things. For visitors fascinated by maps and travel, a visit to the **ADC Map and Travel Center** is essential. This shop has over 5,000 maps from around the world, as well as globes, guidebooks, and language books.

Everything in contemporary products for the home, from kitchenware to furniture, can be found at **Crate & Barrel** in Spring Valley and in Georgetown's **Pottery Barn**. Also in Georgetown is **Restoration Hardware**, which offers everything from decorative door knobs through gardening supplies and lamps, to old fashioned toys and the popular, heavy oak Mission furniture that originated in the Arts and Crafts Movement.

Shoppers browsing in the window of Olsson's bookstore

DIRECTORY

MALLS AND DEPARTMENT STORES

Chevy Chase Pavilion
5335 Wisconsin Ave, NW.
686-5335.

Fashion Center at Pentagon City
1100 South Hayes St,
Arlington, Virginia.
(703) 415-2400.

Georgetown Park
3222 M St, NW.
Map 1B2. 342-8190

Hecht's Department Store
12th & G St, NW.
Map 3C3. 628-6661

Mazza Gallerie Mall
5300 Wisconsin Ave, NW.
966-6114.

Neiman-Marcus
Mazza Gallerie. Map 1B1.
966-9700

Nordstrom
Fashion Center at
Pentagon City.
(703) 415-1121.

Potomac Mills
Dale City, VA.
(800) 826-4557.

Union Station Shops
40 Massachusetts Ave, NE.
Map 4 E3. 371-9441.

GALLERIES, ARTS, AND CRAFTS

Addison/Ripley Gallery
1670 Wisconsin Ave, NW.
Map 1 C2. 338-5180.

Appalachian Spring
1415 Wisconsin Ave, NW.
Map 1C2. 337-5780.

Eastern Market
225 7th St, SE. Map 4 F4.
546-2698.

Torpedo Factory Art Center
105 N. Union Street
Alexandria, VA.
(703) 838-4565.

Zenith Gallery
413 7th St, NW.
Map 3 C2. 783-2963.

ANTIQUES

Bird-in-the-Cage Antiques
110 King St,
Alexandria, VA.
(703) 549-5114.

Emporium at Creekside Antiques
112 E. Patrick St,
Frederick, MD.
(301) 662-7099.

Brass Knob Architectural Antiques
2311 18th St, NW.
Map 3 A1. 332-3370.

Georgetown Flea Market
Wisconsin Ave, between
S & T Sts, NW. Map 1 C3.

SOUVENIRS

Kennedy Center
New Hampshire Ave &
Rock Creek Parkway, NW.
Map 2 D4. 416-8346.

Old Post Office Pavilion
Pennsylvania Ave
& 12th St, NW. Map 3C3.
289-4224.

Washington National Cathedral
Massachusetts &
Wisconsin Ave, NW.
537-6267.

BOOKS AND MUSIC

Barnes and Noble
3040 M St, NW.
Map 2 D2. 965-9880.

Borders
1800 L St, NW.
Map 2 E3. 466-4999.

Kramerbooks & Afterwords Café
1517 Connecticut Ave, NW.
Map 2 E2. 387-1400.

Melody Record Shop
1623 Connecticut Ave, NW.
Map 2 E2. 232-4002.

Olsson's Books and Records
1239 Wisconsin Ave, NW.
Map 1 C2. 338-6712.

Politics & Prose Bookstore
5015 Connecticut Ave, NW.
Map 2 E2. 364-1919.

Second Story Books
2000 P Street, NW.
Map 1B1 659-8884.

Tower Records
2000 Pennsylvania Ave,
NW. Map 2 E3.
331-2400.

MUSEUM SHOPS

Decatur House Museum
1600 H St, NW.
Map 3 A3. 842-1856.

National Building Museum
401 F St, NW. Map 4 D3.
272-7706.

National Gallery of Art
Constitution Ave at
6th St, NW Map 4 D4.
842-6475.

National Museum of African Art
950 Independence Ave,
SW. Map 3 C4.
786-2147.

National Museum of American History
The Mall between 12th
and 14th Sts, NW.
Map 3 B4. 357-1528.

Renwick Gallery
17th & Pennsylvania
Ave, NW. Map 3 A3.
357-1445.

CLOTHES

Betsey Johnson
1319 Wisconsin Ave, NW.
Map 1 C2. 338-4090.

Britches of Georgetown
1247 Wisconsin Ave, NW.
Map 1 C2. 338-3330.

Eddie Bauer
3040 M St, NW.
Map 1 B2. 342-2121.

The Gap
1258 Wisconsin Ave, NW.
Map 1 B1. 333-2657.

Gazelle Ltd.
Chevy Chase Pavilion,
5335 Wisconsin Ave, NW.
686-5656.

Relish
5454 Wisconsin Ave,
Chevy Chase, Md.
(301) 654-9899.

Urban Outfitters
3111 M St, NW.
Map 1 C2. 342-1012.

FOOD AND WINE

Dean & Deluca
3276 M St, NW.
Map 1 C2. 342-2500.

Sutton Place Gourmet
3201 New Mexico Ave, NW.
363-5800.

MISCELLANEOUS

ADC Map and Travel Center
1636 I (Eye) St, NW.
Map 2 F3. 628-2608.

Chocolate Moose
1800 M St, NW.
Map 2 F2. 463-0992.

Crate & Barrel
4820 Massachusetts Ave,
NW. 364-6500.

Pottery Barn
3077 M St, NW.
Map 1 C2. 337-8900.

Little Caledonia
1419 Wisconsin Ave, NW.
Map 1 C1. 333-4700.

Restoration Hardware
1222 Wisconsin Ave, NW.
Map 1 C2. 625-2771.

Wake-Up Little Suzie
3409 Connecticut Ave, NW.
244-0700.

ENTERTAINMENT IN WASHINGTON, DC

VISITORS TO WASHINGTON will never be at a loss for entertainment, from flying a kite in the grounds of the Washington Monument to attending a concert at the Kennedy Center. The city's diverse, international community offers a rich array of choices. If you are looking for swing dancing you will find it; you will also hear different beats around town, including salsa, jazz, and rhythm and blues. Outdoor enthusiasts can

Baseball player

choose from cycling on the Rock Creek bike path to canoeing on the Potomac River. If you are looking for something less active, take in a film at the Smithsonian. Theatergoers have a wide range of choices, from Shakespeare through highly respected repertory companies to Broadway musicals. No matter what your budget is, you will find something to do. There are more free activities in DC than in any other American city.

![Façade of the John F. Kennedy Center for the Performing Arts]

Façade of the John F. Kennedy Center for the Performing Arts

INFORMATION SOURCES

THE BEST PLACE to find information is in the Weekend section of Friday's edition of the *Washington Post*. This lists concerts, plays, movies, children's activities, outdoor recreation, and fairs and festivals. Internet users can check out *Style Live*, the entertainment guide on the *Washington Post* website.

The "Where & When" section in the monthly *Washingtonian* magazine also lists events.

BOOKING TICKETS

TICKETS MAY BE bought in advance at box offices, or by phone, fax, and, in many cases, the Internet. Tickets for all events at the **Kennedy Center** can be obtained by phone through **Instant Charge**. Tickets for the MCI

Center, the Nissan Pavilion, and the Warner Theater can be bought by phone through **Ticketmaster**. For Arena, Lisner Auditorium, Ford's Theatre, Merriweather Post Pavilion, and Woolly Mammoth tickets, contact **Tickets.com**

DISCOUNT TICKETS

MOST THEATERS give group discounts, and several offer student and senior discounts for same-day

Façade of the Shakespeare Theatre on 7th Street

performances. Half-price tickets for seats on the day of the performance may be obtained in person at **Ticketplace**, situated inside the Old Post Office Pavilion.

In addition, theaters offer their own special discounts: The Arena sells a limited number of "Hottix," half-price seats, 30 to 90 minutes before the show. The Shakespeare Theatre offers 20 percent off for senior citizens Sunday through Thursday, 50 percent one hour before curtain rise for students, and discounts for all previews. The Kennedy Center has a limited number of half-price tickets available to students, senior citizens, and anyone with permanent disabilities. These go on sale at noon on the day of the performance (some are available before the first performance). Standing-room tickets may be available if a show is sold out.

FREE EVENTS

THE DAILY newspapers provide up-to-date listings of free lectures, concerts, gallery talks, films, book signings, poetry readings, and shows.

Local artists offer free performances on the Millennium Stage at the Kennedy Center every evening at 6pm.

The **National Symphony Orchestra** gives a free outdoor concert on the West Lawn of the Capitol on Labor Day and Memorial Day weekends, and on the Fourth of July. In

Courtyard concert in the National Gallery of Art

summer, various military bands such as the **United States Marine Band** or the **Army Band** give free concerts at different venues (contact for schedules). From October to June, the **National Gallery of Art** sponsors Sunday evening concerts at 7pm in the West Garden Court. Free lectures and gallery talks are held at the **Library of Congress** and also at the National Gallery of Art. At the Kennedy Center there are music and dance performances every 6pm on the **Millenium Stage**.

OPEN-AIR ENTERTAINMENT

DURING THE summer months at **Wolf Trap Farm Park for the Performing Arts** world-famous performers can

be seen on any night. Check their calendar of events and find your favorite form of entertainment – opera, jazz, Broadway musical, ballet, folk, or country music. You can bring a picnic to enjoy on the lawn.

On Thursday evenings in summer, the **National Zoo** hosts concerts on Lion Tiger Hill. They start at 6:30pm.

If you are in Washington in June try to catch the **Shakespeare Theatre Free for All** held at Carter Barron Amphitheater in Rock Creek Park.

The *Washington Post* lists the local fairs and festivals, held every weekend in warm weather. On the first weekend in May, the **Washington National Cathedral** sponsors the Flowermart, a festival featuring an old-fashioned carousel, children's games, crafts, and good food. The **Smithsonian Folklife Festival**, a two-week extravaganza held on the Mall at the end of June and early July, brings together folk artists

from around the world. For details of other annual events in the city, *see* Washington, DC Through The Year *(pp34–7)*.

FACILITIES FOR THE DISABLED

ALL THE MAJOR theaters in Washington are wheelchair accessible. For information on the Kennedy Center's accessibility services, check its website.

Many theaters, including the Kennedy Center, Ford's Theatre, the Shakespeare Theatre, and Arena Stage, have audio enhancement devices, as well as a limited number of signed performances. For the hearing impaired, TTY phone numbers are listed in the Weekend section of the *Washington Post*.

The National Gallery of Art provides assisted listening devices for lectures. Sign-language interpretation is available with three weeks' notice, and a telecommunications device for the deaf (TDD) can be found near the Concourse Sales Shop. For those with limited sight, the theater Arena Stage offers audio description, touch tours of the set, and program books in large print and Braille.

Cultural Events

For an evening out, Washington has much to offer. A seafood dinner on the waterfront followed by a play at Arena Stage, Washington's oldest repertory company; dancing at one of the new clubs on U Street; jazz in Georgetown; a late-night coffee bar in Dupont Circle; or opening night at the opera at the Kennedy Center and a nightcap in the west end. Or if you are staying downtown and do not want to venture far from your hotel, see a show at the Warner or the National Theater, where the best of Broadway finds a home.

Dancing to live music at the Kennedy Center

Sign on the façade of the Warner Theatre on 13th Street

FILM AND THEATER

For daily screenings of movie classics, as well as film premieres, the **American Film Institute** at the **Kennedy Center** is the place to go. Museums such as **The National Gallery of Art** show films relating to current exhibitions. **The Library of Congress** offers a free film series of documentaries and films related to the exhibits in the museum, shown in the Mary Pickford Theater. The DC Film Festival is based at the Lincoln Theatre.

National touring theater companies bring shows to the **John F. Kennedy Center for the Performing Arts**, the **Warner Theatre**, and the **National Theatre**. For a more intimate setting, try **Ford's Theatre**. **Arena Stage** has a well-established repertory company. **The Studio**, **The Source**, and the **Woolly Mammoth Theatre** produce contemporary works.

The Shakespeare Theatre produces works in a modern, elegant setting. For plays performed in Spanish, seek out the **Gala Hispanic Theater**.

OPERA AND CLASSICAL MUSIC

Based at the Kennedy Center, the **Washington Opera Company** is often considered one of the capital's crown jewels. Although many performances do sell out, standing room tickets are sometimes available. **The National Symphony Orchestra** performs classical and contemporary works.

A rich variety of chamber ensembles and choral groups perform regularly around the city. **The Washington Performing Arts Society** brings internationally renowned performers to DC.

DANCE

The Kennedy Center offers a magnificent ballet and dance season every year, with sell-out productions from the world's finest companies including the Bolshoi, the American Ballet Theater, the Royal Swedish Ballet, and the Dance Theater of Harlem.

Dance Place showcases its own professional modern dance companies, as well as international contemporary dance companies.

If you would prefer to take to the floor yourself, make your way to **Glen Echo Park** where people from ages 7 to 70 enjoy evenings of swing dancing, contra dancing (line dancing), Louisiana Cajun zdeco dancing, and waltzes. The Kennedy Center also occasionally has dancing to live bands.

ROCK, JAZZ, AND BLUES

To see the "biggest names and the hottest newcomers" in jazz, head for **The Kennedy Center Terrace Theater**. Oscar Brown, Jr., Phil Woods, Ernie Watts, and many more are featured here. You can hear international jazz stars at **Blues Alley** in Georgetown, or visit **Madam's Organ** in Adams-Morgan, home to some of the best R&B in Washington.

If you want to hear really big name rock stars or jazz artists, join thousands of fans at the **Merriweather Post Pavilion** in Columbia, Maryland, or at the **Nissan Pavilion** in Manassas, Virginia.

Interior of the highly respected Shakespeare Theatre

CLUBS, BARS, AND CAFÉS

For late night dancing and clubbing, try the U Street neighborhood. Most highly recommended are **Club U** and the **930 Night Club**.

For salsa try the **Rumba Café** in Adams-Morgan. If you fancy a cigar and a martini, then check out **Ozio Martini and Cigar Lounge** downtown. If Irish music is more your thing, head to **Ireland's Four Provinces** in Cleveland Park. **Georgetown Billiards** and other billiard parlors are also popular, as are the city's many coffee bars. **Xando Coffee and Bar** in Dupont Circle serves coffees and cocktails.

GAY CLUBS

Many of the gay bars in DC can be found in the Dupont Circle area. **JR's Bar and Grill** attracts young professionals. **Mr. P's** is one of the city's oldest gay bars. For a good meal, visit **Annie's Paramount Steak House**.

Interior of Rumba Café

DIRECTORY

FILM AND THEATER

Kennedy Center
New Hampshire Ave & Rock Creek Parkway, NW.
Map 2 D4. ☎ 785-4600 or (800) 444-1324.
ⓦ www.kennedycenter.org

Arena Stage
1101 6th St, SW.
Map 4 D5.
☎ 488-3300.
ⓦ www.arenastage.org

Ford's Theatre
511 10th St, NW.
Map 3 C3.
☎ 347-4833.
ⓦ www.fordstheatre.org

Gala Hispanic Theater
1625 Park Rd, NW.
☎ 234-7174.

Library of Congress
Mary Pickford Theater, Madison Building, 101 Independence Ave, SE.
Map 4 E4. ☎ 707-5677.
ⓦ www.loc.gov

National Gallery of Art
Constitution Ave at 6th St, NW. **Map** 4 D3.
☎ 737-4215.
ⓦ www.nga.org

National Theatre
1321 Pennsylvania Ave, NW. **Map** 3 B3.
☎ 628-6161.
ⓦ www.nationaltheatre.org

Shakespeare Theatre
450 7th St, NW.
Map 3 C3.
☎ 547-1122.
ⓦ www.shakespearedc.org

Source Theatre Company
1835 14th St, NW.
☎ 462-1073.
ⓦ sourcetheatre@aol.com

The Studio Theatre
14th & P Sts, NW.
Map 3 B1.
☎ 332-3300.
ⓦ www.studiotheate.org

Warner Theatre
1299 Pennsylvania Ave, NW.
Map 3 C3.
☎ 783-4000.

Woolly Mammoth Theatre
☎ 393-3939.

OPERA AND CLASSICAL MUSIC

National Symphony Orchestra
☎ 467-4600.

Washington Performing Arts Society
☎ 833-9800.

DANCE

Dance Place
3225 8th St, NE.
☎ 269-1600.

Glen Echo Park
Spanish Ballroom, 7300 MacArthur Blvd, Glen Echo, MD.
☎ (301) 492-6229.

ROCK, JAZZ, AND BLUES

Blues Alley
1073 Wisconsin Ave, NW.
Map 1 C3.
☎ 337-4141.

Madam's Organ
2461 18th St, NW.
Map 2 F1.
☎ 667-5370.

Merriweather Post Pavilion
Columbia, MD.
☎ (301) 982-1800 or (703) 218-6500 (Tickets.com) or (800) 955-5566.

Nissan Pavilion
7800 Cellar Door Drive, Haymarket, VA.
☎ (703) 754-6400

CLUBS, BARS, AND CAFÉS

Club U
2000 14th St, NW.
☎ 328-8859.

Georgetown Billiards
3251 Prospect St, NW.
Map 1 C2.
☎ 965-7665.

Ireland's Four Provinces
3412 Connecticut Ave, NW.
☎ 244-0860.

930 Night Club
815 V St, NW.
☎ 393-0930.

Ozio Martini and Cigar Lounge
1813 M St, NW.
Map 3 A1.
☎ 822-6000.

Rumba Café
2443 18th St, NW.
☎ 588-5501.

Xando Coffee and Bar
1647 20th St, NW.
Map 3 A1.
☎ 332-6364.

GAY CLUBS

Annie's Paramount Steak House
1609 17th St, NW.
Map 2 F2.
☎ 232-0395.

JR's Bar and Grill
1519 17th St, NW.
Map 2 F2.
☎ 328-0090.

Mr. P's
2147 P St, NW.
Map 1 C2.
☎ 293-10F

Sports and Outdoor Activities

THE PEOPLE OF WASHINGTON are known for putting in long hours – whether on the floor of the Senate, the office of a federal agency, or in a newsroom. They compensate, however, by taking their leisure hours very seriously by rooting for their favorite teams or spending as much time as possible outdoors. You can join in the fun at the MCI Center or the RFK Stadium, both of which attract hordes of fans. You can meet joggers, cyclists, and in-line skaters on the Mall and around the monuments.

Cyclists enjoying the fine weather outdoors in DC

SPECTATOR SPORTS

FANS OF THE NHL Capitals (National Hockey League), the NBA Wizards (National Basketball Association), and the WNBA Mystics (Women's National Basketball Association) should purchase tickets at the **MCI Center**, an impressive sports arena that opened in December 1997 and has helped revitalize the downtown area.

Depending on the season, you might also see Disney on Ice, the Harlem Globetrotters, or the Ringling Brothers Circus. Visit the MCI's National Sports Gallery, which houses sports memorabilia and interactive sports games. There is plenty to eat at the MCI Center, but you may prefer to slip out to one of the restaurants in Chinatown, which surrounds the MCI Center.

If you are not a season-pass holder, it is very difficult to get a ticket to a Washington Redskins game at the **FedEx Field** stadium, but you can always watch the game from one of Washington's popular sports bars. The DC United team plays soccer at the **RFK Stadium**. College sports are also very popular in DC – you will find Washingtonians cheering either for the **Georgetown Hoyas** or the **Maryland Terrapins**.

FISHING AND BOATING

IF YOU WANT TO spend an hour or perhaps an entire day by the Potomac River, the best place to start is **Fletcher's Boat House** at Canal and Reservoir Roads. You must obtain a permit if you are between 16 and 64, which lasts for a year but does not cost much. You can fish from the riverbank or rent a rowboat or canoe, which are available by the hour or the day.

Redskins team member

In Georgetown there are boats for rent at **Thompson's Boat Center** and **Jack's Boats**. Snacks can be bought at Fletcher's, or you may want to bring a picnic. If you go to Thompson's or Jack's there are cafés and restaurants along the waterfront.

CYCLING

ROCK CREEK PARK is one of Washington's greatest treasures and offers amazing respite from busy city life. Closed to traffic on weekends, it is a great place for cycling. Another popular trail is the Capital Crescent, which starts on the C&O Canal towpath in Georgetown and runs to Maryland.

One of the more beautiful bike trails in the area will take you 16 miles (26 km) to Mount Vernon. Bikes can be rented at Fletcher's Boat House, Thompson's Boat Center, or **Big Wheels** in Georgetown. For maps or trail information call or write to the **Washington Area Bicyclist Association**, or consult one of the bike rental shops in the city.

TENNIS, GOLF, AND HORSEBACK RIDING

SEVERAL NEIGHBORHOOD parks have outdoor tennis courts, available on a first-come, first-served basis. Two public clubs in the city accept reservations: **East Potomac Tennis Club** at Hains Point, and the **Washington Tennis Center**. Both have outdoor and indoor courts.

If you want to take in views of the monuments while walking the golf fairways, go to the **East Potomac Golf Course & Driving Range**. (There is an 18-hole miniature golf course here as well.) Two other courses are open to the public: **Langston Golf Course** on the Anacostia River and

... FK Stadium, cheering on their favorite teams

Rock Creek Golf Course, tucked into Rock Creek Park. You will also find **Rock Creek Park Horse Center**, where you can make reservations for a guided trail ride.

EXPLORING NATURE

FOR AN AMAZING array of trees and plants, visit the **National Arboretum** *(see p138)*, which covers 444 acres in northeast Washington. There is something interesting to see all year round in the arboretum. Special displays, such as the National Bonsai Collection of miniature plants, can be enjoyed at any time of year. To catch the best of the flowering shrubs, the beautiful camellias and magnolias flower in late March through early April, and the stunning, rich colors of the azaleas, rhododendron, and dogwood appear from late April through early May. There is a 1,600-ft (490-m) long "touch and see trail" at the garden for visually impaired visitors.

The beautiful and tranquil grounds of the National Arboretum

An alternative to the arboretum is **Kenilworth Aquatic Gardens**, which has 14 acres of ponds with more than 100,000 water lilies, lotuses, and other plants. It is a good idea to plan a trip early in the day when the blooms are open and before the sun gets too hot. Frogs and turtles can be seen regularly along the footpaths around the ponds. Park naturalists conduct nature walks around the gardens on summer weekends.

One of the most enjoyable ways to spend time outdoors is with a picnic in the park. Visit **Dumbarton Oaks Park** in Georgetown when the wildflowers are in bloom, or visit **Montrose Park**, right next door to Dumbarton Oaks, where you can enjoy the variety of birds and the boxwood maze.

DIRECTORY

SPECTATOR SPORTS

FedEx Field
Raljon Rd,
Landover, MD.
(*(301) 276-6000.*

Georgetown Hoyas
(*687-4692*
(for tickets).

Maryland Terrapins
(*(800) 462-8377*
(for tickets).

MCI Center
601 F St, NW.
Map 4 D3.
(*628-3200.*

RFK Stadium
2400 East Capitol St, SE.
(*547-9077.*

FISHING AND BOATING

Fletcher's Boat House
4940 Canal Rd, NW.
Map 1 A2.
(*244-0461.*

Jack's Boats
3500 K St, NW.
Map 2 D2.
(*337-9642.*

Thompson Boat Center
Rock Creek Parkway
& Virginia Ave, NW.
Map 2 D3.
(*333-9543.*

CYCLING

Big Wheel Bikes
1034 33rd St, NW.
Map 1 C2.
(*337-0254.*

Washington Area Bicyclist Association
733 15th St, NW.
Map 3 B1. (*628-2500.*

TENNIS, GOLF, AND HORSEBACK RIDING

East Potomac Golf Course
972 Ohio Drive, SW at
Hains Point. **Map** 3 A5.
(*554-7660.*

East Potomac Tennis Club
1090 Ohio Drive, SW at
Hains Point. **Map** 3 A5.
(*554-5962.*

Langston Golf Course
26th St & Benning Rd, NE.
(*397-8638.*

Rock Creek Golf Course
16th & Rittenhouse Sts,
NW.
(*882-7332.*

Rock Creek Park Horse Center
Military & Glover Rds, NW.
(*362-0118.*

Washington Tennis Center
16th & Kennedy Sts, NW.
(*722-5949.*

EXPLORING NATURE

Dumbarton Oaks Park
Entrance on Lovers Lane,
off R & 31st Sts, NW.
Map 1 C1.

Kenilworth Aquatic Gardens
1500 Anacostia Ave, SE.
(*426-6905.*

Montrose Park
R & 31st Sts, NW
Map 2 D1.

National Arboretum
New York Ave &
Bladensburg Rd, NE.
(*245-2726.*

Children's Washington, DC

VISITING THE CITY's monuments can be one of the favorite and most memorable activities for children in DC. Call in advance to arrange a tour with a park ranger, during which you take a trip in the elevator to the top of the Washington Monument, then walk down the steps. Young children will like feeding the ducks at the Reflecting Pool or Constitution Gardens. You can view the Jefferson Memorial from a paddleboat on the Tidal Basin, and before you leave Washington be sure to see the monuments lit up against the night-time sky.

Children in front of the National Museum of Natural History

PRACTICAL ADVICE

FOR INFORMATION on specific events for children see the "Saturday's Child" page in the Weekend section of Friday's *Washington Post*.

Food is widely available in DC, whether it is hot dogs from a seller along the Mall, strange space food (such as freeze-dried ice cream) from the **National Air and Space Museum** gift shop (*see pp60–63*), or an impressive star-spangled banana split at the Palm Court café at the **National Museum of American History** (*see pp70–73*).

Sculpture from Children's Museum

OUTDOOR FUN

FOR A TRIP INTO the past, take a ride on *The Georgetown*, a mule-drawn barge on the C&O Canal from April to mid-October (contact the **C&O Canal Visitor Center** for details). Park Service rangers dressed in 19th-century costumes add to the experience.

The beautiful wooded park of the **National Zoo** (*see*

pp132–3) is a good place for a walk, and you can also enjoy watching elephant training and sea lion demonstrations.

For a break from the Mall museums, take a ride on the **Carousel on the Mall**, in front of the Arts and Industries Building. Also worth a visit is the carousel in **Glen Echo Park**, built in 1921. From December to March, ice skaters can head for the outdoor rink at the **National Gallery of Art Sculpture Garden**. Or try **Pershing Park Ice Rink**, located on Pennsylvania Avenue, across from the Willard Hotel. Skate rentals are available.

MUSEUMS

THE DISCOVERY Center, a vast educational complex with an IMAX® theater, is housed in the **National Museum of Natural History** (*see pp66–7*).

If you want to experience outer space, then see "To Fly!" and the Albert Einstein Planetarium at the **National Air and Space Museum**.

A series of children's films and family programs are run by the **National Gallery of Art** (*see pp56–9*). Children can discuss paintings and take part in a range of hands-on activities.

The **Capital Children's Museum** (*see p51*) is a big hit with children – a fun-filled environment with a wide variety of activities.

Dollhouse aficionados will just love the **Washington Doll House and Toy Museum** which is located in Friendship Heights.

Children are always fascinated by the **National Postal Museum** (*see p51*), with its many intriguing hands-on activities.

CHILDREN'S THEATER

THE Arts and Industries Building (*see p64*) houses the **Discovery Theater**, which stages puppet shows and plays. See a puppet show or fairytale production at the **Adventure Theater** in Glen Echo Park.

The **Kennedy Center** (*see p112–3*) and **Wolf Trap Farm Park for the Performing Arts** also provide information on all sorts of children's events in the city.

A LITTLE BIT OF HISTORY

CHILDREN STUDYING American history will be fascinated by a visit to Cedar Hill, once the home of Frederick Douglass, in Anacostia. The video in the visitors' center

Children's tour in Cedar Hill, the historic home of Frederick Douglass

helps to tell the amazing story of this American hero.

You can take a tour of **Ford's Theatre** *(see p90)* where President Lincoln was shot and the house across the street where he died.

On Saturdays **Washington National Cathedral** *(see pp136–7)* runs a Medieval Workshop. This is a hands-on learning center where children can make their own stained-glass windows, create clay gargoyles, or make brass rubbings. The Gargoyle Tour of the Cathedral is particularly interesting; weather permitting, it is possible to touch a gargoyle or two from the cathedral balcony.

Shopping

The **Discovery Channel Stores**, which are located in Union Station and Fashion Central, Pentagon City, sell a range of international merchandise, including science kits, fossils, books, and globes.

The **National Museum of Natural History** *(see pp66–7)* shops stock books, science kits, natural history toys, and games related to sea life, dinosaurs, and nature.

The **National Geographic Society** *(see p128)* has special exhibitions which children find absorbing and fascinating, and the store stocks videos, books, and back issues of its famous magazine.

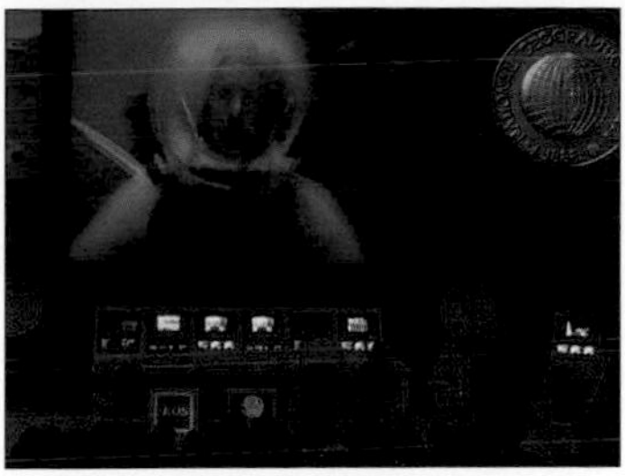

Simulation of sea exploration in the National Geographic Society's Jason Project

Directory

Practical Advice

National Air and Space Museum
6th St & Independence Ave, SW. **Map** 4 D4.
357-2700.

National Museum of American History
Constitution Ave between 12th & 14th Sts, NW.
Map 3 B4. *357-2700.*

Outdoor Fun

C&O Canal Visitor Center
1057 Thomas Jefferson St, NW. **Map** 2 D3.
653-5190.

Carousel on the Mall
Arts and Industries Blg, 900 Jefferson Drive, SW
Map 3 B4. *357-2700.*

Glen Echo Park Carousel
7300 MacArthur Blvd, Glen Echo, MD.
(301) 492-6282.

National Gallery of Art Sculpture Garden Rink
7th St & Constitution Ave, NW. **Map** 4 D4.
371-9359.

National Zoo
3001 Connecticut Ave.
673-4800.

Pershing Park Ice Rink
Pennsylvania Ave & 14th St, NW.
Map 3 B3.
737-6938.

Museums

Capital Children's Museum
3rd & H Sts, NE.
Map 4 F2.
675-4120.
www.ccm.org

National Air and Space Museum
6th St & Independence Ave, SW. **Map** 4 D4.
357-1686 (IMAX® film schedule).

National Gallery of Art
Constitution Ave between 3rd & 7th Sts, NW.
Map 4 D3.
789-4995 (children's film program).
789-3030 (family program).

National Museum of American History
Constitution Ave between 12th & 14th Sts, NW.
Map 3 B4.
357-2700.

National Museum of Natural History
10th St & Constitution Ave, NW.
Map 3 C4.
357-2700 (general information).
633-7400 (IMAX® film schedule).

National Postal Museum
2 Massachusetts Ave, NE.
Map 4 E3.
357-2700.

Washington Doll House and Toy Museum
5236 44th St, NW.
244-0024.

Children's Theater

Adventure Theater
7300 MacArthur Blvd, Glen Echo Park, Md.
(301) 320-5331.

Discovery Theater
900 Jefferson Drive, SW.
Map 3 C4.
357-1500.

Wolf Trap Farm Park for the Performing Arts
1551 Trap Rd, Vienna, VA.
(703) 255-1900.
www.wolftrap.org

A Little Bit of History

Ford's Theatre
511 10th St, NW.
Map 3 C3.
347-4833.
www.fordstheatre.org

Frederick Douglass National Historic Site
1411 W St, SE.
426-5961.

Washington National Cathedral
Massachusetts & Wisconsin Aves, NW.
537-2934 (Medieval workshop).
537-2934 (Gargoyle tour).
www.cathedral.org

Shopping

Discovery Channel Store
Fashion Central, Pentagon City. *(703) 413-3425.*
Union Station.
842-3700.

National Geographic Store
17th & M Sts, NW.
Map 3 B2. *857-7591.*

National Museum of Natural History Shops
Constitution Ave between 12th and 14th Sts, NW.
Map 3 C4. *357-1535.*

SURVIVAL
GUIDE

PRACTICAL INFORMATION

Tour operator sign

WASHINGTON, DC is the heart of the American political world. It is a visitor-friendly place, especially to children and the disabled, since wheelchair accessibility is required almost everywhere. The whole city shuts down on federal holidays as well as anytime the government requires it to, which may be right in the middle of your vacation. With the President of the US and other world leaders often coming and going in the city, unexpected delays and closures can occur. Spring and fall are the best times to visit as the summer can get very hot and the winters very cold.

Visitor Information Center at the Ellipse, near the White House

FOREIGN VISITORS

THE CONDITIONS for entering Washington are the same as for entering other parts of the United States. Citizens of the UK, most western European countries, Australia, New Zealand, and Japan need a valid passport but are not required to have a visa, as long as they stay for less than 90 days, hold a return ticket, and enter the US on an airline in the visa waiver program (which includes all the major carriers). Canadian citizens need only proof of residence. Citizens of all other countries require a valid passport and a tourist visa, which can be obtained from a US consulate or embassy.

TOURIST INFORMATION

THE WASHINGTON area welcomes visitors. Visitor information desks at the airports will provide guides and maps, and staff will be able to answer questions. Major hotels usually have a knowledgeable and helpful guest services desk. There are also a number of other organizations it may be worth contacting before your visit, especially the **Washington, DC Convention and Visitors Association**.

OPENING HOURS

FOR THE MOST PART business hours in DC are from 9am to 5pm. Often malls or department stores will stay open later or have extended hours on a certain day of the week. Shopping on Sundays can be limited, though many gas stations and convenience stores stay open 24 hours. Federal holidays are taken seriously in DC, and many businesses close. Before making arrangements it is worth checking if any such days occur during your stay.

ETIQUETTE

SMOKING IS prohibited in many buildings, restaurants, and stores in the DC area. Check for no-smoking signs before lighting up, or simply smoke outside if you are not sure. Tipping is expected for most services: in restaurants tip 15-20 percent of the bill, give $1.00 per bag to airport and hotel porters, and $2.00 to valet parking attendants. Bartenders expect 50 cents to $1.00 per drink; if you visit a hair salon or barbershop, 10 percent of the bill should suffice.

TAX

IN DC AND the surrounding area be aware that taxes will be added to hotel and restaurant charges, theater tickets, some grocery and store sales, and for almost all other purchases. Be sure to ask whether the tax is included in the price. Sales tax is 5.75 percent, and hotel tax is 14.5 percent.

ALCOHOL AND CIGARETTES

THE LEGAL AGE for drinking alcohol in Washington is 21, and you may need photo identification (I.D.) as proof of your age in order to purchase alcohol and be allowed into bars. It is illegal to drink alcohol in public parks or to carry an open container of alcohol in your car, and penalties for driving under the influence of alcohol are severe. Cigarettes can be purchased by those over 18 years old; proof of age may be required.

ELECTRICITY

Standard US two-prong plug

ELECTRICITY FLOWS at the standard US 110-120 volts, and a two-prong plug is required. For non-US appliances you will need a plug adapter and a voltage converter. Without a voltage converter you will find that powerful electrical appliances such as hairdryers will not only operate poorly but may also overload. You will find that many hotels will provide guests with such items as hairdryers and coffee machines. There are sockets for electrical shavers in most rooms.

International Student Identity Card, accepted as I.D. in America.

STUDENTS

STUDENTS FROM abroad should purchase an International Student I.D. before traveling to Washington, as many discounts are available in the city to students. The ISIC handbook lists places and services in the US that offer discounts to card holders, including accommodations, museums, and theaters. The **Student Advantage Card** is available to all American college undergraduates and offers a range of discounts.

CHILDREN

WASHINGTON IS a very child-friendly city; it even boasts its own children's museum, the Capital Children's Museum *(see p51)*. Many other museums offer exciting hands-on facilities or interesting exhibits for children, such as the collection of 18th- and 19th-century dolls at the Daughters of the American Revolution museum *(see p108)*.

For further information on entertainment for children in Washington, see pp190–91.

Restaurants are becoming increasingly family-oriented, and many provide children's menus or small portions to suit a child's appetite.

SENIOR CITIZENS

ANYONE OVER THE age of 65 is eligible for discounts with the appropriate proof of age. Contact the **American Association of Retired Persons** for further information. Also the Smithsonian produces a free booklet called *Smithsonian Access* with valuable information on parking areas, wheelchair accessibility, and sign language interpreters available around the DC area.

DISABLED VISITORS

WASHINGTON is one of the most convenient cities for people with disabilities. Almost all public buildings, including most hotels and restaurants, are required to be wheelchair accessible. For more information contact the **Society for Accessible Travel and Hospitality** or the Washington, DC Convention and Visitors Association for a free fact sheet on accessibility around the city.

Disabled sign

GUIDED TOURS

THERE ARE MANY city bus tours available in DC. **Tourmobile Sightseeing** has numerous signed pick-up points and extensive routes. But for something a bit different try the **DC Ducks**. Another entertaining option is the **Scandal Tour**, a bus ride around the city to the sites of various political scandals.

The **Old Town Trolley Tours** offer an excellent ride around the main sites in an old-fashioned trolley bus.

DIRECTORY

VISITOR INFORMATION

Washington, DC Convention and Visitors Association
Suite 600, 1212 New York Ave., NW. **Map** 3 C2. [*(202) 789-7000.* [w] www.washington.org

GUIDED TOURS

DC Ducks
Union Station. **Map** 4 E3.
[*(202) 832-9800.*
[w] www.historictours.com

Old Town Trolley Tours
Union Station. **Map** 4 E3.
[*(202) 832-9800.*
[w] www.historictours.com

Scandal Tour
Old Post Office Pavilion, 1100 Pennsylvania Ave. NW. **Map** 3 C3.
[*(800) 758-8687.*

Tourmobile Sightseeing
Union Station. **Map** 4 E3.
[*(202) 554-5100.*

STUDENTS

International Student I.D./Student Advantage Card
280 Summer St., Boston, MA 02110. [*(800) 333-2920.*
[w] www.studentadvantage.com

SENIOR CITIZENS

American Association for Retired Persons (A.A.R.P.)
601 E St. NW. **Map** 4 D3.
[*(800) 424-3410.* [*(703) 739-9220.* [w] www.aarp.org

Smithsonian Institution Information
Smithsonian Institution
Washington, DC, 20560–0010
[*(202) 357-2700.*
[*(202) 357-1729 (TDD).*
[w] www.si.edu

DISABLED VISITORS

Society for Accessible Travel and Hospitality
347 Fifth Ave. Suite 610
New York, NY 10016.
[*(212) 447-7284.*
[w] www.sath.org

A restored 1942 amphibious vehicle used by DC Ducks to tour the city

Personal Security and Health

Park police badge

ALTHOUGH AS in any major city there is crime, Washington has made great efforts in reducing problems and cleaning up its streets, and with great success. If you stick to the tourist areas and avoid straying into outlying areas, you should not run into any trouble. The main sights are located in safe areas where there are lots of people, and major crime is rare. When visiting sights off the beaten track, take a taxi to and from the destination. Most importantly, pay attention to your surroundings.

LAW ENFORCEMENT

THERE ARE nine different police forces in Washington, including the secret service, park rangers, S.W.A.T. (Special Weapons and Tactics) teams, and the more typical M.P.D.C. (Metropolitan Police, Washington, DC) police in blue uniforms.

Because the city is home to the President, whenever he travels, members of the law enforcement agencies follow. When foreign political leaders visit, the police are even more visible than usual: you will see them on horseback, on bicycles, in cars, and even on top of buildings.

As a visitor, should you encounter any trouble, approach any of the blue-uniformed M.P.D.C. officers that regularly patrol the city streets.

GUIDELINES ON SAFETY

SERIOUS CRIME is rarely witnessed in the main sightseeing areas of Washington. However, avoid wandering into areas that you have no reason to visit, either during the day or at night. Pickpockets do operate in the city and will target anyone who looks like a tourist. Police officers regularly patrol the tourist areas, but it is still advisable to prepare the day's itinerary in advance, use common sense, and stay alert. Try not to advertise that you are a tourist; study your map before you set off, avoid wearing expensive jewelry, and carry your camera or camcorder securely. Carry small amounts of cash; credit cards or traveler's checks are a more secure option. Keep these close to your body in a money belt or inside pocket.

Before you leave home, make a photocopy of your important documents, including your passport and visa, and keep them with you, though separate from the originals. Also make a note of your credit card numbers, in case of theft or loss. Keep an eye on your belongings at all times, whether you are checking into or out

of a hotel, standing in the airport, or sitting in a restaurant. Do not allow strangers into your hotel room or give them details of where you are staying. It is a good idea to put any valuables in the hotel safe – do not carry them around with you. Most hotels will not guarantee the security of any belongings that you leave in your room.

LOST PROPERTY

ALTHOUGH THE CHANCES of retrieving lost property are slim, you should report all stolen items to the police. Telephone the **Police Non-Emergency Line** for guidance. Make sure you keep a copy of the police report, which you will need when

Hospital sign

you make your insurance claim. In case of loss, it is useful to have a list of serial numbers or a photocopy of all documents; keep these separate as proof of possession. If you can remember to do so, it is useful to make a mental note of the taxi company or bus route you use; it might make it easier to retrieve lost items.

If your passport is lost or stolen, get in touch with your country's embassy or consulate immediately.

If you lose your credit cards, most card companies have toll-free numbers for reporting a loss or theft, as do Thomas Cook and American Express for lost traveler's checks *(see p199)*.

TRAVEL INSURANCE

TRAVEL INSURANCE is not compulsory but strongly recommended when traveling to the United States. It is particularly important to have insurance for emergency medical and dental care, which can be very expensive in the States. Even with medical coverage you may have to pay for the services, then claim reimbursement from your insurance company. If you take medication, bring a back-up prescription with

M.P.D.C. officer

Park ranger

Police car

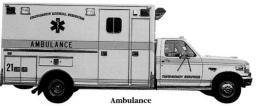

Ambulance

Fire engine

you. In addition, it is advisable to make sure your personal property is insured and obtain coverage for lost or stolen baggage and travel documents, as well as trip cancellation fees, legal advice, and accidental death or injury.

EMERGENCIES

IF YOU ARE involved in a medical emergency, go to a hospital emergency room. Should you need an ambulance, call 911 and one will be sent. Also call 911 for police or fire assistance.

If you have your medical insurance properly arranged, you need not worry about medical costs. Depending on the limitations of your insurance, it is better to avoid the overcrowded city-owned hospitals listed in the phone book Blue Pages, and opt instead for one of the private hospitals listed in the Yellow Pages. Alternatively ask at your hotel desk or at the nearest convenience store for information. Or you can ask your hotel to call a doctor or dentist to visit you in your room.

Fire Department logo

PHARMACIES

IF YOU NEED a prescription dispensed, there are plenty of pharmacies (drugstores) in and around the city, some staying open 24 hours. Ask your hotel for the nearest one.

LEGAL ASSISTANCE

NON-US CITIZENS requiring legal assistance should telephone their embassy. The embassy will not lend you money but can help with advice on legal matters in emergencies. Should you be arrested for any reason, you have the right to remain silent. Do not offer the police money in the form of a bribe; this could land you in jail.

PUBLIC CONVENIENCES

ALL VISITOR'S CENTERS, museums, and galleries have public restrooms, and invariably offer disabled and baby-changing facilities as well. All restaurants and hotels also have restrooms, but may only be available to paying customers.

DIRECTORY

LOST PROPERTY

Police Non-Emergency Line
(727-1010.

MEDICAL MATTERS

CVS 24-Hour Pharmacy
1199 Vermont Ave, NW.
Map 3 B2. (628-0720.

6–7 Dupont Circle, NW.
Map 2 F2. (785-1466.

EMERGENCIES

Police, Fire, Medical (all emergencies)
(Call 911, or dial 0 for the operator.

Medical Services
Dental Referrals
(547-7615.

Medical Referrals
(800 362-8677.

Area Hospitals
(Call 411 for directory assistance.

Crime Victims Line
(232-6682.

EMBASSIES

Australia
1601 Massachusetts Ave, NW.
Map 2 F2. (797-3000.
W www.austemb.org

Canada
501 Pennsylvania Ave, NW.
Map 4 D3. (682-1740.
W www.canadianembassy.org

Ireland
2234 Massachusetts Ave, NW.
Map 3 A1. (462-3939.
W www.irelandemb.org

New Zealand
37 Observatory Circle, NW.
(328-4800.
W www.nzemb.org

United Kingdom
3100 Massachusetts Ave, NW.
(462-1340.
W www.britainusa.org

Banking and Currency

THROUGHOUT WASHINGTON there are various places to access and exchange your money, from banks to cash machines to bureaux de change. The most important thing to remember is not to carry all your money and credit cards with you at once, and have enough cash to get you through Sunday when most banks and currency exchange offices are closed.

ATM for Chevy Chase Bank, one of the popular banks in DC

BANKING

GENERALLY, MOST BANKS are open Monday through Friday from 9am to 2 or 3pm, although some may open earlier and close later. Most banks also open Saturday mornings from 9am to noon or 1pm. All banks are closed on Sundays and Federal holidays (see p37.)

Always ask if there are any special fees before you make your transaction. At most banks, traveler's checks in US dollars can be cashed with any photo identification, although passports are usually required to exchange foreign money. Foreign currency exchange is available at the main branches of large banks; they often have a separate area or teller window specifically for foreign exchange.

ATMs

AUTOMATED TELLER machines (ATMs) are found all over the Washington area, usually near the entrance to banks, or inside many convenience stores and supermarkets.

Widely accepted bank cards include Cirrus, Plus, NYCE, and some credit cards such as VISA or MasterCard. Note that

a fee may be levied on your withdrawal, depending on the bank. Check with your bank which ATMs your card can access and the various fees charged. To minimize the risk of robbery, use ATMs in well-lit, populated areas only. Avoid withdrawing money at night or in isolated areas, and be aware of the people around you.

CREDIT CARDS

AMERICAN EXPRESS, VISA, MasterCard, Diner's Club, and the Discover Card are accepted almost everywhere in Washington, from theaters and hotels to restaurants and shops. Besides being a safer alternative to carrying a lot of cash, many credit cards also offer additional benefits such as insurance on goods purchased and bonus air miles on certain airline carriers. They can also be used to reserve a hotel or rental car.

In emergencies, credit cards are very useful when cash may not be readily available.

American Express credit cards

FOREIGN EXCHANGE

EXCHANGE OFFICES are generally open weekdays from 9am to 5pm, but some, especially those in shopping districts, may have extended opening hours.

Among the best known are **American Express Travel Service** and **Thomas Cook Currency Services**, both of which have branches in DC and the surrounding areas. **Sun Trust Bank** also has a foreign exchange service. For more listings look in the Yellow Pages for the main branch location of any major bank. Most exchange offices charge a fee or commission, so it is worth looking around to get the best value rates. Hotels often charge a higher rate of exchange or commission than currency exchange offices or banks.

TRAVELER'S CHECKS

WHEN BUYING traveler's checks, be sure to get them in US dollars rather than your own currency. It is often simpler to pay by US dollars traveler's checks, where possible, rather than cashing them in advance, and checks issued by American Express and Thomas Cook in US dollars are accepted as payment without a fee by most stores, restaurants, and hotels. However, traveler's checks in foreign currencies can be cashed at a bank or with a cashier at a major hotel. Exchange rates are listed in all daily newspapers and are posted at banks where currency exchange services are offered, and at all exchange offices. A fee or commission is always charged; ask about this before you exchange your money – it is a good idea to shop around for the best deal as commission rates can vary.

Personal checks issued by foreign banks are rarely accepted in the United States so cannot be relied upon as a means of obtaining cash.

Coins

American coins (actual size shown) come in 1-dollar, 50-, 25-, 10-, 5-, and 1-cent pieces. There are also goldtone $1 coins in circulation and State quarters, which feature an historical scene on one side. Each coin has a popular name: 25-cent pieces are called quarters, 10-cent pieces are called dimes, 5-cent pieces are called nickels, and 1-cent pieces called pennies.

25-cent coin (a quarter)

10-cent coin (a dime)

5-cent coin (a nickel)

1-cent coin (a penny)

An American Eagle from old currency

Bills (Bank Notes)

Units of currency in the United States are dollars and cents. There are 100 cents to a dollar. Bills come in $1, $5, $10, $20, $50 and $100s. All bills are the same color, so check the amount carefully. The new $5, $10, $20, $50, and $100 bills (below) are now in circulation; they have very large numbers.

1- dollar bill ($1)

5- dollar bill ($5)

10- dollar bill ($50)

20- dollar bill ($20)

50- dollar bill ($50)

100- dollar bill ($100)

Communications

US Mail stamp

COIN- OR CARD-OPERATED public pay-phones are easy to find on many streets and in restaurants, theaters, bars, department stores, hotel lobbies, and gas stations. Since Washington, DC is the political capital of the United States, news is readily available from newspapers, magazines, television, and radio. For help with the correct postage when sending mail, ask at your hotel or go to one of the many post offices around the city.

PUBLIC TELEPHONES

PUBLIC TELEPHONES are found on street corners all over the DC area. The area code for Washington is 202. When dialing within the district, omit the code. When dialling outside the district from within DC, you will need to use the appropriate area code.

Credit card calls can be made by calling 1-800-CALL-ATT or by having ample change to put in the phone when the charge for using the card is announced. Directory Assistance is 411 and calls are charged as a local rate.

Sign for Western Union

TELEPHONE CHARGES

LOCAL CALLS COST around 35 cents for three minutes from pay phones. Calls made from hotel rooms will cost much more, so it is a good idea to walk to the pay phone in the lobby of your hotel to make a call, rather than using the phone in your room. Operator assistance can be used for making calls, but again, this will cost more. Phone cards of various values can be purchased from most supermarkets, 24-hour stores, newspaper stands, and some branches of **Western Union**.

FAXES

FAX MACHINES can be found in Western Union and **Mailboxes Etc.** stores; they charge per page to send or to receive. Many hotels provide a fax service too, but again charges may be incurred.

CYBERCAFÉS

KEEPING IN TOUCH via the Internet is made easy by visiting any one of the Internet cafés in the city, such as the **Cyberstop Café**. For around $8 an hour you can surf the Net or send e-mails on one of their six computers.

USING A COIN-OPERATED PHONE

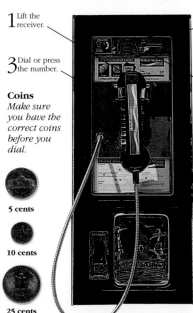

1 Lift the receiver.

3 Dial or press the number.

Coins
Make sure you have the correct coins before you dial.

5 cents

10 cents

25 cents

2 Insert the necessary coin or coins. The coin drops as soon as you insert it.

4 If you do not want to complete your call or it does not get through, retrieve the coin(s) by pressing the coin return.

5 If the call is answered and you talk longer than the allotted three minutes, the operator will interrupt and ask you to deposit more coins. Pay phones do not give change.

USEFUL DIALING CODES

- To make a direct-dial call outside the local area code, but within the US and Canada, dial **1** before the area code. Useful area codes for DC and the surrounding area include: Baltimore **410**; MD **301**; Delaware **302**; Northern Virginia **703**; West Virginia **304**.
- For international direct-dial calls, dial **011** followed by the appropriate country code. Then dial the area code, omitting the first 0, and the local number.
- To make an international call via the operator, dial **01** and then follow the same procedure as detailed above.
- For international operator assistance, dial **01**.
- For local operator assistance, dial **0**.
- For international directory inquiries, dial **00**.
- For local directory inquiries, dial **411**.
- For emergency police, fire, or ambulance services, dial **911**.
- **1-800** and **888** indicate a toll-free number.

POSTAL SERVICE

POST OFFICES ARE open from 9am to 5pm, Mondays through Fridays, and have limited Saturday service, usually 9am to noon. Post offices are closed Sundays and all Federal holidays.

If the correct postage is affixed, you can send a letter by putting it in one of the blue mailboxes found on street corners all over Washington. Times of mail pickup are written inside the mailbox's lid. There are usually several collections a day. Include a zip code to ensure faster delivery of letters within the United States.

Depending on how far the mail needs to travel in the US, it can take from one to five days to arrive at its destination. Send overseas mail via airmail; otherwise it will take weeks to arrive. Express and Priority mail are also available at the post office for a faster, though more expensive, service. If you are a visitor to the city and you wish to receive mail, you can have it sent to you by addressing it care of "General Delivery" at the Main Post Office or any other postal station. They will hold the mail for you to collect.

US Mailbox

Newspaper vendor

TELEVISION AND RADIO

TELEVISIONS ARE everywhere in the United States, from bars and restaurants to hotels and stores. Most have cable hook-up, allowing access to more than 60 different channels. Some of the best to view are CBS (Channel 9), NBC (Channel 4), CNN (Channel 10), ABC (Channel 7), and Fox (Channel 5). For those interested in the political goings-on in the city, tune in to channels C-Span 1 and C-Span 2 to watch the proceedings in Congress as they are broadcast live.

Radios can be found in most hotel rooms, as well as in rental cars, and offer a wide range of music, from country through classical and jazz to rock. Popular radio stations include National Public Radio (WAMU at 90.9 and 88.5), modern rock on WHFS (99.1), and soft rock on Easy 101 (101).

NEWSPAPERS

THE MOST WIDELY read newspaper in the DC area is the *Washington Post*, which is also one of the best newspapers published in the country. The local *Washington Times* is widely available as are *USA Today*, *The Wall Street Journal* and *The New York Times*. Newspapers can be bought in street dispensers (boxes on the sidewalk that dispense newspapers), newsstands, gas stations, convenience stores, hotel lobbies, and bookstores. Newsstands and some bookstores carry newspapers from most large US cities and many foreign countries.

WASHINGTON TIME

Washington is on Eastern Standard Time. Daylight Saving Time begins on the last Sunday in April when clocks are set ahead one hour, and ends on the last Sunday in October when clocks go back one hour.

City and Country	Hours + or - EST	City and Country	Hours + or - EST
Chicago (US)	-1	Moscow (Russia)	+8
Dublin (Ireland)	+5	Paris (France)	+6
London (UK)	+5	Sydney (Australia)	+15
Los Angeles (US)	-3	Tokyo (Japan)	+14
Madrid (Spain)	+6	Vancouver (Canada)	-3

DIRECTORY

PHONE CARDS

Western Union
Branches all over the DC area.
For the nearest one call:
☎ (800) 325-6000.
🌐 www.westernunion.com

FAX FACILITIES

Mailboxes Etc.
4401 Connecticut Ave, NW.
☎ 244-7299.
🌐 www.mbe.com

American University,
4410 Massachusetts Ave, NW
☎ 686-2100.

POST OFFICES

Farragut Station
1800 M St, NW.
Map 2 F2.

Friendship Station
4005 Wisconsin Ave, NW.

Georgetown Station
1215 31st St, NW.
Map 2 D2

Martin Luther King Jr. Station
1400 L St, NW.
Map 2 F3.

National Capitol Station
2 Massachusetts Ave, NE.
Map 4 E3.

Temple Heights Station
1921 Florida Ave, NW. **Map** 2 E1.

For the nearest branch call:
☎ (800) 275-8777.

CYBERCAFÉS

Cyberstop Café
1513 17th St, NW. **Map** 3 B2.
☎ 234-2470.
🌐 www.cyberstopcafe.com
@ feedback@cyberstopcafe.com

GETTING TO WASHINGTON, DC

WASHINGTON is easy to get to via any mode of transportation. Three airports serve the DC area, which in turn are used by most major airlines for domestic and international flights. Two major bus lines also operate to the city,

United Airlines plane

as do the Amtrak trains that arrive at and depart from Union Station, right in the center of Washington. Visitors often tend to travel first to DC, base themselves in the city, and then arrange day or weekend trips into Maryland and Virginia.

Glass-walled interior of Ronald Reagan National Airport

ARRIVING BY AIR

THERE ARE three main airports in the Washington, DC area: **Dulles International Airport**, the **Ronald Reagan Washington National Airport** (known as "National" airport), and **Baltimore-Washington International Airport** (known as BWI). Most of the major carriers, including American Airlines, British Airways, Air France, and United Airlines, fly to at least one of these airports, so visitors to DC have a wide choice in terms of location and cost. The majority of international and overseas flights land at Dulles Airport. Dulles International, situated

26 miles (42 km) west of Washington in Virginia, is DC's main international airport. There is a connecting shuttle service, the **Washington Flyer Coach Service**, to take new arrivals to West Falls Church Metro. The **Super-Shuttle** bus service runs every hour, and a taxi is also an option from Dulles to downtown DC – but make sure the fare is negotiated first.

Although located about 5 miles (8 km) outside the city in Arlington County, Virginia, the Ronald Reagan Washington National Airport is the most convenient airport for central Washington. The city is easily accessible using the Metrorail's yellow and blue lines, or by taking the Super-Shuttle (which runs every 30 minutes), the Washington Flyer Express Bus, or a taxi.

Baltimore-Washington International Airport, situated 30 miles (48 km) northeast of DC, tends to be used by low-cost airlines. **The Maryland Rail Commuter Service (MARC)** is the cheapest way to get from the airport to the city, but it runs only on

weekdays. **Amtrak** offers the next-best train service for just a few dollars more. The SuperShuttle is also available from BWI, but it is more costly and takes longer than a train ride. The taxi fare into central DC is rather expensive.

AIR FARES

THE BUSIEST SEASON for travel to the US is March through June and September through early November. Christmas is also busy. Flights will be at their most expensive during these periods. Flights in June and July are usually the most expensive but there are many discounted accommodations available at this time. Weekend flights are usually less expensive than weekday flights, while Apex tickets are often the best deal but must be booked at least one week in advance, and your visit must include a Saturday night.

Cheap air fares can be obtained by shopping around, so it is worth checking with several airlines and travel agents before you book.

Consolidated tickets (those

The Washington Flyer runs from Dulles to West Falls Church Metro

AIRPORT	ℂ INFORMATION	DISTANCE/TIME TO WASHINGTON, DC	TAXI FARE	SUPERSHUTTLE
Dulles	(703) 572-2700	26 miles (42 km) 40 minutes	$35–47	$20–24
National	(703) 417-8000	10 miles (16 km) 15 minutes	$10–15	$9
BWI	(800) 435-9294	30 miles (48 km) 50 minutes	$55	$30–35

Lining up for tickets at an Amtrak desk

bought from a travel agent) are often considerably cheaper than those bought directly from airlines and can usually offer more flexibility. These can be obtained via the Internet by contacting **NOW Voyager** or in person from **Consolidators: Air Travel's Bargain Basement**.

PACKAGE DEALS

FLY-DRIVE VACATIONS offer a great deal of freedom once you reach your destination and are a popular choice for visitors from outside the US. Information about this and other package deals is available from travel agents. For "romance" and "weekend getaways," as well as family packages, vacations, and special events trips, it is worth contacting the Washington, DC Convention and Visitors Association (see p195).

United Airlines, US Airways, Amtrak, and others also offer their own package deals.

ARRIVING BY TRAIN

AMTRAK IS ONE of the best ways to travel to the DC area. Trains from other cities arrive in Washington at Union Station. Trains are also available from Union Station to Baltimore, Philadelphia, Richmond, and Williamsburg. Amtrak offers a deluxe train service to and from New York City, called the Metroliner, which travels slightly faster and more comfortably than the regular train, but is also more expensive. The "Acela" train is a new high-speed service connecting DC with

New York and Boston. It is also relatively inexpensive. Another train service available is MARC, Maryland's commuter train, which departs on weekdays to Baltimore.

ARRIVING BY CAR

THE CENTER OF Washington, DC is surrounded by Interstates I-95 and I-495, which together form the congested Capital Beltway. Interstate I-66 connects Washington to West Virginia, and Interstate I-50 heads east from DC to Annapolis, Maryland, and the surrounding areas. Beyond the Beltway, Interstate I-95 goes north toward Baltimore, Philadelphia, and New York. Interstate I-270 heads north to Frederick, Maryland.

Greyhound bus, an inexpensive way to see the whole country

ARRIVING BY BUS

TAKING A BUS is the slowest but usually the least expensive way to get to DC. **Greyhound Busline** and **Peter Pan Trailways** both offer routes from around the country, and provide discounts for children and senior citizens. The bus terminals are located in a rather remote part of town, at 1005 1st St, NE at L St. It is advisable to take a taxi from here at night.

DIRECTORY

AIRPORTS

Baltimore-Washington Airport (BWI)
Baltimore, MD.
📞 (800) I-FLY-BWI
📞 (410) 859-7387 (Lost & Found.)
🖥 www.bwiairport.com

Dulles International Airport
Chantilly, VA.
📞 (703) 572-2700.
📞 (703) 572-2954 (Lost & Found.)
🖥 www.metwashairports.com

Ronald Reagan Washington National Airport
Arlington County, VA.
📞 (703) 417-8000
📞 (703) 417-8560 (Lost & Found.)
🖥 www.metwashairports.com

AIR FARES

Consolidators: Air Travel's Bargain Basement
Intrepid Traveler, PO Box 531, Branford, CT 06405.
📞 (203) 488-5341.
🖥 www.intrepidtraveler.com

NOW Voyager
74 Varick St, Suite 307, New York, NY 10013. 📞 (212) 431-1616.
🖥 www.nowvoyagertravel.com

PUBLIC TRANSPORT

Amtrak
Union Station,
50 Massachusetts Ave, NE.
📞 484-7540.
📞 (800) USA-RAIL.
🖥 www.amtrak.com

Maryland Rail Commuter Service (MARC)
📞 (410) 859-7400.
📞 (800) 325 RAIL.

SuperShuttle
1517 K St, NW (bus terminal.)
📞 (800) BLUEVAN.
🖥 www.supershuttle.com

Washington Flyer Coach Service
1517 K St, NW (bus terminal.)
📞 (888) WASH-FLY.
🖥 www.washfly.com

Greyhound Busline
1005 1st St, NE.
📞 (800) 231-2222.
📞 289-5154.
🖥 www.greyhound.com

Peter Pan Trailways
📞 (800) 343-9999.
📞 371-8045.
🖥 www.peterpan-bus.com

Getting Around Washington, DC

WASHINGTON HAS A VERY comprehensive public transportation system. Visitors and locals alike find that it is easier to get around by public transportation than by car, especially as they do not have the aggravation of finding a much coveted parking space. All the major tourist attractions in the capital are accessible on foot, by Metrorail, by Metrobus, or by taxi.

Busy night-time traffic in central DC

PLANNING YOUR TRIP

THE WASHINGTON DC, Maryland, and Virginia tourism departments are all helpful contact points, and hotels should also be able to help guests during their stay.

The **Smithsonian Dial-a-Museum** and **Dial-a-Park** lines are useful resources for finding out about local events. If you plan to visit in winter the weather can be unpredictable, so check with **Weather Update** to find out what the day has in store.

Tourists checking their routes at a tourist information kiosk

GETTING YOUR BEARINGS

WASHINGTON IS a terrific city for walking, as long as you wear comfortable shoes and keep your wits about you. Many of the principal sights are clustered on or around the Mall. In other places, such as Georgetown, walking is undoubtedly the best way to soak up the atmosphere and see the sights.

It is important to know that, with the exception of Georgetown, the city is made up of four quadrants: northeast (NE), northwest (NW), southeast (SE), and southwest (SW), with the US Capitol at the central point. Every address in DC includes the quadrant code (NE, and so on) and, with building numbers running into the thousands on the same street in each quadrant, its use is necessary to distinguish the location.

A useful tip for when you are first trying to find your way around the city is to remember that most numbered streets run North and South, and most lettered streets run East and West. However, be aware that there is no "J," "X," "Y," or "Z" Street, and

that "I" Street is often written as "Eye" Street.

The northwest quadrant contains most of the tourist sights and neighborhoods, with other sights and places of interest located around the Capitol and south of the Mall, in the southwest quadrant.

METRORAIL

A MAP OF THE Metrorail is one of the most important pieces of information visitors will need when trying to get around DC (*see* back endpaper). The system takes some getting used to, and the instructions are in English only, so allow plenty of time when first using the Metrorail (or "Metro," as it is also called.)

The cost of the fare depends on the time and distance you wish to travel, and ranges from \$1.10 to \$3.25.

Tickets, or "farecards," for single or multiple trips can be bought from vending machines. Coins and bills (but no bills over \$20) can be used to pay for the fare; insert the exact change, or add more money if you wish to use the farecard again.

Passengers swipe their farecards through the turnstile at the beginning and end of the trip. If there is any unused fare left at the final destination the ticket will be returned to you; if not, the ticket will be retained. You can top up tickets for further trips, and tickets first purchased with \$20 or more on them get an extra 10 percent free at the time of the original purchase. A rail-to-bus transfer ticket can be bought if you wish to continue your trip by bus. Passes range from one-day (\$5) to 28-days (\$100).

Five Metrorail lines operate in downtown DC: the Orange Line; Blue Line; Red Line; Yellow Line; and the Green Line. Trains run from 5:30am to midnight Monday through Thursday, from 8am to 2am on Friday and Saturday, from 8am to midnight on Sunday.

Gallery Pl–Chinatown Station

Metro si

Washington, DC Metrobus

METROBUS

LIKE THE Metrorail system, Metrobus is a fast and in-expensive way to get around the city. Metrobus stops are frequent – there are 15,800 of them scattered throughout the Metrobus network, which includes Virginia and Maryland.

The standard, off-peak fare on the bus costs around $1.10, with a 25 cent charge for a bus transfer. Discounts are available for disabled travelers and senior citizens. Up to two children under the age of five can travel for free with a fare-paying passenger. Fares can be paid to the driver either with the exact change or with a tourist pass.

Maps of all the bus routes are available in the Metro-rail stations, and maps of specific Metrobus lines are posted at each Metrobus stop. Visitors can write to the **Metrobus** office in advance of their trip to request travel informa-tion and a bus map.

TAXIS

FINDING A TAXI in DC is not difficult. They can usually be hailed from the street corner, but if you need to be some-where at a specific time it is advisable to call a taxi company and arrange a definite pickup time and place in advance. The **DC Taxi Cab Commission** will provide names of cab companies. Fares operate by zone rather than on a meter. Rides within a single zone cost $4 what-ever the distance, but increase when zone boundaries are crossed. For example, a two-zone ride within the city will cost $5.50, and a three-zone ride will cost $6.90, and so on up to $12.50.

Each extra passenger costs $1.50. Bags, rush hour travel, and gas prices can all incur surcharges from 50 cents to $2.00. Always check with the driver to be sure he will take you across zones to your destination without charging.

DRIVING AND PARKING IN THE CITY

DRIVING IN DC need not be stressful as long as you avoid the rush hour (between 6:30 and 9:30 am, and 4 and 7 pm on weekdays.) During these times the direction of traffic flow can change, some roads become one way, and left turns may be forbidden to ease congestion. These changes are usually marked, but always pay close attention to the road. The city's layout is straightforward but drivers can be aggres-sive in heavy traffic.

Curbside parking is hard to find at the more popular locations around the city, and during the rush hour curbside park-ing is illegal in many areas. It is important to keep within your time limit if you are parking at a meter; you could otherwise face a fine or risk being clamped. Parking re-strictions on Sundays and

Road sign

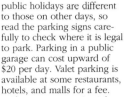

public holidays are different to those on other days, so read the parking signs care-fully to check where it is legal to park. Parking in a public garage can cost upward of $20 per day. Valet parking is available at some restaurants, hotels, and malls for a fee.

Almost every tourist sight is accessible via public trans-portation, and this is recom-mended over driving. If you do decide to drive to Wash-ington, it is worth considering long-term parking in a garage and using the Metro or buses to get around the city. Try www.washington.org or www.downtowndc.org for more information.

Typical Washington, DC taxi cab

Exploring Beyond Washington, DC

THERE IS MUCH TO SEE beyond Washington's city limits, and traveling by car is easy with a good map. Many of the sights are reachable by public transportation, but it is generally easier and quicker to drive. Car rental is widely available but often expensive. Buses and trains are a cheaper alternative, but your choice of destinations may be more limited.

Inline skaters enjoying a clear road

RULES OF THE ROAD

THE HIGHWAY SPEED limit in the DC area is 55 miles per hour (mph) (88 kmph) – much lower than in many European countries. In residential areas the speed limit ranges from 20–35 mph (32–48 kmph), and near schools it can be as low as 15 mph (24 kmph). Roads are generally well-signed but it is still wise to plan your route ahead. It is important to obey the signs, especially "No U-turn" signs, or you risk getting a ticket. If you are pulled over by the police, be courteous or you may face an even greater fine. In addition, all drivers are required to carry a valid drivers' license and be able to produce registration documents for their vehicle.

Roadsign

CAR RENTAL

YOU MUST USUALLY BE at least 25 years old with a valid driving license to rent a car. All agencies require a major credit card or a large cash deposit. Damage and liability insurance is recommended just in case something unexpected should happen. It is advisable always to return the car with a full tank of gas; otherwise you will be required to pay the inflated fuel prices charged by the rental agencies.

It is often less expensive to rent a vehicle at an airport, as car rental taxes are $2 a day more in the city. As rental rates and special deals vary from agency to agency, it is worth checking the offers of more than one company. Agencies with bureaux at the Washington airports include **Alamo**, **Avis**, **Budget**, and **Hertz**.

GASOLINE (PETROL)

GAS COMES IN three grades – regular, super, and premium. There is an extra charge if an attendant serves you, but patrons can fill their own tanks at self-service pumps without incurring an extra fee. Gas is generally cheap in the US, and payment can often be made by credit card or traveler's check, as well as in cash, which is often preferred.

BREAKDOWNS

IN THE UNLUCKY event of a breakdown, the best course of action is to pull completely off the road and put on the hazard lights to alert other drivers that you are stationary. There are emergency phones along some of the major interstate highways, but in other situations breakdown services or even the police can be contacted from land or mobile phones. In case of breakdown, drivers of rental cars should contact the car rental company first.

Members of the American Automobile Association (AAA) can have their vehicle towed to the nearest service station to be fixed.

PARKING

MOST OF THE major sights that lie beyond Washington have adequate parking for visitors, but there may be a charge to use the facility.

In general it is good practice to read all parking notices carefully to avoid fines, being clamped, or being towed away.

Parking sign

CYCLING

THERE ARE SOME great bicycle paths in the Greater Washington, DC area. Bike shops rent out bikes and will be able to suggest routes. They can

Cycling is a pleasant way to see the sights in Washington

Tourmobile bus, one of many sightseeing tour buses available in DC

usually provide route maps.
Better Bikes will deliver a
rental bike to you for a cost
of $25–$50 per day. The company **Bike the Sites, Inc**
offers a selection of tours in
and around the city, including
a one-hour Early Bird Fun Ride
and a 10-mile (16-km) Capital
Sites Ride. They provide riders
with a 21-speed bike, helmet,
water bottle, and a snack.

BUS TOURS

SEVERAL COMPANIES offer bus
tours of DC and its historic
surroundings. **Gray Line** can
take you on the Black Heritage
tour, to Gettysburg, Colonial
Williamsburg, or Monticello,
while **Tourmobile**'s destinations include Mount Vernon,
the Frederick Douglass House,
and Arlington Cemetery.

TRAINS

A MTRAK TRAINS travel from DC's
central Union Station to
New York City and most of the
surrounding areas, including
Williamsburg, Richmond, and
Baltimore. The MARC, Maryland's commuter rail, also runs
from DC to Baltimore on weekdays for a few dollars less.

DIRECTORY

CAR RENTAL AGENCIES

Alamo
[C] (800) 327-9633.
[W] www.goalamo.com

Avis
[C] (800) 331-1212.
[W] www.avis.com

Budget
[C] (800) 527-0700.
[W] www.budget.com

Hertz
[C] (800) 654-3131.
[W] www.hertz.com

BREAKDOWN ASSISTANCE

**American Automobile
Association (AAA)**
701-15th St, NW,
Washington, DC 20005.
[C] 331-3000 (Washington office).
[C] (800) 222-4357 (general breakdown assistance).

BICYCLE RENTAL

Better Bikes
[C] 293-2080.

Bike The Sites, Inc
3417 Quesada St, NW.
[C] 966-8662.
[W] www.bikethesites.com

BUS TOURS

Gray Line
Union Station,
50 Massachusetts Ave.
[C] (800) 862-1400
[C] 289-1995.
[W] www.graydc.com

Tourmobile Sightseeing
1000 Ohio Drive, S.W.,
Washington, D.C. 20024
[C] 554-5100.
[W] www.tourmobile.com

TIPS AND SAFETY FOR DRIVERS

- Traffic moves on the right-hand side of the road.
- Seat belts are compulsory in front seats and suggested in back; children under three must ride in a child seat in back.
- You can turn right at a red light as long as you first come to a complete stop, and if there are no signs that prohibit it.
- A flashing yellow light at an intersection means slow down, look for oncoming traffic, and proceed with caution.
- Passing (overtaking) is allowed on any multi-lane road, and you must pass on the left.
- Crossing a double-yellow line, either by U-turn or by passing the car in front, is illegal, and you will be charged a fine if caught.
- If a school bus stops, all traffic from both sides must stop completely and wait for the bus to drive off.
- Driving while intoxicated (DWI) is a punishable offense that incurs heavy fines or even a jail

sentence. Do not drink if you plan to drive.
- Avoid driving at night if unfamiliar with the area. Washington's streets change from safe to dangerous in a single block, so it is better to take a taxi than your own car if you do not know where you are going.
- Single women should be especially careful driving in unfamiliar territory, day or night.
- Keep all doors locked when driving around. Do not stop in a rural area, or on an unlit block if someone tries to get your attention. If a fellow driver points at your car, suggesting something is wrong, drive to the nearest gas station and get help. Do not get out of your car.
- Avoid sleeping in your car.
- Avoid short cuts and stay on well-traveled roads.
- Avoid looking at a map in a dark, unpopulated place. Drive to the nearest open store or gas station before pulling over.

Street Finder Index

KEY TO THE STREET FINDER

■ Major sight	🅿 Main parking lot	✡ Synagogue
■ Minor sight	ℹ Tourist information office	⊠ Post office
■ Place of interest	✚ Hospital with emergency room	→ One-way street
🚆 Railroad station	🚓 Police station	⚓ Ferry terminal
Ⓜ Metrorail station	✝ Church	
🚌 Bus station	☪ Mosque	0 meters 300 / 0 yards 300 1:20,833

KEY TO ABBREVIATIONS USED IN THE STREET FINDER

Ave	Avenue	Dr	Drive	Pkwy	Parkway	St	Street/Saint
DC	District of Columbia	NE	Northeast	Pl	Place	SW	Southwest
		NW	Northwest	SE	Southeast	VA	Virginia

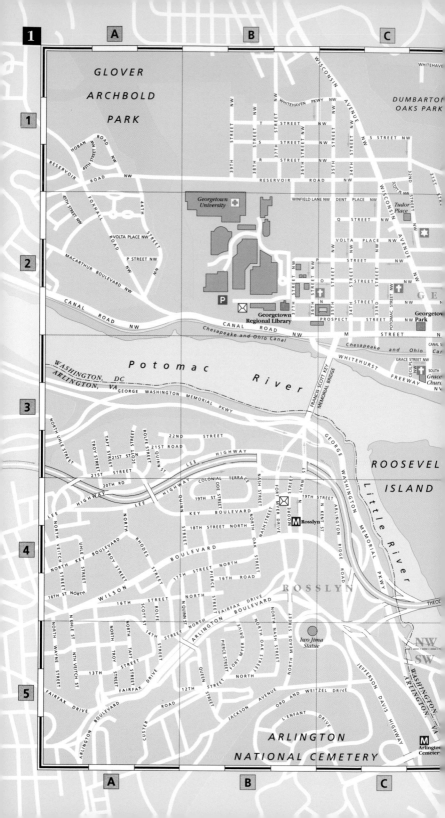

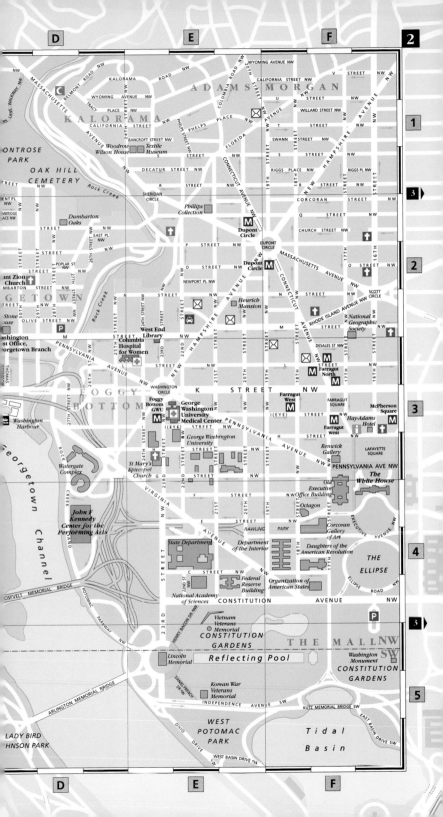

General Index

Acknowledgments

DORLING KINDERSLEY would like to thank the following people whose contributions and assistance have made the preparation of this book possible.

MAIN CONTRIBUTORS
SUSAN BURKE lives in Virginia and works as an editor for the Air Line Pilots Association. She has taught creative writing for many years and has been a freelance editor of a number of books and journals primarily in the fields of sociology, economics, and politics.

ALICE POWERS is a freelance writer living in Washington, DC. She has written many articles for the Washington Post and other newspapers. She has also written several literary anthologies and teaches writing at the Corcoran College of Art and Design.

JENNIFER QUASHA lives in New York City but has a long association with Washington. She has written many articles on subjects ranging from travel to health, and has worked on other Dorling Kindersley books, including *Walking With Dinosaurs*.

KEM SAWYER has lived in Washington for over 20 years and has written children's books, feature articles and book reviews. She particularly enjoys writing about local history.

MANAGING EDITOR
Louise Lang

MANAGING ART EDITOR
Kate Poole

ART DIRECTOR
Gillian Allan

DESIGN AND EDITORIAL ASSISTANCE
Sue Megginson, Johnny Pau, Hugh Thompson.

PROOFREADER
Stewart Wild

INDEXER
Hilary Bird

RESEARCHER
Sarah Miers

SPECIAL ASSISTANCE
Particular thanks go to Kathleen Brooks at the National Air and Space Museum, Jessie Cohen and Leah Overstreet at the National Zoological Park, Julie Heizer at the Washington, DC Convention and Visitors' Association, Sarah Petty and Brennan Rash at the National Museum of American Art, Shannon Roberts at the National Gallery of Art and Morgan Zinsmeister at the National Museum of American Art. Thanks also to Dumbarton House, National Headquarters of The National Society of The Colonial Dames of America.

ADDITIONAL PHOTOGRAPHY: Max Alexander, Frank Greenaway, Tim Mann, Scott Suchman, Matthew Ward, Stephen Whitehorn.

PHOTOGRAPHY PERMISSIONS
Dorling Kindersley would like to thank the following for their assistance and kind permission to photograph at their establishments, as well as all the cathedrals, churches, museums, restaurants, hotels, shops, galleries and other sights too numerous to thank individually.

PICTURE CREDITS
t-top; tl-top left; tlc-top left center; tc-top center; trc-top right center; tr-top right; cla-center left above; ca-center above; cra-center right above; cl-center left; c-center; cr-center right; clb-center left below; cb-center below; crb-
center right below; bl-bottom left; b-bottom; bc-bottom center; bcl-bottom center left; br-bottom right; d-detail

AFP: Stephen Jaffe 23c; Joyce Naltchayan 34c; Mario Tama 26br; ALLSPORT: Doug Pensinger 188c, 188b; ASSOCIATED PRESS AP: Will Morris 127tl; B. SMITH'S RESTAURANT AT UNION STATION: Thomas Townsend 170 br; DAN BEIGEL: 113t; BRIDGEMAN ART LIBRARY, LONDON & NEW YORK: Baynton Williams, London *The Bay of Annapolis*, c. 1880 (litho) by N. Currier (1813–1888) and J. M. Ives (1824–1895) 141 (insert); Freer Gallery, Smithsonian Institution *Sheep and Goat* by Chao Meng Fu 54bl; National Gallery of Art, Washington D. C. *The Alba Madonna* (c. 1510) by Raphael (Raffaello Sanzio of Urbino, 1483–1520) 56cla; National Gallery of Art, Washington D. C., East Building designed by I. M. Pei, 1978, suspended sculpture by Alexander Calder 57b; The Phillips Collection, Washington D. C. *The Luncheon of the Boating Party* 1881 by Pierre Auguste Renoir (1841–1919) 129t; The White House, Washington D. C., *Portrait of Woodrow Wilson* by Sir William Orpen (1878–1931) 25tl.

CORBIS: 19c, 20c, 25cr, 26bra, 27tl, 27crb, 77tl; AFP: 23b; Dave Bartruff: 29cr; Joseph Sohm; Chromosohm Inc. 33tl, 36br, 85bl; Corbis-Bettmann 21c, 22t, 22cl, 23t, 25tr, 26bla, 27cl, 27cra, 27bl, 68b, 85cr, 90t; Corcoran Gallery of Art 14; Jay & Becky Dickman 140-141; Todd Gipstein 191; Hulton Deutsch Collection 21t, 25br; Katherine Karnow 34t, 116b; Kelly-Mooney Photography 190b; Wally McNamee 22cr, 111b; David Muench 144b; Richard T. Nowitz 3 (insert), 36t, 37cr; Moshe Shai 27bc; Bequest of Mrs. Benjamin Ogle Tayloe, Collection of the Corcoran Gallery of Art 24tl; Mark Thiessen 37b; Underwood & Underwood 74tr; UPI 86br; Oscar White 25bcl.

DANITA DELIMONT (AGENT): David R. Frazier Photolibrary/NASM 63c; Karen Huntt Mason 35b; Carol Pratt 186tr; Scott Suchman 131cl, 202c.

PHILIPPE LIMET DEWEZ: 186b, 187.

MARY EVANS PICTURE LIBRARY: 9 (insert), 39 (insert), 159 (insert).

MICHAEL FREEMAN: 38–39, 48bl, 49tl, 60cla, 60br, 61cl, 61cr, 63b, 71b, 72b.

HOTEL GEORGE: 160b.

GRANGER COLLECTION, NEW YORK: 8-9, 15c, 15b, 16t, 16cl, 16b, 17t, 17c, 17b, 18t, 18c, 18b, 19t, 19b, 20t, 20b, 21b, 24tr, 24cl, 24bl, 24bc, 24br, 25cl, 25bl, 45cra, 85t, 85ca, 85cl, 139t, 193 (insert).

ROBERT HARDING PICTURE LIBRARY: Schuster 2–3.

CAPITOL HILTON HOTEL: 160.

IMAGE BANK: Archive Photos 91b; Andrea Pistolesi 48cl, 74bl.

KIPLINGER WASHINGTON COLLECTION: 74tl.

LIBRARY OF CONGRESS: Carol M. Highsmith 44b.

MATISSE RESTAURANT: 170cl; Courtesy Mount Vernon Ladies' Association: 148tl, 148cla.

NATIONAL AIR AND SPACE MUSEUM © SMITHSONIAN INSTITUTION: SI Neg. No. 99-15240-7–29tl.

NATIONAL GALLERY OF ART, WASHINGTON, DC: Samuel H. Kress Collection, Photo: Philip A. Charles *Bust of Lorenzo de' Medici* 55tl; Ailsa Mellon Bruce Fund, Photo: Bob Grove *Ginevra de' Benci* c. 1474 by Leonardo da Vinci 56tr; Samuel H. Kress Collection *A Young Man With His Tutor* by Nicolas de Largilliere, 1685–56clb; Samuel H. Kress Collection *Christ Cleansing the Temple* (d), pre-1570, by El Greco 58t, Samuel H. Kress Collection *Madonna and Child*, 1320–1330 by Giotto 58cl; Collection of Mr. and Mrs. Paul Mellon *Woman with a Parasol*, 1875, by Claude Monet 57t; Harris Whittemore Collection *Symphony in White, No. 1: The White Girl*, 1862, by James McNeill Whistler 57cr; Timken Collection *Diana and Endymion*, c. 1753, by Jean-Honore Fragonard 58b; Chester Dale Collection *Miss Mary Ellison*, 1880, by Mary Cassatt 59b; John Russell Pope (architect) 185.

NATIONAL MUSEUM OF AMERICAN ART/© SMITHSONIAN INSTITUTION: Gift of Mr. and Mrs. Joseph Harrison *Old Bear, a Medicine Man*, 1832, by George Catlin 92br; *Achelous and Hercules*, 1947, © T. H. Benton and R. P. Benton Testamentary Trusts/VAGA, New York/DACS, London 2000 – 92-93c; Bequest of Henry Ward Ranger through the National Academy of Design, *Cliffs of the Upper Colorado River, Wyoming Territory*, 1882, by Thomas Moran 92bl; Gift of John Gellatly *In the Garden (Celia Thaxter in Her Garden)*, 1892, by Childe Hassam 93bl; Gift of the James Renwick Alliance and Museum purchase through the Smithsonian Collections Acquisitions Program, *Game Fish*, 1988 © Larry Fuente 93br; Gift of Herbert Waide Hemphill, Jr. and Museum purchase made possible by Ralph Cross Johnson, *Bottlecap Giraffe* by an unidentified Artist, completed after 1966–94tl; © Untitled Press, Inc/VAGA, New York and DACS, London 2000 *Reservoir*, 1961, by Robert Rauschenberg 94cr; Gift of Anonymous Donors *The Throne of the Third Heaven of the Nations Millenium General Assembly*, c. 1950–1954, by James Hampton 94bl. NATIONAL MUSEUM OF AMERICAN HISTORY/© SMITHSONIAN INSTITUTION: 70t, 70bl, 71t, 73c, 73b (detail); Eric Long 70br; Laurie Minor 74t; NATIONAL MUSEUM OF NATURAL HISTORY/© SMITHSONIAN INSTITUTION: 66b; Dane Penland 67t; NATIONAL PARK SERVICE: Rick Latoff, courtesy www.Parkphotos.com 65b; Mary McLeod Bethune Council House NHS, Washington D.C. 134c.

NATIONAL PORTRAIT GALLERY/© SMITHSONIAN INSTITUTION: Gift of The Morris and Gwendolyn Cafritz Foundation and Smithsonian Institution Trust Fund *Selfportrait*, 1780–1784, by John Singleton Copley 93ca; Gift of Friends of President and Mrs. Reagan, *Ronald Wilson Reagan*, 1989, © Henry C. Casselli 95c; *Diana Ross and the Supremes*, 1965, © Bruce Davidson/Magnum 95b; Transfer from the National Gallery of Art, Gift of Andrew W. Mellon, 1942, *Pocahontas*, Un-identified artist, English school, after the 1616 engraving by Simon van de Passe, after 1616 – 95tl; Gift of the Morris and Gwendolyn Cafritz Foundation and the Regents' Major

Acquisitions Fund, Smithsonian Institution *Mary Cassatt* , 1880–1884, by Edgar Degas 93tl; Courtesy National Portrait Gallery *"Casey" Stengel* , 1981 cast after 1965 plaster by © Rhoda Sherbell 93tr.

NATIONAL POSTAL MUSEUM/ © SMITHSONIAN INSTITUTION: Jim O'Donnell 51c.

NATIONAL ZOOLOGICAL PARK/© SMITHSONIAN INSTITUTION: Jessie Cohen 132tl, 132cl, 132br, 133tl, 133tr, 133crb; PETER NEWARK'S AMERICAN PICTURES: 26tl.

DAVID NOBLE: 1, 52, 158-159.

RICHARD T. NOWITZ: 61b, 77crb; Abe Nowitz 35c.

OCTAGON MUSEUM/AMERICAN ARCHITECTURAL FOUNDATION, WASHINGTON DC: 109b. OXFORD SCIENTIFIC FILMS: James Robinson 153br.

PHILLIPS COLLECTION: 129c; © Mondrian/Holtzman Trust c/o Beeldrecht, Amsterdam, Holland & DACS, London 2000 *Composition No. 33*, 1921–1926, by Piet Mondrian 129b.

POPPERFOTO: Reuters 26cl, 26cr.

PRIVATE COLLECTION: Kevin Ryan 180t.

REX FEATURES: 25tc; SIPA Press/Trippett 25bcr.

MAE SCANLAN: 29cla, 30t, 34b, 60bl, 73t, 98, 190t. SCIENCE PHOTO LIBRARY: US Geological Survey 10. FRANK SPOONER PICTURES: Markel-Liaison 85br;

TEXTILE MUSEUM: Gift of Mrs.Charles Putnam 130t.

TOPHAM PICTUREPOINT: 119clb.

TRH PICTURES: National Air and Space Museum 61t, 62t.

UNITED AIRLINES: 202t; UNIVERSITY OF VIRGINIA: Library Special Collections Department, Manuscript Print Collection 121tl; UNITED STATES HOLOCAUST MEMORIAL MUSEUM: 77cra.

WESTERN UNION: 200c; WHITE HOUSE COLLECTION, COURTESY WHITE HOUSE HISTORICAL ASSOCIATION: 102cl/b, 103t/c/bl/br, 104b, 105c/b; WOODFIN CAMP & ASSOCIATES, INC: Katherine Karnow, National Air and Space Museum 62b.

FRONT ENDPAPER: All special photography except David Noble br; Mae Scanlan tl.

BACK ENDPAPER: © 1998 Washington Metropolitan Area Transit Authority.

JACKET
Front - CORBIS: Ron Watts cb; DK PICTURE LIBRARY: Giles Stroke br; GETTY IMAGES: Eric Meola bl; POWERSTOCK: Sandra Baker main image. Back - DK PICTURE LIBRARY: Giles Stroke t, b. Spine - POWERSTOCK: Sandra Baker.

All other images © Dorling Kindersley. See www.dkimages.com for more information.

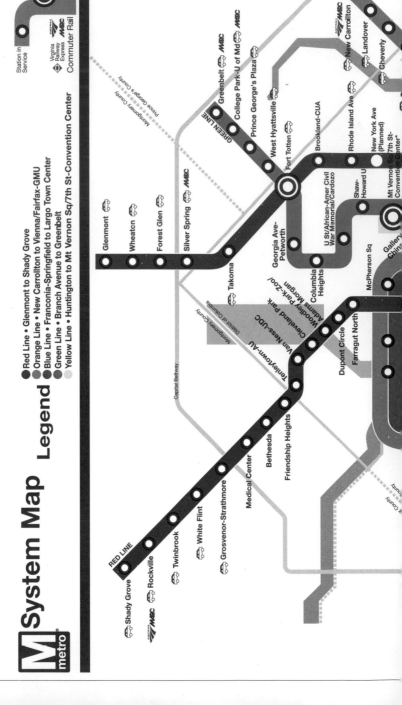

M System Map

Legend

- ● Red Line • Glenmont to Shady Grove
- ● Orange Line • New Carrollton to Vienna/Fairfax-GMU
- ● Blue Line • Franconia-Springfield to Largo Town Center
- ● Green Line • Branch Avenue to Greenbelt
- ● Yellow Line • Huntington to Mt Vernon Sq/7th St-Convention Center

Station in Service
Planned Station
Transfer Station
Parking

Virginia Railway Express
MARC Commuter Rail

RED LINE

Shady Grove
Rockville
Twinbrook
White Flint
Grosvenor-Strathmore
Medical Center
Bethesda
Friendship Heights
Tenleytown-AU
Van Ness-UDC
Cleveland Park
Woodley Park/Zoo/Adams Morgan
Dupont Circle
Farragut North

Glenmont
Wheaton
Forest Glen
Silver Spring
Takoma
Georgia Ave-Petworth
Columbia Heights

GREEN LINE

Greenbelt
College Park-U of Md
Prince George's Plaza
West Hyattsville
Fort Totten
Brookland-CUA
Rhode Island Ave
New York Ave (Planned)
U St/African-Amer Civil War Memorial/Cardozo
Shaw-Howard U
Mt Vernon Sq/7th St-Convention Center*

New Carrollton
Landover
Cheverly

McPherson Sq
Gallery Pl-Chinatown

Capital Beltway
Montgomery County
Prince George's County
District of Columbia

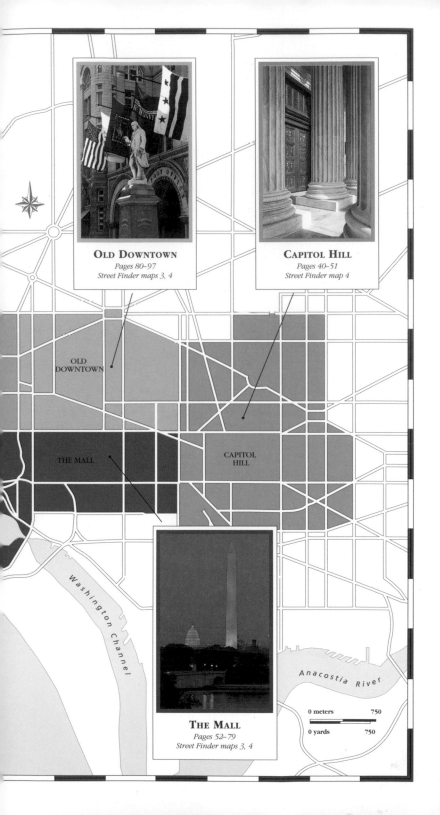

OLD DOWNTOWN
Pages 80–97
Street Finder maps 3, 4

CAPITOL HILL
Pages 40–51
Street Finder map 4

OLD
DOWNTOWN

THE MALL

CAPITOL
HILL

Washington Channel

Anacostia River

THE MALL
Pages 52–79
Street Finder maps 3, 4

| 0 meters | 750 |
| 0 yards | 750 |

EYEWITNESS TRAVEL GUIDES

WASHINGTON, DC